Victorian and Early 20th Century Baby Farming

Victorian and Early 20th Century Baby Farming

The Darkest Business

Eve Bacon

First published in Great Britain in 2024 by
Pen & Sword History
An imprint of Pen & Sword Books Limited
Yorkshire – Philadelphia

Copyright © Eve Bacon 2024

ISBN 978 1 03611 056 7

The right of Eve Bacon to be identified as
Author of this Work has been asserted by her in accordance
with the Copyright, Designs and Patents Act 1988.

A CIP catalogue record for this book is
available from the British Library

All rights reserved. No part of this book may be reproduced or
transmitted in any form or by any means, electronic or mechanical
including photocopying, recording or by any information storage and
retrieval system, without permission from the Publisher in writing.

Typeset by Mac Style
Printed in the UK by CPI Group (UK) Ltd, Croydon, CR0 4YY.

Pen & Sword Books Limited incorporates the imprints of After
the Battle, Atlas, Archaeology, Aviation, Discovery, Family History,
Fiction, History, Maritime, Military, Military Classics, Politics,
Select, Transport, True Crime, Air World, Frontline Publishing, Leo
Cooper, Remember When, Seaforth Publishing, The Praetorian Press,
Wharncliffe Local History, Wharncliffe Transport, Wharncliffe True
Crime and White Owl.

For a complete list of Pen & Sword titles please contact

PEN & SWORD BOOKS LIMITED
47 Church Street, Barnsley, South Yorkshire, S70 2AS, England
E-mail: enquiries@pen-and-sword.co.uk
Website: www.pen-and-sword.co.uk
or
PEN AND SWORD BOOKS
1950 Lawrence Road, Havertown, PA 19083, USA
E-mail: uspen-and-sword@casematepublishers.com
Website: www.penandswordbooks.com

I dedicate this to my husband, Steve, who has lived with baby farmers for so many years, and to Neil R. Storey, without whom this book would never have been started.

Contents

Acknowledgements		viii
Foreword		ix
Introduction		x
Chapter 1	Reasons for the Rise of Baby Farms	1
Chapter 2	Good Baby Farmers	10
Chapter 3	The Role of the Midwife	16
Chapter 4	The Role of the Coroner	19
Chapter 5	Contravention of Infant Life Protection Act 1872	52
Chapter 6	Abandonment	60
Chapter 7	Children's Homes	66
Chapter 8	Fraud	75
Chapter 9	Cruelty	87
Chapter 10	Manslaughter	107
Chapter 11	Murder	132
Chapter 12	The Fight to Protect Children	200
Notes		207
Bibliography		218
Index		221

Acknowledgements

Thanks to Neil R. Storey; Neil Bell; staff at Bristol Records Office; staff at Berkshire Records Office; Angela Buckley; Eleanor McCann; Colin Boyes of the Thames Valley Police Museum; Alan Williams, Martin (Ed) Hewines, Jane Filshie, Alan Beaty, Jon Hewines (family of Eva Muriel Grundy); Jacqueline Nott for the photo of Buckingham St, Wolverton; Michael Welsh, Records Officer, NSPCC; Dan Bogart, for use of railway maps; Dave Powers, Railway Enthusiasts Club; Alan Moss, Keith Skinner, Paul Bickley, Metropolitan Police Museum; John O'Connor, Totterdown History; and Louise Argent, Bristol and Avon Family History Society.

Foreword

Before my interest in baby farmers began, a cousin visited me with a puzzle to solve. She had been researching her family history and had found a several times great-grandfather had been born in Newgate prison. Where could she find details of his mother? Together we searched online and discovered both the baby's parents had been jailed for the manslaughter of an infant, which they had been paid to mind. Later, when I started researching baby farming, I began to wonder if my cousin was descended from such creatures. I have found no evidence that these two 'cared' for more than the one unfortunate child, but I started to think that baby farmers could be present in the murky depths of many family histories. The other startling revelation was that most of the witnesses at the trial of these two did not appear in any census records, either before or after the trial. This led me to realise that, before the advent of income tax, welfare payments or universal health care, there was no reason for a lower-class citizen to maintain one identity. A name could be a transitory thing rooted in a particular time and place and to be altered whenever it suited the individual and so I have found throughout my research that many of these women who were involved, both as 'carers' and as the mothers of the unfortunate infants, in the murky business of baby farming were frequently difficult to trace through time. They often appear and disappear through the records that are now available. Women who claim to be married cannot be found in marriage records as many, my cousin's ancestors included, did not go through the formal marriage ceremony but cohabited together as common-law man and wife. I have, therefore, done my best to give a background to the women and, sometimes, men that have appeared in my research but there are many cases where these people just appear and disappear in an instant.

Introduction

When many of us think of Britain during the Victorian era, we think of wealthy aristocrats and businessmen. We think of industry making a nation that led the world. We think of the making of an empire that, they thought, improved the lives of conquered peoples. We see pictures of women in elaborately beautiful clothes surrounded by hordes of loved, cared for and wanted children. These ideals of family life were epitomised by the royal family: Queen Victoria and Prince Albert were frequently depicted surrounded by their children and, later, grandchildren. Their children's arms and legs were carved in marble, and these can still be seen at Osborne House, their home on the Isle of Wight.

Children were revered even in death, which was all too frequent in Victorian Britain. Mothers and babies were at risk during birth and those children that survived this gruelling procedure continued to fight diseases that we now use vaccines, antibiotics and other medicines to alleviate. Deathbed photographs were taken of beloved children and overly sentimental grave furniture was erected.

There is also the image of a workforce that lived a hard life on the edge of poverty; of large families where children worked from a young age in order to earn a few pence to help subsidise the household's income.

This poverty trap and the social mores of the time were the melting pot that encouraged the darkest business of the baby farmer.

Charles Dickens writes of the poverty and cruelty inflicted on many children during this time and in his novel *Oliver Twist* we see the eponymous hero sent after birth into the care of 'Mrs Mann', a baby farmer. Oliver is one of the fortunate babies: he survives! Many were not as lucky, as Dickens points out:

> The parish authorities inquired with dignity of the workhouse authorities, whether there was no female then domiciled in 'the house' who was in a

situation to impart to Oliver Twist, the consolation and nourishment of which he stood in need. The workhouse authorities replied with humility, that there was not. Upon this, the parish authorities magnanimously and humanely resolved, that Oliver should be 'farmed', or, in other words, that he should be dispatched to a branch-workhouse some three miles off, where twenty or thirty other juvenile offenders against the poor-laws, rolled about the floor all day, without the inconvenience of too much food or too much clothing, under the parental supervision of an elderly female, who received the culprits at and for the consideration of sevenpence-halfpenny per small head per week. Sevenpence-halfpenny's worth per week is a good round diet for a child; a great deal may be got for sevenpence-halfpenny, quite enough to overload its stomach, and make it uncomfortable. The elderly woman of wisdom and experience; she knew what was good for children; and she had a very accurate perception of what was good for herself. So she appropriated the greater part of the weekly stipend to her own use, and consigned the rising parochial generation to an even shorter allowance than was originally provided for them. Thereby finding in the lowest depth a deeper still; and proving herself a very great experimental philosopher.

Everybody knows the story of another experimental philosopher who had a great theory about a horse being able to live without eating, and who demonstrated it so well, that he had got his own horse down to a straw a day, and would unquestionably have rendered him a very spirited and rampacious animal on nothing at all, if he had not died, four-and-twenty hours before he was to have had his first bait of air. Unfortunately for, the experimental philosophy of the female to whose protective care Oliver Twist was delivered over, a similar result usually attended the operation of her system; for at the very moment when the child had contrived to exist upon the smallest possible food, it did perversely happen in eight and a half cases out of ten, either that it sickened from want and cold, or fell into the fire from neglect, or got half-smothered by accident; in any one of which cases, the miserable little being was usually summoned to another world, and there gathered to the fathers it had never known in this.

Occasionally, when there was some more than usually interested inquest upon a parish child who had been overlooked in turning a bedstead, or inadvertently scalded to death – though the latter accident was very scarce, anything approaching to a washing being a rare occurrence in the farm – the jury would take it into their heads to ask troublesome questions, or the parishioners would rebelliously affix their signatures to a remonstrance. But these impertinences were speedily checked by the evidence of the surgeon, and the testimony of the beadle; the former of whom had always opened the body and found nothing inside (which was very probably indeed).[1]

It was not only workhouses that used the services of baby farms. Mothers of illegitimate babies had few choices available to them. Some may have had families that could encompassed an extra child into the care of family members, as was the case with many of my ancestors, while other women may have been sent away to avoid shame being brought upon the family. These women needed to find a home for the unwanted infant before being taken back, unencumbered, into the more well-to-do family. Other women were required to work in order earn enough to live on, or face life in the workhouse, and would be unable to do so with a baby in tow. Some married women, for one reason or another, were unable to care for yet another mouth to feed. This need to find homes for babies allowed the business of baby farming to flourish.

This juxtaposition of ideas about babies can be seen in the *Penny Illustrated* newspaper of 2 July 1870,[2] where an article about babies dying after leaving the Brixton baby farm of Margaret Waters was followed by an advertisement for a baby show.

PRIZE BABY SHOWS are announced for the 11th at Highbury Barn, and for the 18th at the North Woolwich Gardens.

Advertisement for a baby show. (Penny Illustrated, *2 July 1870*)

It may be wondered why this development occurred during the Victorian period. Probably it had been present earlier but the 1834 Poor Law Amendment Act brought in sweeping changes that made bringing up an illegitimate child by its mother more difficult and so the options for women in that position became more limited. Despite the argument that more infant desertions and infanticide would happen, fathers were no longer held responsible for financial arrangements to be put in place with regard to their illegitimate offspring and all expenses incurred by the child should be the responsibility of the mother. Neither could a single mother leave her child with the parish.[3] This alone made it imperative that a single mother should be able to earn a living. In addition to this, the 1834 Act was designed to deter scroungers and the previous custom of parishes providing out-relief – money given to the parish paupers who continued to live in their own homes – now stopped and parishes were obliged to provide only in-house relief, whereby a pauper was taken into the parish workhouse. Should a woman go into the workhouse to give birth to an illegitimate child, she would, within days, be removed from her baby and be transferred to the 'able-bodied' ward, where she would be required to work, and often she would encounter treatment that was harsher than that meted out to other paupers.[4] The child would be cared for by the pauper 'nurse', or, as in the case of Oliver Twist, sent out to be nursed in a baby farm.

There is also ambivalence during the Victorian period about infanticide: on one hand children were cherished, but on the other, there was a tacit blinkered approach to the deaths of small babies, particularly the illegitimate. In August 1865, the *Pall Mall Gazette* published an article pointing out that infanticide is still murder, although many people, including juries, were inclined to overlook this and make excuses to allow the perpetrators to go unpunished. It suggested that hospitals or asylums be set up to take unwanted babies where both mother and father pay towards the child's keep. The writer of the article believes that this system would stop the killing of innocent children. Although this idea was not taken up, it could be said that the employment of nurses, or baby farmers, was an unofficial way of adopting this system – with consequences not thought of by the author of the article but possibly initially in keeping with the Victorian turning a blind eye to infanticide.[5]

These issues were all reasons why mothers would seek out someone who purported to want to care for the child, whether on a weekly basis, or to 'adopt' the baby, and the baby farmers would ask for a fee, or premium, to take the child 'as their own', thereby giving the farmer an income, and a reason not to keep the child, particularly those that had been 'adopted as their own'.

While Dickens referred to Oliver Twist being 'farmed' in his 1837 publication, the term 'baby farming' only seems to have come into more widespread use after 1867 when a number of young bodies were discovered around London and the police started investigating the matter. However, we can find cases of baby farming taking place prior to the 1867, the most notorious being of Charlotte Winsor in 1864, the first baby farmer to be sentenced to death.

One wonders what the motivation was for these women to treat babies so badly. The answer was money! Taking babies for a premium of a few pounds that may have seemed a lot of money to the poor mothers but was nowhere near sufficient to keep a child for life. While some women truly did adopt the little mites, as in the case of Eva Muriel Grundy, who was adopted by the Carter family having been passed on by baby farmer Jane Arnold, there were other women who wanted to be released from the responsibility of caring for a baby as quickly as possible. Many ways were used to ensure the money paid was not taken up by the baby. Insufficient feeding allowed the child to 'waste away'; abandonment; 'sweating' babies was the practice of advertising for children only to answer similar adverts and thereby pass the child from one baby farmer to another, no doubt for a smaller premium each time; and, of course, suffocating or strangling the child. Once the child was out of the way, the premium could be spent on other things, although, interestingly, few baby farmers appear to have become wealthy.

Each case of baby farming relies on a societal acquiescence to allow the business to take place, regardless of the outcry amongst many to stop the practice. Newspapers continued to accept the advertisements, changes in the law only came about slowly, baby farmers worked in tandem with others carrying out the same business, and even the police, who in many cases set up task forces to find the culprits, didn't follow up on all the leads presented to them in the form of letters found in the homes of those arrested. Consequently, this darkest business continued to flourish for over half a century.

Chapter 1

Reasons for the Rise of Baby Farms

The Victorian era saw a rise in incidents of baby farming. What caused this proliferation to become so apparent? As with all things, there was no single incident that was the cause but a series of changes that made this career choice easier to carry out.

Illegitimacy has always existed. Some families, if not welcoming the new family member, opened their arms to care for the infant, sometimes passing off the child as the offspring of the grandparents or a married aunt, sometimes acknowledging the birth mother but living with a family member, either with or without the mother being present at the same address. This has not always been the case. Some women hid their pregnancy from family and friends, leaving the area where they were known to live until their confinement in rented accommodation well away from prying eyes. In other cases, family members supported the pregnant woman but required the child to live elsewhere. In some cases, women could manage to support themselves with the help of the child's father, or with the help of parish outdoor relief, thereby allowing the child and mother financial support until the child was old enough to allow the mother to support herself and the child.

All this changed in 1834. The Poor Law Amendment Act which was passed that year required each parish to set up a Board of Guardians that had a workhouse. No longer would parishes be able to give financial support to those unable to support themselves. Instead, the destitute were to be taken into the workhouse and this included mothers and their illegitimate children. Children over 12 months were separated from their mothers. Women may well find they had no option but to put their children into the workhouse while working themselves at jobs that paid too little to support both themselves and their children. Workhouses were reluctant to accept illegitimate children who came from outside their own parish. Even so, as a result, workhouses found themselves with an abundance of children and needed to find accommodation for them elsewhere.[1] Dickens writes in the late 1830s about one such placement that infant Oliver Twist is sent to. Mrs Mann, the baby farmer, takes children in from the workhouse and feeds them barely enough for survival in order to keep as much money given for their support for herself.[2] By 1849, the case of Drouet's Juvenile Pauper Asylum appears. Various workhouse guardians sent children to this establishment in Tooting, London, and others like it, where it was said up to 1,500 children were under the care of Bartholomew Peter Drouet, each child's food, clothes and lodging paid for at the cost of 4 shillings and sixpence per week by the workhouse guardians.[3] An outbreak of cholera hit Drouet's establishment and 150 children died. At the time, the cause of cholera was in dispute; the general belief was that it was caused by miasma – bad air – but arguments were starting to appear suggesting it was a water-born illness. Although this children's home had had inspections and had been deemed a well-conducted institution, the outbreak of such a devastating illness highlighted the inadequacies in the care given to the children: up to six boys slept in one bed, food was insufficient, with the potatoes sometimes being rotten and in consequence not eaten, and their clothing was too thin to keep the children warm. Bartholomew Drouet was charged with feloniously killing the boy, James Anderson, but after a trial at the Crown Court, the judges recommended that the jury should find him not guilty as there was no evidence that the boy would have survived cholera had he not been in Drouet's establishment.[4] Clearly workhouses could not be the solution to the problems faced by the mothers of illegitimate children.

Why, you may ask, were so many children being sent to workhouses? Of course, family poverty is one reason, but this is not the whole reason. The 1834 Act's bastardy clauses also stopped the requirement that the fathers of illegitimate children should pay for the child's keep. Prior to this, a mother only needed to name the father of the child, with no other evidence, to have a magistrate order him to pay maintenance to the mother. In many cases the father would be obliged to marry the woman. Once this was removed, the women became vulnerable to poverty.[5] Fathers did appear to have been more accommodating when asked to provide a 'one off' payment that provided the mother with a premium to pay to an adoptive family.

As dangerous as abortions were, prior to 1861, when the Offences Against the Persons Act came into force, desperate women may have been tempted to obtain an abortion without evoking the wrath of the law, but in 1861 this avenue became illegal for both the mother and the abortionist. Although abortions were still carried out, they became more difficult, and probably more expensive, to obtain, and the risk was not only to the woman's health but also to her liberty.

Given all these restraints on expectant mothers, many had little choice but to rely on the seemingly kind women who wanted to care for the illegitimate child. Some midwives, such as Mary Ann Hall who was convicted of fraud, or Amelia Sach who was hanged for murder, may be able to suggest a person who would take the child for a small sum of money. Otherwise, the women needn't look far to find advertisements in newspapers purporting to be from childless couples or women looking to nurse babies.

> A MARRIED COUPLE, of good position, without children, living in a beautiful country house, wish to ADOPT an INFANT CHILD of good birth, or TAKE CHARGE of a WARD in CHANCERY. Well-appointed house; carriage and horses kept; liberal terms expected.—J. C. G., May's advertising office, 159, Piccadilly, London.
>
> WANTED, a Child, to nurse or adopt; premium required.—Address A. E., Western Mail Office, Swansea. 966i10
>
> A Married Couple are willing to ADOPT a CHILD as their own. No objection to sox. A premium required.—Address O P, 42, Chatsworth-street, Edge-hill. 24sc29
>
> ADOPTION.— A respectable couple, without children, wish to ADOPT ONE OUT of ARMS. A small premium required.—Address W. M., the post-office, Broadway, London-fields, Hackney, London.

Advertisments for baby farmers (Morning Post 6.11.1883, Western Mail 5.1.1881, Liverpool Mercury 25.8.1866, The Standard 19.11.1867).

These seemingly innocuous adverts tempted many women to pay a premium for their offspring to be adopted into caring, loving families, when, in fact, they were probably handing the baby over to a person only interested in keeping the premium, not the child.

One of the other changes that came about during the Victorian era that aided the baby farming industry was the growth of the railway system. Many baby farmers used the British railway system to travel around the country or to meet mothers who have travelled from other areas. Prior to the coming of the railway, this meeting of strangers in an anonymous place would have been much more difficult.

If we compare the development of the railway system from 1844 to 1911, we can see how much easier travel becomes between not just the cities but

4 Victorian and Early 20th Century Baby Farming

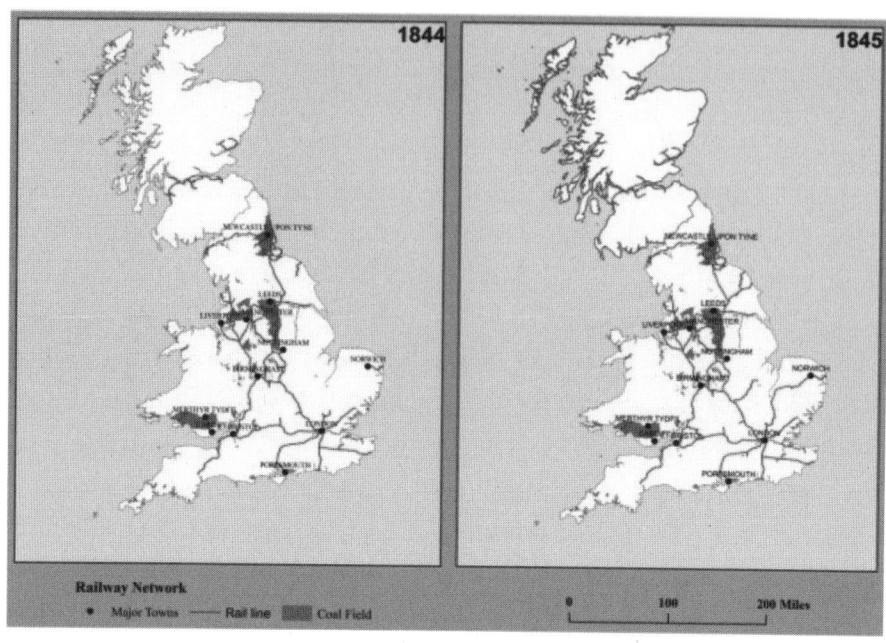

British Railway System 1844 and 1845. (*Dan Bogart, Leigh Shaw-Taylor and Xuesheng You, 'The development of the railway network in Britain 1825–1911', www.campop.geog.cam.ac.uk, 2018*)

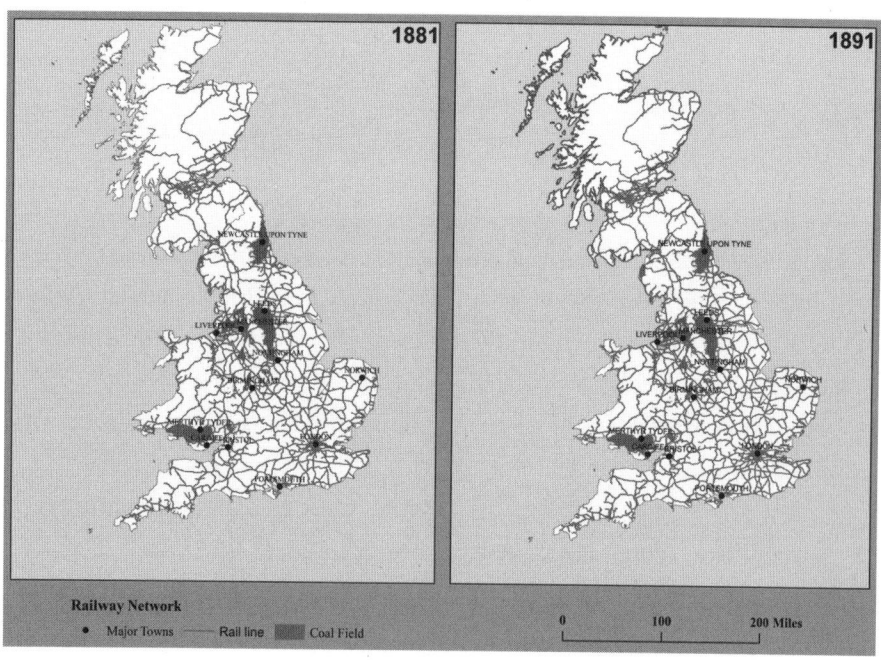

British railway system 1881 and 1891. (*Dan Bogart, Leigh Shaw-Taylor and Xuesheng You, 'The development of the railway network in Britain 1825–1911', www.campop.geog.cam.ac.uk, 2018*)

Reasons for the Rise of Baby Farms 5

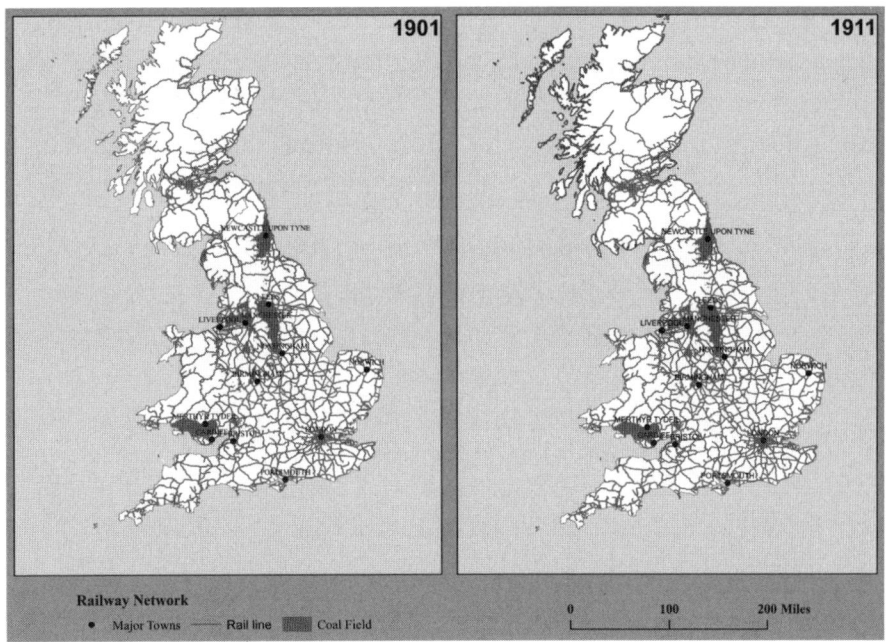

British railway system 1901 and 1911. (*Dan Bogart, Leigh Shaw-Taylor and Xuesheng You, 'The development of the railway network in Britain 1825–1911', www.campop.geog.cam.ac.uk, 2018*)

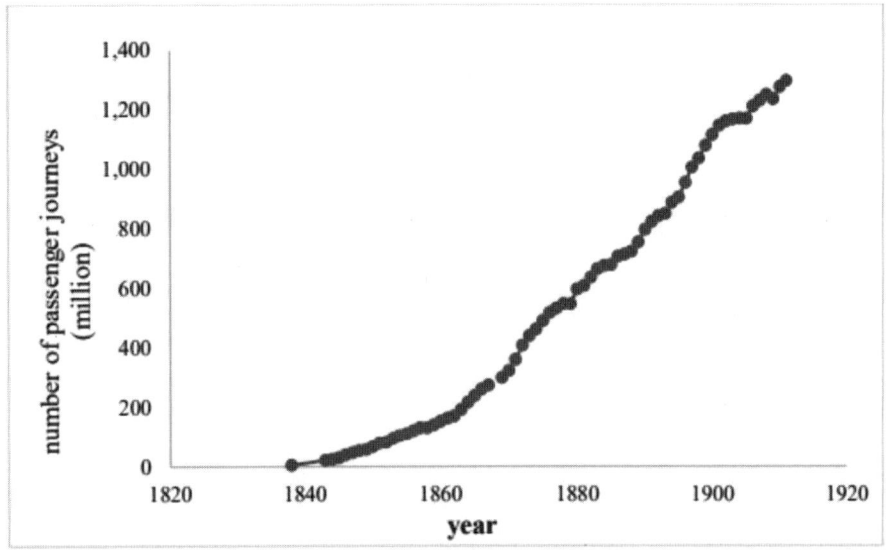

Number of passenger railway journeys 1838–1911. (*Dan Bogart, Leigh Shaw-Taylor and Xuesheng You, 'The development of the railway network in Britain 1825–1911', www.campop.geog.cam.ac.uk, 2018*)

also between more rural areas. This means that unmarried women who found themselves expecting a child could move to areas where they were unknown while awaiting the birth of the baby. Then they were able to use the railway to travel to yet another town to meet the woman who would take that child from them in an obvious meeting place at the station under a clock or in a waiting room.

Gladstone's Railway Act of 1844 allowed third-class travel at the cost of no more than one penny per mile and from the 1870s third-class accommodation became more comfortable, making the option more attractive to the working classes. In response to this, the number of railway passenger journeys increased considerably from 1838 to 1911.[6] The railways made travelling from one part of Britain to another quick and inexpensive, thus allowing the transfer of children to be far more anonymous than was previously possible.

If we look at known baby farmers, we find that many of them use the railways extensively.

1870 – In London, John Cowan's grandfather met Margaret Waters at Brixton Station and later the baby was handed to Waters at Walworth Road Railway Station. Waters' sister, Sarah Ellis, met Sergeant Relf at Camberwell New Road Station and this meeting led to the arrest of both women.[7]

1874 – Ann Kay received Herbert Cayshe from his mother at Birkenhead Station.[8]

1877 – Alice Rodenhurst handed over her daughter to John and Catherine Barnes at Hereford Railway Station. The Barneses were observed by police after arranging a meeting at the First-Class Room, Exchange Station, Liverpool.[9]

1888 – Jane Arnold lived in the railway town of Wolverton, Buckinghamshire. Her husband worked at the railway works.[10] Wolverton Station has a direct line Euston Station, London where Jane could have access to women in London to whom she passed children.

1890 – Ellen Barnard received baby Albert Weston from Sarah Baker at the waiting room of Victoria Station, London.[11]

From 1869 to 1896, Amelia Dyer, her daughter and son-in-law, the Palmers, are known to have connections to Bristol, Reading, Cardiff, Plymouth, Newton Abbot and possibly Newcastle-upon-Tyne and Stafford, and collected children from Cheltenham station, Gloucester, and Paddington Station.[12] In 1898, Polly and Arthur Palmer left a baby on a train at Newton Abbot.[13]

1897 – Ada Chard-Williams met the mother of Selina Jones at Woolwich Railway Station.[14]

1898 – Elizabeth Heley received Louise Steinhauer's daughter at the cloakroom of Liverpool Street Station, London.[15]

1902 – Although Annie Walters was known to travel by omnibus, she was apprehended outside South Kensington Underground Station.[16]

We can be sure that although not all baby farmers used the railways to collect and deliver babies, those mentioned above were only a few of those who did.

In addition to the known meeting places, we see from letters found in the homes of baby farmers that their clients came from towns far removed from their own. The railway system from Liverpool to Hull is shown in the case of John and Catherine Barnes, where communications were received from Wigan, Bradford, Leeds and Hull in addition to those down the western side of England from Hereford, Bristol and Bath.[17]

Today most of us hold insurance in one form or another: car, house, home contents, travel and life insurance policies are valued by most of us just in case the worst should happen, but there were occasions in the past when insurance benefits were seen as a way to financial reward and baby farmers were not adverse to taking advantage of this way to make easy money.

The Friendly Societies Act of 1793 allowed insurance to be regulated and the taking out of insurance by the working classes increased considerably. Lionel Rose states in *Massacre of the Innocents: Infanticide in Great Britain 1800–1939* that 'by 1858 there were over 20,000 *registered* societies in England and Wales with over 20,000 members'.[18]

Most societies offered more than just funeral benefits at a relatively high weekly fee; however, some offered just funeral benefits at a cheap subscription, maybe a penny or halfpenny a week, this was well within the reach of many poorer families. By 1854, commercial insurance companies had seized the opportunity to sell to the working classes these insurances designed to cover the cost of funerals.

In 1856, the Prudential started recruiting collectors who would visit clients on a weekly basis to collect the subscriptions, thus making payments simple for the client, and in 1860 the Prudential extended its portfolio to include infant life insurance. Friendly Societies had already been selling just such policies. All put conditions on the age children could start to be insured and required a certain amount to have been paid in prior to the child's death when a small payout could be expected. This was partly due to the high death rate amongst young children and partly to avoid accusations that these policies encouraged infanticide. These modest benefits were designed to help with funeral costs, not to completely cover the cost. However. beneficiaries were inclined to take out several policies covering a single child, thus allowing for a substantial profit to be made from the death of a child.

The Prudential led the field for infant life policies. According to Rose, by the end of the 1880s, £13,000,000 was the total value of child life insurance among commercial companies, of which £9,500,000 was held by the Prudential and £1,400,000 held by the Pearl Life Assurance Company. The Prudential refused to insure the lives of illegitimate children below the age of 3 years as they were considered to be a bad risk; nevertheless, due to the company's policy of paying commission to its collectors, many illegitimate children were insured. It was easy for baby farmers to insure children as their own by calling themselves 'parents' or 'guardians'. The Friendly Societies Act of 1875 and the Trade Union Amendment Act of 1876 brought all societies under the same rules regarding claims procedures and insurable limits, yet this still allowed 'parents or personal representatives' to be lawful claimants. In the case of George and Mary Hayes, who were convicted under contravention of the Infant Life Protection Act in 1888, the agent from the Victoria Legal Friendly Society insured all children in their care for a halfpenny a week, each using 'personal representatives' to allow them to qualify.[19]

The coroner for Surrey, Mr Athelston Braxton Hicks, took a keen interest in the deaths of children – this could be due to his father being the eminent obstetric physician, John Braxton Hicks – and wrote a detailed letter to *The Times* in February 1889 outlining amendments to the 1875 Act that would make it less advantageous for those who insure the lives of children to seek the early death of the insured.[20]

By the 1908 Children's Bill, it became punishable by a fine of £25, or six months in prison, to insure the life of a child under 7 years who was in the care of a paid minder. Not only could the minder be punished but so could the insurance officials involved should they be aware that the insurer was a paid minder.[21]

Baby farmers found to have insured their charges:

- Mark and Mary Jane James – Bournemouth – see Chapter 5.
- Holliday and Leonard – Bristol – see Chapter 9.
- William and Elizabeth Pearson – Stockport – see Chapter 9.
- Annie and Thomas Pavitt (an insurance agent) – Eastbourne – see Chapter 9.

All of these circumstances came together to make baby farming easier for those mothers who had few options when it came to the care of their children, and for the baby farmers who earnt a living caring for the same children. Although many baby farmers at best cut corners when it came to spending on the children, and at worst took steps to ensure the child had a short life, there were also a great number of women who did their best to care for the infants in their care, often bringing them up as loved family members, as the Carter family did with young Eva Muriel Grundy.

Chapter 2

Good Baby Farmers

Not all baby farmers were cruel to the children they cared for, many of them tried their best for children in their care.

Mrs Fletcher

In 1867, a case came before Marlborough Street court where a respectably dressed widow, Mrs Fletcher, from Normanton said she had started looking after a little boy about four years previously when she lived in Camden Town.

She had been visited by a lady and gentleman who said they were the unmarried parents of a 3-year-old boy and asked if she would look after the boy for a fee. This arrangement had continued with the mother paying the fee regularly, even after the widow had moved to Normanton, until about twelve months ago when she wrote to the father who lived in George St, Hanover Square but she received no answer. She then contacted a friend, Mr Jeffs, who visited the father, Mr Redpath, but was told the man did not know the boy until Mr Jeffs produced a photograph of the child, when Mr Redpath admitted the child looked like him. Shortly afterwards, Mrs Fletcher received a lawyer's letter accusing her of attempted extortion. She said she had simply told Mr Redpath that if she did not get money for the maintenance of the boy she would have to contact the magistrates; however, she had discovered that Mr Redpath had been married a year earlier, but not to the boy's mother.

She had actually approached the Mayor of Retford, who had advised her to go to London to place the case before a magistrate there. The magistrate said he didn't know what was to be done but that Mrs Fletcher should return to the court in a couple of days when something may have been decided.[1] At this point our information ends and we have no way of knowing what happened to either Mrs Fletcher or the baby.

Jane Clarke

Just months after the conviction of Margaret Waters in 1870, the Metropolitan Police received information about a baby farm at 44 Palmerston St, Battersea Fields being run by Mrs Clarke, a widow. Chief Inspector George Clarke reported to Superintendent Williamson that enquiries had been made and it was found that Mrs Clarke had five children in her care: Rosa Kettley, 10, Mercer Kettley, 7, and Frank Kettley, 3½, whose father was employed at Lloyd's newspaper office and paid 10 shillings a week for their keep; Fredrick Giles, 14 months, for whom she received 8 shillings a week from a gentleman signing himself K. L. M. from the Army and Navy Club; and Bertie Church, 6, who was supported by his grandfather, who worked at Chatham Dockyard; however, Mr Church had lost his employment and was now unable to pay for the boy. He had suggested the child be taken to the workhouse, but Mrs Clarke had become fond of young Bertie and had kept him in her care. All the children were well fed and decently clothed. Rosa said, when questioned, that she was kindly treated. Mrs Price, a neighbour, saw the children playing both in the street and in the garden and believed them to be properly cared for. The landlord, Mr Chaplin, lived opposite and had frequently seen the children and was of the opinion that they were well cared for by a respectable woman.

Mrs Clarke said she had been taking children in for the last eight years as a means of support and had only had one death, which had been two years previously.[2]

Sarah Murrant

In 1871, respectable-looking widow Sarah Murrant, of 6 Albert Buildings, Vauxhall, found herself charged with causing the death of 5-week-old William Beard after the sickly child died whilst in her care.

Surgeon Mr John Scott had refused to issue a death certificate for the child as he considered its death had been caused by the lack of food. Sergeant Mullard visited Mrs Murrant's home and asked about the death of the baby and he was shown the emaciated body of the boy in a coffin in the back room.

When giving evidence, Mr Scott stated that he knew the prisoner as she had brought other sickly children to him, two of which had later died.

The boy's mother, Emily Beard, had been staying at a home for fallen girls and had given birth to the illegitimate William at Queen Charlotte Lying-in Hospital, where the baby had been the smallest child to be born there. The superintendent of the home, Mrs Bagshaw, had prevailed on Mrs Murrant to take the tiny child despite Mrs Murrant's reluctance to do so as she already had one nurse child and didn't like to have two at the same time.

The judge, Mr Chance, commended Mrs Bagshaw for coming forward as he had considered it suspicious that three children had recently died whilst in Mrs Murrant's care. He then stated that it had been a very proper enquiry and discharged the prisoner.[3]

Charlotte Higgs

Charlotte Higgs of Byfield Road, Isleworth comes to our attention in October 1871 when a boy, 5-month-old John Finn, who had been in her care before going into the workhouse, died, and Dr McKinley refused to issue a death certificate due to a mark on the child's head. An inquest was conducted, and it was concluded that the cause of death was accidental, the mark having been caused by a fall. No one was blamed for this, and it was said that Mrs Higgs had treated the boy kindly. Mrs Higgs was the widow of market garden labourer George Higgs. They had lived in Walkers Cottages, Worton Lane, Isleworth for twenty-four years and for the last fourteen years, after George died, Charlotte had been taking in nurse children. She had adopted a 9-year-old girl, who had been one of her nurse children and, at the time of the inquest, had three others in her care, although two further children had been taken away by their parents after receiving an anonymous letter suggesting the children were being ill-used. Charlotte does not appear to follow the usual modus operandi of baby farmers in that she does not move house frequently, and, in the 1871 census, she states her occupation as 'Taking in nurse children'. Clearly Mrs Higgs is proud of her calling.[4]

Mrs Tarbeth

Was this a case of baby farming or not? That was what much of the discussion was about at the inquest called into the death of 1-year-old Ernest Atack.

Mrs Tarbeth was living in Malvern, Worcestershire when she replied to an advertisement in a London newspaper asking for a nurse for a young baby.

Ernest Atack was born in 1879 in Ramsgate, Kent where his unmarried mother had taken lodgings while awaiting the birth of her baby before returning to London.

Mrs Tarbeth received the baby when he was just a few weeks old, along with a substantial eighty pounds and some baby clothes. While in Malvern, Ernest was vaccinated and attended by a doctor for an unconnected illness. On hearing this, the jury said they thought no blame could be laid upon Mrs Tarbeth for the baby's death. The Tarbeths moved to Nottingham and Ernest's mother continued to correspond with them, sending more clothes and enquiring after his health, which was not always the best. However, on 4 August 1880, Ernest died unexpectedly. As a doctor had not seen the baby prior to his death, a post-mortem was called. Dr Brown Sim concluded that he died of a rupture to the stomach that had been full of gruel.

It appears that at an earlier hearing Mrs Tarbeth had been rather evasive in her answers, apparently in order to conceal the name of the boy's mother, which had led to the adjournment while the coroner tried to locate the mother. The jury criticised the coroner for not reading letters he had in his possession at the earlier hearing and one juror said he thought it gave the wrong impression of Mrs Tarbeth to refer to her as a baby farmer. The coroner, Mr M. Browne, stood by his words and stated that he believed this to be a baby farming case as the woman caring for the child was not its mother. In answer to a juror who said that the mother could not be in the wrong for getting another person to look after the baby if she was not in a position to do so herself, Mr Browne said that the mother should attend to it herself at any sacrifice. He also said that Mrs Tarbeth would gain from the baby's death as she would keep the money given to her for his keep. Clearly, he was annoyed that Mrs Tarbeth had given evasive answers. Mr Tarbeth asked that Mr Browne withdraw his assertion about baby farming as that involved caring for more than one child at a time but, again, Mr Browne refused. Mr Browne's mood was not improved when he heard that the child's mother had been in Nottingham just a few days earlier in order to bring more baby clothes as he would have liked to have spoken to her. The whole inquest appears to have turned into a bit of a bun fight and the proceedings were then terminated when the coroner asserted that no blame could fall on Mrs Tarbeth, but that she had been party to wrongdoing on the part of the mother.[5]

Mrs Iredale

Given the need for childcare in the nineteenth century, it is understandable that the business of baby farming flourished, but what did a baby farmer do if the payments dried up?

Clearly Mrs Iredale's client had no intention of paying for the baby girl put into her care. What was she to do?

Mrs Iredale of Cirons Road, Gospel Oak Fields, London, had been contacted by a gentleman who had replied to an advertisement for a nurse child that had been inserted by her friend and fellow baby farmer, Mrs Cale, saying his daughter had been widowed and wished to find a nurse for her child. The following day, a lady came with the baby girl and negotiated a fee of 10s. per week. The lady gave the name Mrs Morgan and an address in St John's Wood and said Mrs Iredale should call there for clothes for the child. However, when Mrs Iredale visited the address she had been given, she found neither the lady or gentleman were known at that address or anywhere nearby.

She then went to Mr Tisley, the relieving officer for the district, demanding that the child be entered into the workhouse. Mr Tisley refused and referred her to the relief committee, who in turn said she should go before the Board of Guardians of St Pancras. And so it was that Mrs Iredale found herself, accompanied by Mrs Cale and the unfortunate 2- or 3-month-old infant, standing in front of the Board in November 1870.

The Board were less than helpful and, after refusing to take the child, decided to take Mrs Iredale to the Police Magistrate. Mrs Iredale, being less than pleased by this turn of events, became abusive while pointing out that if she were put into prison, the Board would have to take the child into the workhouse. Both women then became so abusive they were forcibly removed.

Mrs Iredale then tried to leave the little girl in an anteroom and run from the building, but she was apprehended by the officers, taken back and forced to take the baby with her. However, her parting shot was that the Guardians should have the child somehow before the night was out.

There is no record of the fate of the child.[6]

Mrs Kirby

Mrs Kirby of Wandsworth Lodge, Tooting answered an advertisement in the *Daily Telegraph* in July 1870 signed H. R., The Post Office, Sloane St, Chelsea. Mrs Roberts then arrived, carrying a 4-month-old baby girl, at Mrs Kirby's home. Although the baby was only dressed in a nightgown and shirt and appeared to be undernourished, weighing only 8 lb, an arrangement was made that Mrs Kirby would be paid 5 shillings a week to nurse the child, and Mrs Roberts said she would return the following week with clothing, etc. However, that was the last Mrs Kirby saw of Mrs Roberts. As she had no allowance for the child, she took it to Wandsworth Workhouse, where it remained.[7]

Chapter 3

The Role of the Midwife

Midwifes and baby farmers were often inextricably linked. Many baby farmers also offered accouchement services and advertised as certified midwives, and it is easy to see that, in these days before efficient contraception, a midwife's role could slide into that of baby farmer, or, at least, the supplier of unwanted infants.

Certainly, some of the most notorious baby farmers, Amelia Dyer and Amelia Sach, were nurses. Mrs Dyer seems to have offered accouchement services and Mrs Sach advertised her house as a lying-in home with the services of a certified midwife.

However, other midwives were associated with baby farmers. During the late 1860s and 1870s, Mrs Castle, Mrs Hall and Mrs Martin came to the notice of the authorities.

Mrs Hall's story is related elsewhere as a case of fraud.

Mrs Castle's establishment in Camberwell was under surveillance for some time in relation to the investigation led by Sergeant Relf into the source of the babies' bodies being deposited around Brixton in 1870. Mrs Castle was the midwife who attended Robert Cowan's daughter, Jannette, when she gave birth to her son who became one of the child victims of Margaret Waters.[1] Suspicion into the goings-on in Mrs Castle's house and her involvement in illegal activities continued throughout the 1870s, with a series of letters sent to the police from the Rev. Richard Thorpe, of Christ Church, Camberwell, naming her as being involved with baby farming.[2] Her name was also mentioned by Sophia Todd when she was questioned after her conviction for murder, and this, along with other names mentioned, elicited the attention of the Home Secretary.[3] Nevertheless, no evidence was ever found against Maria Castle.

Mrs Louisa Martin caused outrage in the late 1860s. In 1869 she advertised her house at 33 Dean St., Soho, London as an accouchement home and herself as a certified midwife.[4] She had certainly been living at this address for some time as in 1861 as she is shown on the census along with her husband, Charles, daughter and son, in addition to two servants and four other females; two of whom are unmarried patients.[5]

During 1869, a series of anonymous letters, all in the same handwriting, containing much underlining and many apostrophes, were sent to *The Lancet*, *The Telegraph* and a Col. Henderson, which were forwarded to the police. All the letters claimed that Mrs Martin openly carried out abortions, or drowned live births, and said she had admitted to over 500 such offences over the course of a year. One of the letters stated that Mrs Martin had also taken a large house in Tulse Hill, where she intended to use in addition to the Dean St house.[6]

The Daily News reported that Mrs Martin told a prospective client that 'if you are confined here you will never see the child. I place them in the Foundling; but most likely it will die.' The article states that this was not intended to drive custom away but that women who had found themselves in this predicament wanted to be helped out of their unhappy situation.[7]

The police took this accusation seriously and set out to investigate, using two women to act as 'clients'. They found that Mrs Martin insisted that patients should come into the house for a fortnight and she charged between £20 and £50 depending on the circumstances of the woman. She did offer one of the women a dose of medicine once payment was made but refused to allow the drug to be removed from the house.

Claims were made that so much money was being made by Mrs Martin that, although her estranged husband was only a painter and decorator, she was using a Brougham carriage driven by a 'flunky' called George.

The police were fairly certain that illegal activities were taking place in the Soho house but getting proof was virtually impossible. No one else would be present when the offence was committed and neither party would wish to give evidence as both the abortionist and the patient could be prosecuted.

In light of the press attention, customers were shy of attending Dean St, so Mrs Martin took the Railway Hotel, Woking where she intended to continue her trade using Dean St for introductions only. However, in December 1869, she died suddenly at Woking of apoplexy.[8]

One would expect the case would now be closed except a year later a letter signed Sarah Tilson was received. In this the writer suggested there was a link between the Dean St address, now lived in by Mrs Martin's widower and her son, and the baby farming cases that were being unearthed in London at the time. After investigation, it was decided that there was no foundation to this as the lower part of the house was now operating as a ham and beef shop.[9]

As an interesting aside, Joseph Rogers, a surgeon who improved conditions in workhouse infirmaries, particularly for women who had just given birth, also lived at 33 Dean St at the same time, and there is now a blue plaque attached to the house in his honour.[10]

As can be seen, midwives running accouchement establishments seemed to be walking a careful line between the caring profession of midwife and the hated baby farmers, however financially beneficial the trade might be.

Webs of Baby Farmers

It is impossible to be completely sure of how many links were forged between baby farmers; however, some names crop up in relation to the stories of others. Rarely would a baby farmer work without coming across another working in the same field.

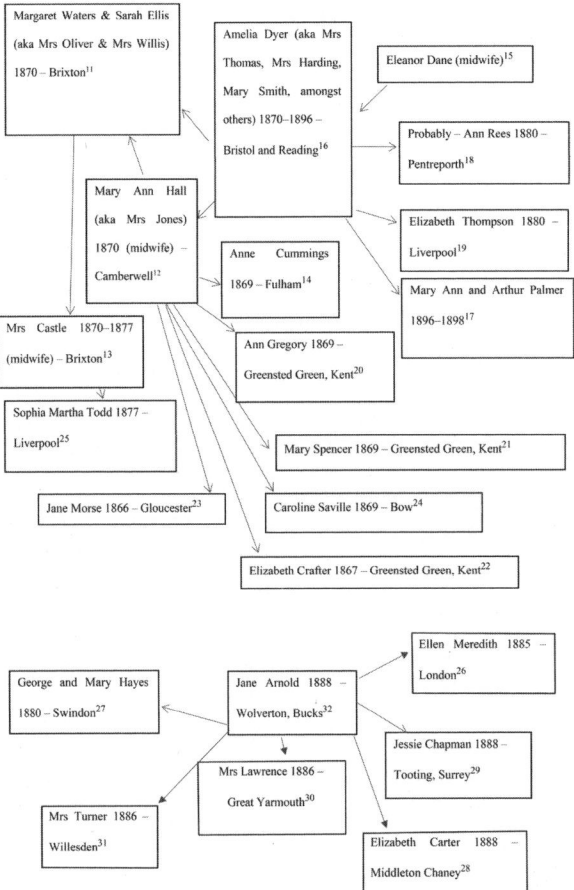

Chapter 4

The Role of the Coroner

The 1836 Birth and Death Registration Act allowed for registrars to refer doubtful cases to the coroner and in the 1874 Act registrars were obliged to refer all deaths that were due to violence or had suspicious circumstances to the coroner, whether or not a medical certificate was present.[1]

The area in which a coroner had jurisdiction varied in size, population and number of inquests held. This may account for why some areas appear not to have had any cases of baby farming appearing while other areas had many cases.

The 1887 Coroner's Act required coroners to conduct inquests in all cases where the cause of death stated was 'unknown' or a sudden death that was not accompanied by a certificate.[2]

Until the late nineteenth century, coroners' inquests were often held in a local public house or prison. As the century progressed, and in order to easily facilitate the implementation of the Coroner's Act, purpose-built coroners' courts were built, particularly in larger towns or cities, although in smaller towns, town halls, police stations or other dignified locations were used for the task. These newly built courts were often located close to a mortuary, or with a mortuary built behind the court itself, as it was mandatory to view the body prior to the start of the inquest.

Coroners were either of a medical or legal background and had the task of summoning the jury of twelve men chosen from the parliamentary voting lists, witnesses and a doctor to perform post-mortem examinations.[3]

Results of Coroner's Inquests into the Deaths of Children in Baby Farms

September 1867 – Tottenham, London – Coroner: Mr John Humphries – Baby Farmer: Caroline Jagger, 41 – Child's Name: Mary Stevens – Mother's Name: Unknown
A girl named Mary Stevens, aged about 3 or 4 months, was taken to be cared for by Mrs Caroline Jagger of Tottenham by Mrs Stevens. The name

of the mother of baby Mary was never revealed in court; it was said if it were, the woman would commit suicide. Mrs Jagger was to be paid 6s a week to look after the child. The money was paid to her via a solicitor, Mr Raines. Mary had lived with Mrs Jagger for about one year and three months. After suckling the child for two months, Mrs Jagger had fed her on bread, milk, raw eggs and port wine, which the child had eaten ravenously. The little girl was often sick but had not had any medicine.

One witness, Mr Raines, the solicitor's clerk, knew of Mrs Jagger through her advertisements in newspapers.

The coroner stated that he had presided over the inquests of two other children who had been cared for by Mrs Jagger.

The post-mortem discovered Mary's body to be emaciated with no fat on it and, although the stomach was healthy, it was nearly empty. There was disease of the mesenteric glands. It was stated that the child must have been badly fed. The doctor, Mr F. W. Watson, had attended two other children at Mrs Jagger's house the day before the girl died but had not been asked to look at Mary.

When questioned, Mrs Jagger was asked why she had taken the girl to the German Hospital and it was pointed out that the local doctor, Dr Niblett, had told her: 'I have had enough of you; go to someone else.' She also admitted that she advertised for children to be put in her care and agreed that she might have had forty children in her care over the last three years. She said she had received the child at 'Mr Chilton's, my bakers, at Hornsey'. In a letter to *The Standard* on 27 September 1867, Mr Chilton denied this and said he never knew Mrs Jagger.[4]

> **BABY FARMING.**
>
> **TO THE EDITOR.**
>
> SIR,—In your report of this case it is stated that Mrs. Jagger, in reply to a question from the coroner, said, "I received the child at Mr. Chilton's, my baker's, at Hornsey." That is entirely false. I do not even know such a person as Mrs. Jagger, and I am not aware that she ever entered my shop.
>
> As such a statement is likely to do me serious injury in my business, I must ask the favour of an insertion of this denial.—I remain, Sir, yours, respectfully,
>
> F. CHILTON, Baker.
>
> Hornsey.

Letter denying knowledge of Mrs Jagger. (The Standard, *27 September 1867*)

The jury decided the girl had died from 'disease of the glands' but censured Mrs Jagger for not calling a medical man and for her behaviour in court (she had screamed and frequently burst into tears during the proceedings).[5]

Despite Caroline Jagger not being tried for any crime, her name continued to be mentioned for many years as the epitome of a cruel, heartless baby farmer.

December 1867 – Bethnal Green – Coroner: Mr Richards – Baby Farmer: Mr and Mrs William Cooper – Child's Name: Unknown – Mother's Name: Unknown
This is a strange case. Dr John Chambers was called to the house of brush maker's carman, William James Cooper, at 10 Nelson Street, Bethnal Green, to see Mrs Cooper who was suffering from the effects of premature labour. As he was leaving, Mr Cooper mentioned to him that his child was dead. The doctor was surprised as he had been told that the Coopers had not had any children, but he followed Mr Cooper into another room where there was the body of a beautiful boy of about 2 years old. Indications suggested that the boy had died of suffocation. Mr Cooper said the child had been found dead that morning. Neither of the Coopers knew who the mother of the child was. It transpired that they had advertised in the *Clerkenwell News* in March for a child to adopt using their own name and address. After an exchange of letters signed J. C. L., an agreement was made that the 14-month-old boy should be given to them along with £10 and some clothes. The boy was delivered to them by a woman in her early 20s who said the child was her illegitimate child, he had no name and had not been baptised. He had been kept secret from friends but she intended to marry the father and emigrate to Australia. She asked if she could visit the boy once prior to her leaving and this was agreed; however, she had not been in contact with the Coopers since. Subsequent enquiries discovered that the child had been with a nurse in Islington from a few weeks old until now. Although the Coopers lived in a poor neighbourhood, the clothes brought with the child had been of the highest quality with unusually rich embroidery.

Coroner Mr Richards pointed out that the newspaper mentioned carried several advertisements for adoptions and that once the premium had been paid, the adoptive parents could register the child in their own name. He reminded the court that a fine of £50 was payable for misrepresentations to the registrar but that it was in all parties' interests in these cases to keep the transaction a secret, so the penalty was rarely enforced. He carried on to suggest that a registration was needed of all persons taking children to nurse or to adopt, and of the children themselves.[6]

December 1867 – Newbury, Berks – Coroner: Mr Joseph Bunny – Baby Farmer: Mrs Hamblin – Child's Name: Unknown – Mother's Name: Sarah Ann Fryers
Sarah Ann Fryers gave birth to illegitimate child which she left in the care of Mrs Box of Speen near Newbury. She now lived with friends in Gloucestershire. Some months later Mrs Box, who now had three nurse children, received the permission of Miss Fryers to relocate the baby to Mrs Hamblin of Newbury. During the past year, Mrs Hamblin had received four children, of which three had died.

Mrs Hamblin's daughter said the child (now 7 months old) was fed five times a day with arrowroot and oatmeal.

The coroner stated that it was improper that children should be left in an area when their mothers departed and become a drain on the local ratepayers. He criticised mothers who left an area and had no contact with their children. He continued, saying that the system of caring for children in this manner was a vicious one and the mortality of children in the care of Mrs Hamblin was very great.

The jury decided the child had died during convulsions due to teething but commented that the food given to the child was improper.

There appears to have been no censure of Mrs Hamblin.[7]

December 1867 – St Luke's, London – Coroner: Mr J. Humphreys – Baby Farmer: Matilda Thorne – Child's Name: Alfred Johnson – Mother's Name: Mary Ann Johnson
This case shows just how hard life was for young mothers at this time. Wages were low and trying to make ends meet was extremely difficult.

Widow Matilda Thorne of Regent St, St Luke's, London needed to make money in order to pay her rent of 3 shillings and sixpence a week and feed and clothe both herself and her son. The solution to this problem was to take in children to nurse on a weekly basis, usually for 5 shillings a week. She advertised in *Clerkenwell News* to find children to nurse and generally took no more than three children.

We come across Mrs Thorne when a child in her care died suddenly.

Mary Anne Johnson was a paper bag maker and, in 1867, had an illegitimate son, Alfred, by a soldier who was stationed in Ireland. While she kept 4-month-old Alfred with her, she could earn 7 shillings a week. Her rent was 2 shillings and threepence a week and she required 4 shillings and ninepence a week to support herself, let alone the child. If she put Alfred to a nurse, she could earn 12 shillings a week if she worked until ten or twelve at night. As a consequence, she answered Mrs Thorne's advertisement and handed Alfred over, while still visiting the little boy twice a week. Even after paying Mrs Thorne 5 shillings a week to look after Alfred, she only just had enough left to live on.

Mrs Thorne was also living on the breadline; she had three nurse children, earning herself 16 shillings a week to pay for her own rent and the keep of herself, three nurse children and her own son. The foreman of the coroner's jury stated that someone must suffer as the pittance she received was not enough to support so many.

During the Christmas night, Mrs Thorne was woken by a child crying and she found Alfred to be in a poor way. She held him in her arms until six in the morning when she went to his mother's home, but she found no one in as Miss Johnson had been working all night. She had hoped Miss Johnson would be able to contact the doctor who had previously given the child medicine, but, by this time, the child had died, and Dr Steadman was sent for.

Dr Steadman stated that no marks of violence could be seen on the child, but it was in an emaciated condition, and had died of congestion to the lungs. He said he had been called to Mrs Thorne's home on numerous occasions to see children in her care and he thought she looked after them as well as she could; however, she had a lot of children in her care.

The jury decided that Alfred had died from congestion of the lungs, want of nourishment and lack of care due to the number of children Mrs Thorne was caring for. They also stated the opinion that something should be done about baby farming and requested that the coroner should write to the Home Secretary outlining this case.[8]

April 1869 – Bow – Coroner: Mr Richards – Baby Farmer: Mrs Caroline Savill – Child's Name: Frederick Wood – Mother's Name: Miss Ann Wood
The sickly Frederick Wood, aged 1 year 5 months, was taken by his 23-year-old mother, Ann Wood, to Mrs Savill ten months before his death. She paid 4 shillings and sixpence a week for his keep. Miss Wood was satisfied with the care given to her son, although she had not been to see him for five weeks. Mrs Savill had eleven babies at the home in Swayton Road, Bow, she shared with her porter husband. Of the eleven, five had died and the people of the locality were taking a great interest in the case.

Asked if she ran a baby farm, Mrs Savill said, 'I leave that to the generosity of the jury.'

Young Frederick was put to bed in an egg box with straw for a mattress by Mrs Savill at 9 o'clock at night and when she went to him at 8.30 the following morning, he was dead. A juror stated that the egg box was a short one and only 16 inches wide and the child had been unable to turn in it, but Mrs Savill said the end had been cut out and the child slept with his knees tucked up. It was also stated that Mrs Savill never tied the child's legs together.

The previous October she had been taking him up to bed when the boots she was wearing made her slip and she fell onto the child, breaking his thigh. Although he had cried, she had not noticed the damage until the following morning when she called the doctor.

Dr Atkins said the child had a malformed chest and had much congestion of the lungs. He had died from an effusion of serum on the brain produced by natural causes and not by neglect or accelerated by the damage to the thigh.

The jury consulted for a long time before returning the verdict of 'death by natural causes' but they had wanted the coroner to add a censure, which he refused to do.[9]

Later in 1869, James Greenwood wrote his *Seven Curses of London*, in which he attacks the business of baby farming and Caroline Savill in particular and cites the plight of little Frederick Wood as an opportunity for legislation to be brought in to protect such children.[10]

It is interesting to note that a Caroline Savill gives evidence at the trial of Mary Ann Hall.

May 1869 – Limehouse, London – Coroner: Mr Richards – Baby Farmer: Mrs Amy Gathard – Child's Name: Unknown – Mother's Name: Unknown
Mrs Gathard of 3 Kirk's Place, Limehouse placed an advertisement for a child. The following day she agreed to nurse a child from a respectable-looking woman. She agreed a payment of 7 shillings a week after refusing to adopt the day-old baby. The woman paid 14 shillings and arranged to return or write the following week. Mrs Gathard never heard from her again. Some days later, the child became ill and Dr Forster was called. The baby died from inflammation of the lungs from natural causes. The only clue to the family of the dead baby was a white handkerchief with 'M Watters, 2, 66' written on it. The coroner referred the matter to the police who, should they find the mother of the child, would prosecute for abandonment.[11]

August 1869 – Bethnal Green, London – Coroner: Mr Richards – Baby Farmer: Mrs Sarah/Susannah Smith – Child's Name: Arthur Fuller Gibson – Mother's Name: Mrs Louisa Gilroy
Mrs Gilroy had been married to comedian Fras Gilroy. When Fras died at the end of December 1868, his widow was left with three children to support and, as he had not been a member of the Royal Dramatic College, she had been compelled to work as a forewoman in a shop in order to support her family. However, six months later she gave birth to Arthur and paid Mrs Sarah Smith 4 shillings a week to look after him (Mrs Smith had wanted 7 shillings a week) as she needed to continue working or her other children would have starved. Mrs Smith lived with her husband at Miss Burdett Coutts Model Lodging House in Colombia Square.

Mrs Smith started breastfeeding Arthur but after two weeks found she was unable to feed him and her own child, Graham Ebeneezer, so she continued to breastfeed her own child but fed Arthur milk and cornflour. At the time of his death, Arthur was 7 weeks old and Graham 10 months old. Graham was so well fed, and Mrs Smith was so proud of him, that she entered him for the Great Baby Show at North Woolwich Gardens. While she was at the baby show for four days, she had left Arthur with another woman.

Mrs Gilroy had visited Arthur twice a week and said he had always been nothing but skin and bone.

When Mrs Smith took the stand, she was recognised as the person who had taken another baby to care for who had died within five weeks. She stated she had never advertised in a newspaper for babies to look after.

Mr H. B. Lillie MRCS stated that Arthur weighed just 4½ lb when he died and there was little fluid in his stomach. He said the baby had died from exhaustion and diarrhoea and was a pitiable object before death.

The jury returned the verdict that the cause of death was the effects of exhaustion and, after some very strong remarks from the jury, it was decided that Mrs Smith had not done anything that was contrary to the present law on baby farming, and she should not be censured.[12]

November 1869 – Haggerstone, London – Coroner: Mr Humphries – Baby Farmer: Mrs Corbett – Child's Name: Unknown – Mother's Name: Louisa Fincham
A woman who called herself Mrs Leslie went to Mrs Walker's house at 16 King Street, Haggerstone where she gave birth to a little girl. When the child was 2 weeks old, Mrs Leslie left to go to Sussex and left the child in the care of Mrs Corbett. While she was away, the baby died and Dr Simpson was called. When he arrived, the baby was cold. A post-mortem showed the cause of death to be an effusion of serum to the ventricles of the brain that was brought on by exhaustion produced by want of food. The mother of the baby was called as a witness and she stated that she was unmarried, and her name was not Mrs Leslie but Louisa Fincham. The jury's verdict was that the child died from exhaustion brought on by lack of food. It is not recorded that any further action was taken against Mrs Corbett.[13]

April 1871 – Clerkenwell, London – Coroner: Dr Hardwicke – Baby Farmer: Elizabeth Russell – Child's Name: Unknown – Mother's Name: Jane Mansfield
Eccentric, slight officer's daughter Miss Elizabeth Russell formally kept a school but, due to bad luck, she now took in children to nurse. She had been doing this for ten years, having up to ten children, when the baby boy died whilst in her care. Miss Russell refused to admit she was a baby farmer and stated that she did not live in an underground kitchen but now lodged in a room at 4 Little Bath Street, Clerkenwell that once had curtains and a pianoforte, but those days were long gone; now she didn't even possess a bed but slept on two chairs pushed together.

She advertised for a nurse child and had hoped to get more than the 2 shillings she received from 19-year-old Miss Jane Mansfield as she had emphasised what respectable hands were nursing the baby; however, she never saw the child's mother again. She had heard that Miss Mansfield had been admitted to Westminster Hospital with smallpox.

When the baby developed a rash, she gave him some medicine and powder and asked for an order to see the parish doctor, Dr Edwin Dyer. When Dr Dyer attended the child, he found the child dead in a small, dirty, foul-smelling room. During the post-mortem examination he noted the child was small, emaciated, exossated (deprived of bones), filthy dirty and marked with smallpox. The child had not been vaccinated. The cause of death was exhaustion due to lack of nourishment and smallpox.

When Miss Russell was asked if she had ever washed the child, she said, 'How dare you talk so? You make me feel quite ill. I must have a cup of tea after this.' This comment was met with laughter from the court.

Mrs Catherine Mary Tulletti, Miss Russell's landlady, stated that Miss Russell received 1 shilling and sixpence and a loaf of bread each week from the parish. She thought neighbours had washed the baby but could not be sure.

The jury decided the child had died from smallpox, accelerated by the want of proper nourishment.

It was asked if steps had been taken to disinfect the house as it may cause spread the disease all over London. He was assured by Dr Dyer that the officer of health's attention had been drawn to the house.[14]

April 1871 – Oakhill, Somerset – Coroner: Mr Garland – Baby Farmer: Louisa Wotton – Child's Name: Jessie Clifford – Mother's Name: Jessie Clifford Cartner
Louisa Wotton was a woman who was used by the local Board of Guardians to care for children from the workhouse. In January 1871, she was approached by a medical man, Robert Augustus Major, who, although he was not a qualified surgeon, practised in the neighbourhood, to take a newborn baby girl to nurse. Mrs Wotton agreed to do this for a charge of 2 shillings and sixpence a week. Jessie Clifford was brought to Mrs Wotton late at night by Mr Major along with a bundle of clothes and eleven weeks' payment. Mr Major said the child's mother was called Eliza Clifford and came from Bristol.

When some weeks later the baby became unwell, Mrs Wotton called Mr Major, who gave her some medicine, but the child continued to decline and Mrs Wotton, fearing the child would die, called the qualified surgeon Mr Thomas Stephen Baker, as he would be able to supply a death certificate. Mr Baker gave the infant calomel and magnesia, but baby Jessie died two days later. Mr Major then supplied a coffin for the infant to be buried in.

The matter would have stopped there but local gossip about the way the child had been delivered to Mrs Wotton came to the ears of the police, who ordered a post-mortem and inquest. Mr Baker carried out the examination and found no signs of violence and decided that the child had died for the lack of natural feeding.

During the inquest, Mr Major was asked for the identity of the mother but he refused to divulge the information and was imprisoned for a week for contempt of court. However, he was released later that same night as a woman had visited the coroner and made herself known to him as the child's mother.

When the inquest was reconvened, the disclosure of the mother's name caused a sensation in the court.

When summing up, Mr Garland, the coroner, addressed an objection that had been brought by the solicitor working for Mr Major and Mrs Wotton, saying that the inquest was legal, and that the solicitor had tried to confuse the jury into thinking the inquest should not have been asked for. He said that he knew why the inquest had been convened and that Mrs Wotton should have realised that baby had not been brought from Bristol as it was only about an hour old when it arrived at her house and must, therefore, have been born locally. He doubted the 2 shillings and sixpence allowed for the child's maintenance was sufficient but had no reason to believe the baby had not been well cared for.

The jury returned a verdict of death by natural causes but questioned the wisdom of Mr Baker when giving calomel to such a young baby.

Throughout the neighbourhood, Mr Baker was the subject of a great deal of ill feeling and Mr Major was considered to have been unjustly treated by the court.[15]

Interestingly if we look at the 1871 census, we can find Mr Major lodging with the widow of his former teacher – Susan J. Cartner! Perhaps this explains a lot about the furore caused locally by this case.[16]

December 1871 – Liverpool – Coroner: Mr Clarke Aspinall – Baby Farmer: Ann Kimberton and Ellen Cunningham – Child's Name: John Henry Thompson – Mother's Name: Hannah Thompson

Hannah Thompson had nursed her illegitimate son for ten months when she decided to put him out to nurse with Ann Kimberton for a payment of 2 shillings and sixpence a week. When she went to visit him, she thought he had been neglected and, although she had provided him with two sets of clothes, he had been wrapped in a piece of flannel while Mrs Kimberton, the worse for drink, was washing one set of his clothes, having pawned the others. Mrs Kimberton stated the boy had been in a declining state when she received him and a doctor had advised her to feed him milk and cornflour, but she had fed the infant on a penny-halfpence worth of milk a day, although a witness stated that she had been feeding him on flour and water. Hannah removed him and placed him with Mrs Cunningham, who had care of him for six weeks until his death, with the instruction to spare no expense. The week before his demise, he was taken to Dr Butters, who observed the boy to be emaciated and thought he had been unwell for a long time. He stated the baby had died from atrophy and debility from lack of proper food and care.

The jury upheld the cause of death noted by Dr Butters and stated that this had started whilst he was in Mrs Kimberton's care. They also took the opportunity to comment on the ills of the baby farming system but appreciated that this was brought about by the proliferation of illegitimate births.[17]

December 1871 – Newport, South Wales – Coroner: Mr W. H. Brewer – Baby Farmer: Mrs Hannah Price – Child's Name: Unknown – Mother's Name: Unknown

Midwife Mrs Price arrived at the house of Mrs Pritchard on Tuesday night with a baby boy. Mrs Price said an unknown well-dressed woman had arrived on her doorstep in labour and she needed to find a nurse for the baby for a fortnight. Mrs Pritchard and her lodger Mrs Mary Ann Edmunds agreed to care for the child for 4 shillings a week. The baby was fed cornflour, flour, milk and brandy. After two days, the baby died despite being kept warm and washed. After the mother had been with Mrs Price for a week, she left, having paid for her confinement and 8 shillings for the care of the boy. Mrs Price had supposed that when the money ran out, the child would have been given to the Union Workhouse.

The post-mortem showed the infant to have food in his stomach, but his lungs were congested. The doctor, Dr Benjamin Davies, said that had the mother suckled the baby, it might have lived. The jury decided that the child had died of natural causes but strongly condemned Mrs Price for keeping the name of the mother secret.

Mr Brewer, coroner, stated that Mrs Price should organise the infant's burial. Mrs Price initially refused to do this, saying that it was the responsibility of the parish, but Mr Brewer said that the parish should not bear the cost and Mrs Price reluctantly agreed to pay for the burial.[18]

November 1873 – Loose, Kent – Coroner: J. N. Dudlow Esq. – Baby Farmer: Mrs Spurgeon – Child's Name: Maud Thompson – Mother's Name: Elizabeth Thompson

Mrs Spurgeon, living in the pretty village of Loose, near Maidstone, already had several children in her charge, three of whom had already died, when she advertised in the *Christian World*. The advertisement was seen by a married woman, Mrs Thompson, whose husband had recently deserted her, and she entrusted Mrs Spurgeon with the care of her fat, healthy young daughter for a payment of 4 shillings and sixpence per week, payable monthly. Just seven weeks later, 3-month-old Maud was dead. Mrs Spurgeon asked Dr Owen of Coxheath to certify the child's death but, being unconvinced by her story, he refused and instead carried out a post-mortem. He found the body to be very much emaciated, but he could not be sure of the cause of death.

The jury returned the verdict of 'death from natural causes' but stated that houses of this type should be under police surveillance. Mrs Spurgeon was cautioned as to her future conduct.[19]

July? 1874 – Tilston, Cheshire – Coroner: Mr H. Churton – Baby Farmer: Mrs Bithell – Child's Name: Unknown – Mother's Name: Martha Jones

Widow Mrs Bithell of Tilston near Malpas, Cheshire, was in the habit of looking after illegitimate babies when she received into her care the illegitimate daughter of Martha Jones. When the baby died, after wasting away over several weeks, she was unable to get Dr Proudlove, the district registrar, to sign the burial certificate as no doctor had seen the child for several weeks. Mrs Bithell then went to the registrar and said the child had died in a fit of convulsions and a certificate was provided. The child was buried four days after it had died. However, rumours abounded as to the cause of the baby's death and these came to the ears of the rector of Tilston, Rev. A. Wright, who was so concerned that a certificate had been provided without a doctor seeing the child that he asked the constable to contact the coroner. Mr H. Churton, the coroner, ordered an exhumation and the post-mortem, carried out by surgeon Mr Parker, could find no reason why the child should have died from natural causes. He believed the baby girl had died after being fed improper food that had caused irritation of the bowels and diarrhoea and that this had continued for some time, leading to the child becoming a mere skeleton.

The coroner stated in his summing up that registrars should not give certificates to illegitimate children when a doctor has not been present as this could lead to cases of infanticide taking place.

The jury decided the baby had died from the effects of an improper diet and they censured the registrar.

It appears that no action was taken against Mrs Bithell, although it was noted in the *Cheshire Observer* that three weeks earlier another emaciated baby had died at Mrs Bithell's home.[20]

May 1875 – Wavertree – Coroner: Mr Driffield – Baby Farmer: Ann Kay – Child's Name: Herbert Cayshe – Mother's Name: Ellen Cayshe
In the summer of 1874, Ellen Cayshe placed an advertisement in the *Liverpool Mercury* for someone to nurse her month-old son, Herbert. Ann Kay, wife of a journeyman stonemason, answered this advert and, after an exchange of letters, Mrs Kay agreed to nurse him for 16 shillings a month, although she later stated she had been paid £1 per month. She took charge of young Herbert at Birkenhead Station at the beginning of August 1874 and for a while the mother had visited once a month, but these visits had ceased just before Christmas when the mother had 'gone away'.

The child appears to have been of a sickly nature, for soon after going into Mrs Kay's care she was obliged to visit Dr Harvey with him. The child was only half conscious and Dr Harvey told Mrs Kay to take the child home and give him brandy, water and milk. Mrs Kay telegraphed the boy's mother, who arrived the following day from Wrexham. Dr Harvey saw Herbert on 4 and 5 January 1875 with an abscess on his neck. Dr Harvey gave her a prescription that she took to the chemist, Mr Fingland, but she failed to collect the medicine because the abscess had then burst. When another abscess appeared, Mrs Kay treated this herself.

Sometime later, the child became ill again and died the following day. When Mrs Kay went to Dr Harvey for a death certificate, he stated that he hadn't seen the child recently and sent her to the registrar, Mr Morgan. Mr Morgan said it was difficult to register the death without a certificate, but he began to fill in the book and asked her to sign. Being confused, she signed as 'Ann Cayshe' and, while not saying the child was hers, she failed to mention it was a nurse child.

Dr Harvey did carry out a post-mortem and found no signs of violence, but Herbert weighed only 6½ lbs. The only trace of food was in the lower bowel. There was no sign of disease in any of the organs except the lungs, which showed sign of pneumonia of no more than nine days standing. The cause of death must have been the pneumonia, but this could have been caused by the child's weakly state, which was caused by insufficient food.

A police sergeant, Igoe, stated that the house was in a filthy state and that ducks were kept in one room. There was little furniture and, in the bedrooms, only dirty mattresses and no bed coverings, just old sacks and rags.

The foreman of the jury, Mr Fingland, the chemist, said he thought this was a case of gross neglect. The coroner concurred with the foreman and stated that Mrs Kay should have called in medical assistance but said in her favour that she had provided medicine from her own pocket, even if this had been injudicious. He also said that it gave the case 'a very ugly appearance' that she had misrepresented herself to the registrar and that this might be dealt with elsewhere.

The jury returned the verdict that Herbert had died as a result of pneumonia brought on by lack of proper and nutritious food.

Interestingly there was another ailing nurse child found in Mrs Kay's establishment.[21]

June 1876 – Chew Magna, Somerset – Coroner: Unknown – Baby Farmer: Mrs Hinam – Child's Name: Clara Ada Knight Thomson – Mother's Name: Unknown
Mrs Hinam ran a house registered to nurse babies in Chew Magna, Somerset. On 27 May 1876, she noticed an advertisement placed by a woman wishing to have her month-old daughter nursed. After being in Mrs Hinam's care

for three weeks, the child died in an emaciated condition. The inquest was adjourned to allow time for the mother to be found. It was said she had corresponded from Weston-super-Mare and the child had been sent from Taunton. No more information is available about this case.[22]

September 1877 – Ladywell, Lewishan, London – Coroner: Unknown – Baby Farmer: Mrs Burroughs – Child's Name: Unknown – Mother's Name: Unknown
In September 1877, an inquest was held on the bodies of several illegitimate children that died shortly after being taken from the house of an unregistered baby farm run by Mrs Burroughs. The jury found the deaths were caused by inanition (starvation) but, remarkably, no one could be held responsible for the deaths, although they were far from thinking that those involved with the children were innocent.

This discovery follows finding many infant bodies in the area of Lewisham, Blackheath, Peckham, Brixton and Camberwell. Many of these had appeared to have died from starvation but some had marks of violence.[23]

June 1880 – Pentreporth – Coroner: W. H. Brewer – Baby Farmer: Ann Rees – Child's Name: Linda May – Mother's Name: Mary May (Naye)
Ann Rees advertised in the *Christian World* for a nurse child. She had a reply and travelled to Reading to collect baby Linda May. Linda died on 31 May, nine weeks after the baby came into her care, and at the first inquest Ann Rees gave evidence that was contradicted by her husband. At the second inquest, held after the post-mortem examination, Mrs Rees changed her story. She had received £13 to look after the 10-day-old baby but she had been told she would get £20, although this had not been forthcoming. She did not know the mother of the child and, should the infant not survive, she was to advertise her demise in the *Christian World*.

Next-door neighbour Ann Thomas said she had looked after the baby once and had thought the child had not looked healthy. She stated that Mrs Rees had not kept the baby as clean as she should have, and the infant had frequently been looked after by a 9-year-old girl.

Surgeon Dr Robert Cooke said the child was 'an exceedingly scrofulous child' who had had congestion of the bowels and had died of starvation but had been fed. He said the baby had a disease that would mean the child would always be hungry and would not thrive, but the neglect would have accelerated her death.

Police Inspector Sheppard had found a letter in the house of Mrs Rees that was sent from 153 Sussex Place, Kings Road, Reading by a Mrs E. Griffiths who advertised in the name of E. Jones. He had written to the police at Reading who had discovered the name of the child's mother was Mrs Naye, not May, from Yew Tree Farm, Westerham, Kent whose husband was in a lunatic asylum, and she had now gone to Antwerp.[24]

The jury decided Linda May had died from consumption of the bowels but thought Ann Rees should be prosecuted for perjury.

It is interesting to note that in his evidence at the first inquest, Mrs Rees's husband, Alfred, mentions the author of the letter from Reading had moved to London and that Mrs Rees had mentioned meeting the child's mother in Bristol in the middle of May. These locations are places associated with the notorious Amelia Dyer. It would not be unreasonable to think that baby Linda May might have started life in the care of Mrs Dyer.[25]

October 1880 – St Pancras, London – Coroner: Dr Hardwick – Baby Farmer: Mary Ann Sheppard – Child's Name: Edward Rayner – Mother's Name: Alice Rayner

Eighteen months earlier, Alice Rayner had given birth to her son, Edward, at Queen Charlotte's Hospital, London. As she was leaving hospital, she saw a card advertising for a nurse child. On investigating further, she visited Mary Ann Sheppard at 64 Whitfield St and arranged that Mrs Sheppard should have care of the infant, sometimes on a daily basis and sometimes weekly. In February 1880, she left Edward with Mrs Sheppard all the time and visited him two or three times a week. Alice stated that she had noticed the child had a cold when she saw him the week before he died but she had no indication he was dying.

When Mr Thomas Murphy, divisional police surgeon, visited the house, he noticed how small the room was, only 14' x 12' x 8'8". In this space there were Mrs Sheppard, two other women and two farmed children, one 18 months old and the other just a few weeks old. When carrying out the post-mortem, he discovered that Edward had a mass of tubercule on the lungs and must have been unwell for some time. He concluded that illness had been accelerated by the lack of fresh air and overcrowding.

Mrs Sheppard stated that the two young women who were with her had been children she had nursed, and they were now 17 and 19 years old. On being questioned, she answered that she had looked after over 200 children and had never had an inquest on any of them. She said that up until six weeks before Edward's demise she had paid a dispensary doctor to look after him but that he had not been seen by a doctor since. When asked if she had ever been licensed under the Infant Life Protection Act, she replied that she had many years ago, but when the coroner, Dr Hardwick, pointed out that the Act had only been in force for a few years, she changed her story and admitted she had never been licensed but had applied and been turned down due to her room being too small. Dr Hardwick stated that Mrs Sheppard had been very cunning as she only kept one child under 18 months old and the Act stated the need to register only if more than one was nursed and that the Act needed to be amended to rectify this loophole.

The jury found the child had died from disease of the lungs that had been accelerated by bad air and overcrowding. They also declared that the inspector for the Infant Life Protection Act should take an interest in Mrs Sheppard's baby farm.

Dr Hardwick then told Mrs Sheppard she had had a narrow escape from the charge of manslaughter.[26]

March 1881 – Southampton, Hampshire – Coroner: Mr W. Coxwell – Baby Farmer: Mary Ann Dawkins – Child's Name: Unknown – Mother's Name: Laura Louise Ellman

Dressmaker Laura Ellman was a young woman who farmed her illegitimate baby out for 8, and later 6, shillings a week to mother of nine Mary Ann Dawkins. When, on Friday evening, the baby became unwell with symptoms of bronchitis, Mrs Dawkins sent for Miss Ellman. Miss Ellman thought she would send for the doctor the following morning, but the child died overnight. The inquest jury decided the child had died from natural causes but, under the direction of the coroner, censured Mrs Dawkins for having sent for the mother and not a doctor. They stated that Miss Ellman was too young to make the decision to call the doctor, but that Mrs Dawkins was experienced enough to know that medical assistance was required.[27]

December 1884 – Tremain, Davidstowe, Cornwall – Coroner: Mr E. G. Hambly – Baby Farmer: Mary Cook – Child's Name: Unknown – Mother's Name: Mary Jane Pluess

Mary Jane Pluess gave birth to her fifth illegitimate child in Camelford Workhouse. None of her previous children had survived but the newborn baby was a large, 11 lb healthy boy. After her confinement, she left the workhouse and took the baby to Mary Cook who, for 2 shillings and sixpence a week, would care for the child. After three weeks, Mrs Cook's husband Tom called on Mary Jane to tell her the infant was ill, and she needed to come to see him. The child was taken to Mary Jane's father's house. Dr Pearce was called, and he instructed Mary Jane to take the baby to the workhouse, where it was noticed that the boy's eyes had sunken, and he had the appearance of an old man. His weight was found to have dropped to 9 lb 4½ oz before he died.

At the inquest it was said that Mrs Cook had fed the baby on bread, water, sugar and milk and occasionally she would suckle it. She had a 20-month-old child of her own and another child that she farmed.

Dr Pearce said Tremain was an area of Cornwall well known for baby farmers and he believed the farmers were ignorant of the correct food to give the babies, although he had instructed them on many occasions. He said that this way of baby farming was no less than 'a legalised way of murdering children'.

The jury found that the child had died due to exhaustion due to the lack of food and condemned the practice of putting young children out to nurse.

The coroner reprimanded both Mary Jane Pluess and Mary Cook and the case had been watched by the local police who were taking an interest in the baby farming business around Tremain.[28]

August 1888 – Wandsworth, London – Coroner: Mr Braxton Hicks – Baby Farmer: Jane Arnold and Jessie Chapman – Child's Name: Isaac Arnold and Others – Mother's Name: Unknown

Women who found homes for illegitimate babies often had a wide range of contacts, several aliases and frequently told lies, and so it was with Jane Arnold. Although Jane was never convicted, she came to the attention of the authorities on more than one occasion and I'm sure she can be classed as a baby farmer.

Mrs Arnold was the daughter of builder Robert Walpole. She was born in July 1850 in Leicestershire[29] but, by 1871, the family had moved to Stony Stratford, Buckinghamshire, where Robert employed four men and three boys and Jane was living with her parents and her husband, Isaac Arnold.[30] In the 1881 census, Isaac and Jane can be seen living at 21 Buckingham Street, Wolverton, which is within walking distance of the railway station, and Isaac worked in the local railway works as a carpenter.[31]

She first appears as a baby farmer in August 1888 when an inquest is held in Wandsworth, Surrey on the death of Isaac Arnold, aged 6 months. Baby Isaac had been in the care of an unmarried woman, Jessie Chapman of Tooting, Surrey at the time of his death. Miss Chapman was registered under the Infant Life Protection Act. She had been caring for children for two years and had received the baby on Wednesday, 22 August 1888 from Jane Arnold with a payment of 7 shillings a week. She had believed the child to have been Mrs Arnold's own baby and had been told that Mrs Arnold's mother was seriously ill in Bournemouth and that she need to go and nurse her, so was unable to care for the baby and would be glad if Miss Chapman would care for the child until she returned, but it transpired that Mrs Arnold had collected this child from a Mrs Bailey at Euston, along with £30 and articles of clothing. The boy's birth had been registered as John Bailey, son of John Bailey and Elizabeth Bailey, although witnesses had said the boy's mother was unmarried and that she had another child who was already cared for by others (interestingly an Elizabeth Bailey was convicted of cruelty at Gosport in 1894). Along with the baby, Mrs Arnold had given Miss Chapman a tin of food with instructions to give the child some at night. This had been the second child Miss Chapman had received from Mrs Arnold, the first being Edward Lovell, who was said to be the child of Mrs Arnold's niece that she had taken care of for eighteen months. Miss Chapman had another three children in her care, but these had not come from Mrs Arnold.

On Friday, 24 August, Miss Chapman gave baby Isaac and another child some of the tinned food according to the instructions on the tin. She claimed the tin had already been opened and half of the contents used before she had been given it. Both children were sick as soon as they had eaten. Neither had been unwell prior to this. That evening Isaac had a convulsion and on Sunday Dr Taylor was called, just a few hours before Isaac died, and he saw a baby suffering from convulsions with abnormally dilated pupils. The post-mortem revealed the child had shown evidence of convulsions. The stomach contents had been kept for analysis.

When giving evidence, Mrs Arnold denied that the tin had been previously opened. It was at this point that she admitted the baby was not her own but claimed she had lost a little boy and had wanted one to replace him, so she had placed an advertisement in the *Christian World*: 'Adoption – Nice healthy child wanted. State premium given. Or would take care of one. Nice home, every comfort. – Mrs James Baker, 3 Albert Terrace, Blackheath-hill, Kent.'

The advertisement was answered, and she arranged to take a baby boy from a lady living in Holloway on 22 August. She was due to keep the child for a month and should it prove to be successful she would receive a premium of £30. On the same day, she had given the boy to Miss Chapman along with the tin of food given to her by the mother. She did not think the tin had been opened. She said she had told Miss Chapman that the baby was hers as she thought it would receive better care and that she had intended to have the child christened in her husband's name. She said she had not received any money and had written to the mother twice but had not had an answer. She also admitted that the other child in Miss Chapman's care, Ernest Lovell, was not her niece's child but her cousin's and she had not advertised for that one, but it had been a private agreement.

Jane Arnold initially said she had advertised several times but had not taken any other babies as they had not suited. She then agreed she had taken one other child that she had given to a Mrs Hayes to nurse. Mrs Hayes of Ashton Keynes, Oxon had got so fond of the child she had not wanted to part with it, so Mrs Arnold had paid her off with more than she had received for the baby. She denied having given Mrs Hayes four children. She also denied having given a child to a Mrs Turner of Willesden in 1886.

The inquest into Isaac Arnold, aka John Bailey's death was adjourned in order to await the results of the examination of the child's stomach.

When the inquest resumed, Mrs Arnold had engaged a solicitor, Mr T. Bore, to defend her. At this time, the coroner demanded that Mrs Arnold should state the names of the parents of the child as the letters she had written were so contradictory she could not be believed.

Mr Charles Henry Laurence of Great Yarmouth gave evidence that Mrs Arnold had sent two children to him and his wife: Ernest William Williamson, who had been called Arthur, and Matilda Florence Laurence

Richardson, aka Mary Ann Miller. Both had come with a premium and Mrs Arnold had also given a bottle of Mother Siegle's Syrup to give to the little girl. When given the syrup, the child turned black in the face and became ill. The syrup was tasted, and found to be hot, pungent and burned the chest. A doctor was called to the child and he declared she may have had an irritant poison. This evidence is interesting as there is a possibility that the tin of food given to Miss Chapman was tainted and that that had been the cause of the child's death.

Elizabeth Carter, wife of a carpenter and wheelwright of Middleton Chaney, Northants said that in September 1886 she been given baby Eva Muriel Grundy by Mrs Arnold, who had replied to an advertisement Mrs Carter had put in a weekly newspaper. In this case, Mrs Carter had been told the baby was Mrs Arnold's mother's niece's and that the father was dead. Mrs Carter was to receive 5 shillings a week from Mrs Arnold's mother. Mrs Carter had previously taken young Constance Hall from Mrs Arnold. Mrs Arnold also had three children living with her who believed she was their mother but one of these was now living with Mrs Carter; this was possibly the boy that Mrs Carter had been told was Constance's brother, Bertie (who was later named as Bertie Arnold), and that their parents had died, but this story, too, had changed in that their mother was now said to want them back. Mrs Carter said she was owed £8 and 10 shillings for the care of the children.

Mrs Arnold had entrusted a Mrs Ellen Meredith with the care of Ernest William Arnold for a weekly sum of 6 shillings, although this had now reduced to 5 shillings and, at the time of the inquest of Isaac Arnold, Mrs Meredith was owed £6 or £8. Mrs Meredith had no other income and was reliant on the payments from Mrs Arnold. She had now applied for outdoor relief and had been refused. She was reliant on the money given to her by friends and had continued to care for young Ernest even though she had not heard from Mrs Arnold for two years. The coroner told Mrs Meredith that she could sue Mrs Arnold, or send the boy back to her, or send him to the workhouse, where they would ensure Mrs Arnold paid for him. He said that others who were in a similar position could do the same.

These children were not the only ones Mrs Arnold had passed on; it appears that Mrs Arnold had been advertising for babies for the previous four years in the *Christian World* newspaper using a variety of aliases: Mrs Walpole and Jane Hall in addition to Mrs James Baker and letters sent to her in reply had been received by Mary Ann Saunders, who sometimes passed on dozens of letters in reply to one advertisement. Mrs Saunders had also taken charge of a month-old child named Eva from Mrs Arnold for the fee of 10 shillings per week after Mrs Arnold had arrived unannounced at her door at 9 o'clock in the evening. This arrangement was due to last just a month but, despite frequent requests and many excuses from Mrs Arnold, the child was taken by another woman, said to be the child's aunt, who had arrived with Mrs Arnold some weeks later. Mrs Arnold later claimed that the child's mother was a servant in Penge and that the child had now gone to a Mrs Watford in Ashford, Kent. This was followed up and proved to be true; however, the address in Penge was actually a post office where letters addressed in Mrs Arnold's handwriting were found to be waiting for collection by a person named Savage.

After claiming that all the children she had placed with others were being well cared for, it came as a surprise to Mrs Arnold that Mrs Hayes, with whom she had placed a child by the name of Peploe, although she had denied placing four children here, was now serving a sentence of two years' hard labour for neglecting several children (could this be the same Mrs Hayes from Swindon we shall meet elsewhere in this book?). She claimed that, on the whole, she had done a great deal of good. It became apparent that Jane Arnold had been trafficking babies around the country and the coroner claimed that he knew of twenty-four children Mrs Arnold had had dealings with.

The coroner continued to question Jane Arnold about the parentage of fourteen children. For most of these children, Mrs Arnold denied knowing who the parents were, although the coroner refused to believe her, threatening her with prosecution for perjury.

Dr Thomas Stevenson, a government analyst, had examined the contents of young Isaac's stomach and the remains of the food from the tin and had found nothing amiss. He suggested the death had been caused by the change of food and recommended that such tinned baby food should not be given until the child reached the age of 7 months, and then only sparingly.

The coroner was clearly exasperated by Jane Arnold and, in his summing up, claimed that she was involved in baby farming, or more correctly, 'sweating', which appears to be the system of taking children with premiums paid for them, then putting them out on hire in order to see how much money she could make on the transactions. He thanked the police in various counties for the assistance they had given with this case. He also stated that the Infant Life Protection Act was totally inadequate when dealing with the likes of Jane Arnold.

The jury returned the verdict of 'death by natural causes' but asked that Mrs Arnold be censured for her part in this matter, that Mrs Arnold be referred to the Public Prosecutor and that there should be amendments made to the Baby Farming Act.[32]

Jane Arnold seems to have avoided any further trouble related to this case but in May the following year, 1889, she was involved in another inquest, this time in Newport Pagnell, Buckinghamshire, where Mrs Arnold had moved to from Wolverton.

The child in question this time was 2-and-a-half-year-old Ernest Alexander Lovell, the boy Mrs Arnold had passed to Jessie Chapman, initially saying this boy was Mrs Arnold's niece's child then changed her story to say it was her cousin's boy. Miss Chapman had cared for young Ernest for most of his life and had frequently taken him to St Bartholomew's Hospital as he had always had poor health. Miss Chapman had taken the baby for 25 shillings a month, but this had later been reduced to 5 shillings and she was now owed £2 and 17 shillings. Miss Chapman was assured of the child's fitness to travel to Newport Pagnell by a medical practitioner, even though the boy was still unable to walk.

When questioned, Mrs Arnold stated that she did not know who the mother of Ernest was, and she had been given him by a man who called himself Mr Williams at Clapham Junction. She said that when she received the boy from Miss Chapman, he had weighed just 11½ lb and that the bruises found on his little body were due to him falling, which he often did.

The coroner adjourned the inquest to await analysis on the contents of the child's stomach.[33]

On the resumption of the inquest, Mr N. M. Fisher, county analyst, stated he could find no evidence of poison in the child's stomach. The jury then found the cause of death to be in accordance with the medical evidence but felt there had been gross neglect in this case; however, there was not enough to affix criminal responsibility to any one person. They added that further legislation was needed to deal with cases of this nature.[34]

For all her changes of story about where she got the children from, their names, their parentage, how much she had received in premiums for them, etc., Jane Arnold appears to have escaped prosecution. She then vanishes; her husband is seen in later census returns to be living with his relatives and there is no mention of Jane or any children.

This case has shown the demise of two of the babies that passed through Jane Arnold's hands, but Mrs Arnold did say during the first inquest she had done a lot of good, and in at least one case, this seems to have been true. I'm grateful to the family of Eva Grundy, who have generously shared information with me about Eva's later life. Eva Muriel Grundy went to live in Middleton Chaney with Mr and Mrs Carter. Eva continues to be found on the next three census returns, even moving to Bournemouth with Elizabeth Carter after Mr Carter's death.[35] She became a teacher, married a fellow teacher and they set up their own school outside Bournemouth. They had three children, all of whom attended university. In her later years, she always spoke fondly of her 'Carter family' who had treated her as one of their own. Eva died in 1964.[36]

December 1889 – Bromley – Coroner: Mr Baxter – Baby Farmer: Mary Ann Short – Child's Name: Eveline Martin – Mother's Name: Evelina Martin
Servant Evelina Martin came from the country with her sister in order to be confined in the house of nurse Mrs Eleanor Walters. When her illegitimate daughter was born, she trusted Mrs Walters to find a nurse for the child, who was placed in the care of Mary Ann Short, a known baby farmer, for 5 shillings a week. Evelina then returned to Norfolk.

Mrs Short, wife of a dock labourer, had two other children in her care at the time of the inquest on baby Eveline and the coroner was particularly interested in this case as he had carried out another inquest on a child from the same baby farm that week. Asked if she was registered under the Infant Life Protection Act, she stated that she wasn't but had applied for registration and was awaiting the receipt of it. When she was asked if she called for medical attendance for the children in her care, she stated that although she had in the past, she found that to do this made her out of pocket, so she no longer did. She did tell the court that she had kept a baby farm for fourteen years and had only had five children die in that time. She was also asked if she insured the life of the children, and she assured the court that she didn't.

Regardless of Mrs Short's testimony that she didn't call in doctors to attend her charges, it appears that 2-month-old Eveline was attended before her death by Drs O'Brien and Taylor, who did their best to save the life of the infant; however, Eveline died from malnutrition. The jury returned a verdict in accordance with the medical evidence, and nothing more appears to have been done with Mrs Short.[37]

March 1890 – Bow – Coroner: Dr MacDonald – Baby Farmer: Caroline Brightwell – Child's Name: Percy Fellows – Mother's Name: Fanny Fellows
Three-month-old Percy Fellows, illegitimate son of Fanny Fellows, died whilst in the care of Caroline Brightwell, who received 5 shillings a week for this service. Miss Brightwell was housekeeper to chemist Mr Pridgeon of Roman Road, Bow. It appears that Fanny was a friend of Mr Pridgeon and had stayed at his home for ten weeks prior to giving birth to baby Percy. When Fanny left three weeks later to go to Swansea, she left Percy behind. Percy had never been a healthy child and over the last three weeks he had been seen to dwindle away. Miss Brightwell had seen the boy when she went to bed but on waking the following morning, she had found him dead beside her. The coroner noted that Percy's life had not been insured. Despite stating that the baby was thin and emaciated, Dr Frederick Mercer, who had attended the house and found Percy dead, declared that the cause of death was suffocation. The coroner remarked that there didn't appear to be any sign of neglect on the part of Miss Brightwell and the jury found in line with the medical evidence.[38]

May 1890 – Upper Broughton, Leicestershire – Coroner: Unknown – Baby Farmer: Eva Stevenson – Child's Name: Unknown – Mother's Name: Unknown
Wife of a railway porter, Eva Stevenson, advertised for a baby to adopt, stating she and her husband had no children of their own. As a result of this, she took an illegitimate child from his Norwich servant girl mother for a premium of £10. This case appeared before a coroner's inquest when the child died within a fortnight. Mrs Stevenson's assertion that she was childless was not untrue; however, it was found that they had five children, ranging in age from 5 years old to 14 months, in their care, all living in one room and never seen outdoors. These children came from London, Leicester and Leeds for premiums between £5 and £15. No result of this inquest has been found.[39]

August 1894 – Acton – Coroner: Mr G. P. Wyatt – Baby Farmer: Charlotte Blackburn – Child's Name: Dorothy Cannell – Mother's Name: Barbara Cannell
Charlotte Blackburn of Berrymead Gardens, Acton, London had featured in three inquests into the deaths of children in her care prior to the inquest into 11-month-old Dorothy Cannell in August 1894. Dorothy, daughter of lady's maid Barbara Cannell, had been with Mrs Blackburn since the previous October and Miss Cannell had paid 24 shillings a month for the baby's upkeep. The baby's mother had frequently visited, and the little girl seemed to be doing well until five weeks ago when the baby looked thin and unwell. When questioned, Mrs Blackburn said the child was teething and this was the cause of the problem, but sometime later Miss Cannell received a letter saying Dorothy was unwell. On visiting, the baby was seen to be in an awful state and when returning a few days later, the child's head was bandaged. Dorothy was then removed from Mrs Blackburn's care and taken to Walcord Ave., Walworth, where the child died a week later. Dr G. A. Mitchell attended the child while she was at Walworth and noticed that she was severely underweight and had signs of neglect. However, he was unable to say whether the emaciation was due to the lack of food or the inability of the baby to process food. The immediate cause of death was a convulsive fit. The coroner's officer had visited the Acton address but had discovered that Mrs Blackburn had moved to an unknown destination the previous Thursday and he had been unable to locate her.

The jury returned a verdict in line with the medical evidence but stated that Mrs Blackburn's actions had appeared to be very suspicious. We will see Mrs Blackburn's name appear in a later inquest.[40]

October 1894 – Tottenham – Coroner: Mr Hodgkinson – Baby Farmer: Charlotte Spicer – Child's Name: Mary Natali – Mother's Name: Caroline Natali
Registered under the Infant Child Protection Act, widow Charlotte Spicer had been taking in babies to nurse for twenty years and had had as many as eleven children in her care. She was given Mary Natali to nurse by the baby's mother, who gave the name of Caroline Cook, in July 1894. Mary was actually the illegitimate daughter of Caroline Natali, a dressmaker, and her fiancé, a Mr Cook from Forest Hill. Caroline had lodged with Mrs Spicer until August, when she disappeared. Mary had been fed on tinned milk, a few drops of brandy and some lime water, but the child had gradually wasted

away even though Mrs Spicer had kept the child warm and had sent for a doctor. As Mrs Spicer was no longer receiving payment for young Mary, she decided to visit the home of a Mr Natali in Woodlands Park Road, Tottenham but had not had any satisfaction so she went to the workhouse intending to give baby Mary over. This is what Mrs Spicer did whenever payment for children she was caring for stopped and she had been unable to give them back to their families. However, on this occasion the workhouse refused to take 7-month-old Mary Natali. On returning to the Natalis' house with the baby, she was greeted by servant Edith West. Mrs Spicer attempted to hand the baby to Edith, who refused to take her. Edith was then sent to fetch the police by Mr Howard Natali. Mrs Spice told Mr Natali that she could no longer keep the baby and he had given her five minutes to leave the house. When Edith returned, Mrs Spicer had gone but had left the baby.

Dr Donbavaed stated that death had been caused by lack of nourishment (inanition) due to improper feeding. On hearing this, Mr Hodgkinson, the coroner, adjourned the inquest to allow further investigation. On the resumption of the inquest, the jury found that young Mary had died from inanition but attached no blame to Mrs Spicer. A rider was added that the workhouse should not have refused to take baby Mary.[41]

January 1895 – West Kensington – Coroner: Mr C. Luxmore Drew – Baby Farmer: Mrs Cox – Child's Name: Unknown – Mother's Name: Florence Brunger
On a cold, foggy January morning, Mrs Cox, wife of a vestry employee from Caxton Road, West Kensington, London, received a message to attend the Shepherd's Bush home of midwife Mary Bouchier to collect a newborn baby boy, son of domestic servant Florence Brunger. The boy had been born just an hour prior to Mrs Cox's arrival at the house and an hour later he was to leave with Mrs Cox without ever having been fed. Mrs Cox was to be paid 6 shillings a week to care for the little mite.

Mary Bouchier was a registered midwife. She was an Englishwoman who admitted her name was actually Mary Butcher but felt that Bouchier was more appropriate for her profession. She had sometimes arranged for nurses to be found for the babies and she received 10 shillings as an arrangement fee. Mrs Bouchier is the link between this case and a previous one, as she was the midwife who had sent children to Mrs Blackburn, some of them just hours old.

Mrs Cox arrived home with the tiny boy and put him near the fire as it was so cold, but two days later the child died. It was said he had died from acute congestion of the lungs caused by exposure to the cold air.

When giving evidence, Florence Brunger said the boy was her first child and she had lived at Mrs Bouchier's for thirteen weeks while waiting for her confinement. During her time there, there had been five other women who had been confined and another five were waiting for their confinements.

Mr Samuel Babey, inspector for the Infant Life Protection Act, said there was no legislation to cover lying-in houses but that he did visit them on occasions. Mrs Bouchier had been registered under the Act from February 1890 to February 1891, when she had been living in Clapham. He also stated that he had seen nurses who had received children from Mrs Bouchier and had complained that the babies had not been properly attended at birth.

Dr Augustus Joseph Pepper had examined the body of the baby boy and noted there was no food in its stomach. He was surprised the child had lasted as long as he had as he thought just taking such a young baby out in such weather, even to cross the road, would be fatal.

The jury returned the verdict of death by exposure as they did not think the evidence strong enough to warrant a verdict of manslaughter but severely censured Mrs Bouchier and asked that depositions be laid before the Treasury to license such establishments.[42]

January 1898 – Tottenham – Coroner: Mr Alfred Hodgkinson – Baby Farmer: Elizabeth Heley – Child's Name: May Steinhauer – Mother's Name: Louise Steinhauer

On 12 September 1897, Miss Louise Steinhauer handed over her 22-month-old daughter to Elizabeth Heley of Tottenham in the cloakroom of Liverpool Street Station along with a bundle of clothing and £13. In return, she received an agreement that had been signed by Mrs Heley's husband, William, saying that the child would be adopted by the Heleys. When asked what she knew of Mrs Heley, she replied that she knew nothing about her. One of the jurors commented that the child had been sold like a side of meat. The coroner appears to have agreed and questioned the mother about whether she cared about the way the child was treated. Miss Steinhauer said she trusted the signed agreement. It rather went against the mother that she had initially lied about her involvement with the child, as did her mother and a Mrs Potter, who had been present at the birth and when the girl had been given to Mrs Heley.

On being asked if she had any other nurse children, Mrs Heley said she had one other and refused to say how much she had received with that child until she was threatened with imprisonment, when she admitted to having been given £25. She then said she had had another child some time before, but it had died. Had it lived, she was due to get £20 a year for that one. She also had a boy named Ernest but his mother had taken him away. It appears that Mrs Heley had not always been so honest with the coroner and that she had previously told him that she hadn't received any money for the child. She also claimed that she did not know she should be registered under the Infant Life Protection Act.

Dr Daniel Mowat said he had attended May for ten days prior to her death and that she had had rickets and bronchitis. During the autopsy, he ascertained that she weighed about a third of that expected of a child of her age. The cause of her death was rickets and bronchitis.

The jury returned a verdict in accordance with the medical evidence and Mr Hodgkinson stated that he expected there would be prosecutions by the proper authorities, and he disallowed the witnesses' expenses. There is no evidence that any further action was taken against Mrs Heley.[43]

April 1898 – Tottenham – Coroner: Mr Alfred Hodgkinson – Baby Farmer: Ann Spinks – Children's Names: Winifred Maundrell and Winifred Kips – Mothers' Names: Unknown

In March 1898, Ann Spinks of Greenfield Road, Tottenham contacted the Salvation Army Home at Hackney, wishing to nurse one or two children. She was given 2-month-old Winifred Maundrell, illegitimate daughter of a domestic servant, to nurse and, two days later she was given Winifred Kips, also 2 months old, whose parents had separated. Two weeks later, Dr O'Meare was called in to look at baby Maundrell, only to find her in a dreadful state of emaciation. When she died the following morning, the coroner was informed. During the course of enquiries, baby Kips was seen; however, when enquired after the following day, the officer was told that baby Kips was all right when, in fact, the child was lying dead in an upstairs room. It appears that a different doctor had been called just prior to the baby's death, and being unaware of the previous case, had signed a death certificate whereby the child was hurriedly buried in Chingford, a different jurisdiction, before the inquest into baby Maundrell's death.

When on oath at the inquest Mrs Spinks revealed the fate of baby Kips, Mr Hodgkinson stated that baby farming was becoming too prevalent in Tottenham and that on a previous occasion (the case of Elizabeth Heley?) he had been grossly misled and it had caused no end of trouble. In that case he had discharged the baby farmer with a caution but, in this case, Mrs Spinks had obstructed the coroner in his duty and had buried the Kips baby outside his jurisdiction, and he would, therefore, fine her 20 shillings. He thought both of these children had probably died due to neglect and that too many illegitimate children were being 'done away with' without the facts coming to the notice of the coroner and, should another such case come before him, he would send them to prison without the option of a fine.[44]

August 1899 – Edmonton – Coroner: Mr Arthur C. Langham – Baby Farmer: Mary Packer – Children's Names: William Clarence Stutter and Arthur Henry Baker – Mothers' Names: Rose Stutter and Mary Baker
Over the course of four years, eighteen children had died whilst in the care of certified nurse Mrs Packer, so it was surprising to hear that many of these unfortunate children had been placed with her by the Salvation Army maternity homes.

When appearing at the coroner's inquest, widow Mrs Packer, who was licensed to care for five children, wore the auxiliary dress of the Salvation Army. She stated that William Clarence Stutter (2 years, 11 months old) had been a weak child when she received him from the Edmonton Union Workhouse and that all the children had contracted measles and diarrhoea prior to the deaths of these two. She said she had received 4 shillings a week from the mothers of the children she looked after and had never received a premium for any of the children. If they were deserted, she continued to keep the children as she liked them so much. It seems she classed all the children she 'adopted' as her own. She said she had fed the younger children on bread and butter and milk, and the older ones ate the same as she did.

William's mother, servant Rose Stutter, said that William had been in Mrs Packer's care for two years and she had paid 16 shillings a month. Rose visited often and said she had seen all the children in the house over that time, but that Mrs Packer had never had more than five children there, although she had two grown-up children of her own and three younger ones that she had adopted when their mothers had deserted them. As far as she was aware, Mrs Packer had taken care of toddler William.

Domestic servant Mary Baker said that her son, Arthur, had been born in Edmonton Workhouse and that the matron, Mrs Graham, had sent Arthur (3 years of age) to Mrs Packer. She believed that Arthur had been well cared for by Mrs Packer.

A juror asked if the council that registered Mrs Packer knew of the number of children that had died whilst in the care. The coroner replied that this would not have been his business as the deaths had been registered without an inquest.

The inquest continued by questioning Mrs Graham to confirm that both boys had been sent to Mrs Packer from the workhouse.

Dr F. Johnson said he had been called to the Packer house to examine William and Arthur on 4 or 6 August and had found them to be thin and weakly and suffering from diarrhoea, which he treated. When he returned ten days later, William was in a state of collapse and died the following morning, while he was at the house, and, although Arthur had rallied, he relapsed and died at almost the same time as William. The post-mortem found that the cause of death in both cases was exhaustion due to gastroenteritis. He was questioned as to why he hadn't given a certificate and he replied that, as there had been an inquest on another child earlier that month, he felt that the coroner would want an inquest on these two deaths. It was agreed that the illness could have been caused by the hot weather making the milk go sour.

The coroner said that the inquest had been necessary due to the large number of deaths that had occurred over the previous four years and that these had been due to the small amount of money paid to Mrs Packer. He calculated that her income was 32 or 34 shillings a week; from that she paid 7 shillings and sixpence a week rent and had to keep twelve people on the residue. He opined that the registering authorities should look at the means of the people they registered. The jury found the deaths to have been caused by natural causes but agreed that the authorities should have been more aware of Mrs Packer's circumstances when issuing her with a licence.[45]

Ellen Daisy Chivers – The Woman Who Avoided the Coroner's Inquest!

Fifty-seven-year-old Ellen Daisy Chivers was the proprietress of a register office in Brighton, Sussex. She was also well known to gain an income by baby farming and had frequently been brought before the Board of Guardians for taking more children than she was allowed. It appears that she had been baby farming for some years as she is shown on the 1911 census for Southsea with an adopted 6-year-old girl, Ella Rich, and a nurse child, 6-month-old Donald John Cameron.

When in December 1926 Mary Grace Rogers signed an agreement with Chivers, who was using the name 'Mrs Beagley', to take her daughter's son, baby Donald Rogers, for £50 and a good supply of clothing, she said her daughter had gone to Canada. In March the following year, the 5-month-old boy developed a bad cold. Chivers was advised by her sister, Mrs Agnes Beagley, to call in a doctor to see him as he looked thin and miserable; however, she replied that doctors were expensive on a Sunday and refused to call one in. Besides, she had managed to pull babies around when they looked worse than this. The real reason for her reticence was because Donald was not one of the children registered with the Guardians, with whom she had already been in trouble for keeping too many children. Around noon the following day, young Donald died. Mrs Chivers now had the problem of what to do with the baby's body. She wrapped it in a paper parcel and stored it for three days behind the piano. Eventually, Chivers placed the parcel in a perambulator with another, living baby and took it to another house that she rented in Ditchling Road. A large fire was made up in the scullery grate and the parcel was placed on it. When the fire was cold, the ashes were taken to Moulscombe, near Brighton and scattered to the winds.

Chivers was charged with killing Donald by neglecting the baby and preventing the coroner from calling an inquest by burning the body.

Evidence was given by domestic servant Ada Goose that Chivers rented a number of houses or parts of houses around Brighton. Mrs Goose said she met Mrs Chivers in 1925 when Chivers had five children being looked after. The Guardians had sent her notice and, subsequently, had taken two children into care.

Chivers claimed it was Mrs Goose who had suggested burning the body as there would be no trace left of it, whereas Chivers would have preferred to bury the child. Although she admitted lighting the fire, she claimed Goose had placed the parcel on the flames and had later looked through the ashes to ascertain nothing was left. Together they had gone to scatter the ashes. It seems clear that both women were complicit in the disposal of baby Donald's body.

Chivers pleaded guilty to destroying the body of Donald Rogers with intent to prevent an inquest being held.

It was stated that Chivers had had inquests on the bodies of two children who were in her care in 1913 at Portsmouth and that she had been censured by the coroner in those cases.

When passing sentence, Mr Justice Horridge said that Chivers was 'a very wicked woman' and sentenced her to nine months' imprisonment with hard labour.[46]

Chapter 5

Contravention of Infant Life Protection Act 1872

Despite the passing of the Infant Life Protection Act in 1872, many authorities ignored it; the first prosecution under the Act seems to have been in 1878. A comment at the trial of John and Catherine Barnes in 1879 stated that the Act was 'all but dead in the water' in Cheshire.[1]

In London, Samuel Braby was an inspector appointed under the Infant Life Protection Act.[2]

One notable prosecution was that of Amelia Dyer in 1879,[3] but that is dealt with elsewhere in this book.

Mary Ann Waller – 1878 – Worship St, London

Samuel Braby (or Babey) visited a dirty house, unfit for habitation, in Rivington St, Shoreditch on 20 February 1878. There he found Mary Ann Waller, her 12-year-old daughter, two infants and the body of an illegitimate baby, approximately 6 months old, that was lying in a coffin. The dead child was named as William Harry Goodes and Waller had received 5 shillings and sixpence a week to care for the child. Waller claimed the two infants belonged to herself and her sister, Mrs Beach, who lived at the same address.

On 2 March, Mr Braby again visited the house and this time found the body of another infant, George Dugoy. George's mother, Mrs Emma Dugoy, gave her healthy baby boy into the care of Mary Ann Waller on 12 February that same year. She had seen George once afterwards when he had been very ill, and she had been informed of his death on 25 February. The other two infants that Mr Braby had seen previously were still alive in the house, but he doubted that they were the children of Mrs Waller and her sister. Enquiries were made as to where the two had been born and where they were registered but no trace of either their births or registration could be found.

Middle-aged Mary Ann Waller was charged with receiving for hire or reward more than one child under the age of 1 year, for the purpose of maintaining such children away from their parents without being licensed. The case was remanded as the mother of William Goodes had not attended the trial and it was thought this case was so dreadful in character that it should be thoroughly examined.

When the case resumed it was found that a third child from the house had died while Mrs Waller was on remand and the mothers of the two children that had been claimed by Waller and Beach as their own offspring had been found. Mrs Beach said that over the course of eighteen months she could not swear how many children had been taken in, she did not think it were as many as fifteen but could have been ten. She thought Mrs Waller had done her duty by the children and thought only two had died. The case was again remanded as it was felt children had been unaccounted for.

After the police had investigated fully, the case resumed again, and it was stated that Mrs Waller and her mother had carried out a baby farming business some years previously, but it had been discontinued for some time. All the children that had been in the care of Mrs Waller over the previous eighteen months had now been accounted for and were living with their proper guardians. An inquest had been carried out on the body of the third baby, infant Chislett, and it was said that the child had died of natural causes. The case was adjourned yet again.

On the resumption of the case, Mr Bushby stated that he had been considering whether the case should be heard in a higher court on the charges of manslaughter due to neglect, but the evidence did not indicate the children had died due to being in the care of Mrs Waller, even though the premises that were used were inadequate for the purpose. The lies told by the prisoner indicated that she was well aware of the law concerning baby farming. Given this, Mrs Waller was sentenced to six months' imprisonment.[4]

Elizabeth Thompson – 1880 – Liverpool

Elizabeth Thompson, middle aged and respectable looking, was living apart from her husband in Stonehill Street, Liverpool when a child she was nursing died in November 1879. Attempts were made to find the mother of the child to no avail. When, a month later, another child died whilst under Mrs Thompson's care, the doctor refused to issue a death certificate until the coroner had been informed. The police cautioned Mrs Thompson about keeping nurse children without being registered under the Infant Life Protection Act, so when she was visited on 11 March 1880 and found to be caring for two infants under 12 months and an older child, all of whom seems to be in delicate health, she was prosecuted. She was fined 40 shillings and costs or a month's hard labour.[5] It was discovered that Mrs Thompson received babies from intermediaries, one of whom was a 'Mary Smith' from Totterdown.[6] This was one of the names used by the later notorious Amelia Dyer.

George and Mary Hayes – 1888 – Swindon

After a visit to the home of George and Mary Hayes by the bailiffs, where the stench had been so great that one or two of the men were overcome both by the smell and by the cruelty they saw inflicted upon the children, the Society for the Prevention of Cruelty to Children was alerted. A visit was paid to them by an officer where he found seven children living in filthy conditions with no furniture and only soiled rags for coverings. He had been unable to find any food in the house, except a few crumbs on the floor. Some of these children were unable to walk due to constant neglect. All of the children had been given into the care of Mrs Hayes for lump sums of money and four of them had their lives insured with the Liverpool Victoria Legal Friendly Society. Comments were made in court about how these insurances encouraged the perpetration of murder and should have been made illegal some time previously. George Hayes, 57, was sentenced to nine months' imprisonment and his wife, Mary, 52, to two years' imprisonment.[7]

This case is related to another mentioned elsewhere in this book: that of Jane Arnold. It appears that one of the children sent to Mr and Mrs Hayes came via Jane Arnold.[8]

Ann Marsh – 1890 – Brixton, London

Ann Marsh was living with her husband in one room in Effra Parade, Brixton when she was visited by Mr Braby, who found three infants. Mrs Marsh was no stranger to Mr Braby as he had cautioned her many times about keeping children without being registered, so this time she was taken to court and fined £5.[9]

Susan Pearce – 1890 – Stockwell, London

Elderly Susan Pearce of Fenwick Place, Stockwell had been cautioned by an inspector under the Act and had been given a form to complete to allow her to apply for registration; however, she had failed to do so and continued to keep infants. The two found in her care were 'farmed' for 7 and 8 shillings and, although the babies were treated kindly and carefully, Susan was prosecuted and fined £5 plus 2 shillings costs and warned that she could have been imprisoned for six months.[10]

Emily Clark – 1890 – Peckham, London

Emily Clark of Linnell Street, Peckham had applied for registration but had been refused due to circumstances that had come to the notice of the authorities and had prevented registration. Mrs Clark continued to farm infants and she was fined £3 plus costs and warned that, should she continue, she would receive a much heavier penalty.[11]

Eve Nicholson – 1890 – Fulham, London

When Eve Nicholson moved into 31 Coomber Road, Fulham she knew that she had been registered under the Infant Life Protection Act to have five children in her home, so when she was visited on 13 March 1890 by an inspector who had seen her advertisement for children, she was not concerned. Of the five children in her home that day, three were over the prescribed age and one of the younger children had died the previous day. Unfortunately, her registration was in Uxbridge, Middlesex and, therefore not applicable to her new address. She was cautioned about her registration. On returning on the 29th of the month, the inspector noticed that she had taken in another baby and was told that she expected to receive £200 for its adoption. The inspector noted that Nicholson slept in the back room with all five children and that the size of this room was smaller than the 250 cubic feet required by the regulations. She was summoned to appear in court on two charges.

Due to her claim that she was registered in Uxbridge, Nicholson's first appearance was adjourned. At the resumed session, the clerk of the magistrate's court in Uxbridge appeared and stated that Nicholson was registered in Uxbridge and the registration was not due to expire until

November. Unfortunately, this registration was not valid in Fulham, but it was thought that this might make a difference to the first summons relating to the visit on 13 March, especially as she had, she claimed, visited the police station in Fulham to make enquiries about the situation. The police had no record of this visit. It was decided that a technical offence had been committed in this case and Nicholson was fined 3 shillings with 2 shillings costs, but the second offence was more serious as she had been cautioned by the inspector and had still taken in another child. For this she was fined 40 shillings with 2 shillings costs. An application was made to reduce the fine as she was a poor woman but, as she was receiving 6 shillings a week for each child and a promise of £200 for the adoption of the youngest child, this was refused.

The inspector said he would be making an early visit to the house and, given the present accommodation, a licence would not be granted. Nicholson was allowed time to pay the fine and costs.[12]

Mary Ann Lamb – 1891 – Driffield, East Yorkshire

Fourteen-week-old Gertrude Bryan had been living with widow Mary Ann Lamb for eight weeks, for which she had been paid 4 shillings a week by the baby's single mother. The little girl had been in good health. Mrs Lamb had advertised in newspapers for children to nurse. As well as baby Gertrude, Mrs Lamb had two other children to care for. As she had not intended to keep the children for so long, she hadn't been registered for a licence. All the children slept in the same bed as Mrs Lamb. She slept well that night but when she got up at seven the next morning in order to feed the children with a bottle she had kept all night, she found baby Gertrude to be dead and quite cold. The baby had never been given any medicine or seen a doctor, but it was noted that the child had suffered from a bad case of eczema, although this was not thought to be the cause of death. The coroner pointed out that Mrs Lamb could face six months' imprisonment for not having been licensed to keep a baby farm, but he exonerated her from any neglect in this case. The jury returned the verdict that the child had died from a fit of convulsions, accelerated by its surroundings, but offered no censure to Mrs Lamb.[13]

Davis and Stephens – 1896 – Battersea

German lady's maid Miss Grass gave birth to a healthy daughter weighing 7 lb 12 oz at a Clapham maternity home in May 1896. When the baby, Marie, was 5 weeks old on 30 June, she was taken to Miss Caroline Davis's home that she shared with her sister, Mary Ann Stephens, at Amies St, Battersea. Although the house was scantily furnished, Miss Grass was keen to return to service and, needing to put baby Marie out to a nurse, she left the child there for the sum of 5 shillings a week. There were no other children in the house during Miss Grass's first visit but later she saw two other babies and was told there were others in the house. When she commented that the baby looked unwell, she was told that Miss Davis had altered the food she was providing, and mention had been made of a doctor. Knowing she was to return to Germany, Miss Grass paid three months' fee in advance to the sisters.

The house in Amies Street had been registered as a baby farm for three children but the registration had lapsed in June 1896, and it was known that a mysterious death had occurred there previously.

Dr Alfred Dudley Edgington, of High St, Battersea, said that on 21 July the baby and two others were taken to see him by Mrs Stephens suffering with diarrhoea and looking thin, emaciated and smelling badly. He had provided a large bottle of medicine that had been sufficient for all three babies. Two days later, baby Grass and one other child had returned, both much wasted. Mrs Stephens had had with her a foul-smelling feeding bottle, which he had remonstrated with her about. Both of these babies had since died. Dr Edgington visited the house and discovered a lack of furniture, a foul smell and the floor covered in dirt. During the post-mortem of baby Marie, Dr Eginton found her weight to be just 5 lb 11 oz and marks on her skin that showed she had not had her clothes change frequently enough. Death was due to exhaustion following diarrhoea and gastroenteritis that had been caused by the unwholesome surroundings.

Miss Isobel Smith, inspector under the Infant Life Protection Act, visited the house frequently and had warned Mrs Stephens and Miss Davis that they were infringing the law. She stated that the house was no longer registered and that eight children had been kept there, five of whom had died. It was later found that there had been fourteen children in the house and eight had died.

The coroner, Mr Braxton Hicks, said he did not believe there was sufficient evidence to return a verdict of manslaughter but hoped the London County Council would take the case further as there had be a gross contravention of the law.

In October, the case was taken to the South-western Police Court by the London County Council where it was said that when Miss Smith visited the house, she felt children were being concealed from her and she had recommended that a doctor be called to some of the children, but this did not happen. She later returned, with the assistance of Mr Newlands, another inspector, and while searching the house they found a dying child. Two sick children were removed as was another, who was very dirty. The council had refused to renew the registration of the house. At the conclusion of this evidence, both defendants fainted, and the case was adjourned until they had recovered.

At the resumption of the case, the defence put was one of ignorance and that the two women had believed the renewal would be given.

The magistrate, Mr Francis, had said he needed to consider this case for a week due to the gravity of the charge. When sentencing, he complimented the council for bringing it into court and sentenced both women to six weeks' hard labour.[14]

Mark and Mary Jane James – 1897 – Bournemouth

On 1 May 1897, PC New had discovered there had been the death of a child in the house and that the child had been insured for £3 and £1 15s by two insurance offices and was also in a doctor's club. Two children under the age of 12 months were in the house and one-legged Mark and Mary Jane James were being paid 4 shillings a week for their keep.

When Mr and Mrs James appeared in court charged with failing to be licensed under the Infant Life Protection Act, they were carrying the children with them. They pleaded ignorance of the need to be licensed. However, when they had been visited by PC New, Mr James had said the licence was being kept by the superintendent, Mr Drewitt, who denied this was the case.

When asked if Mrs James was a nurse or in any way qualified, PC New answered that she wasn't and that she was 'quite incompetent'.

The fact that the couple had never been charged before was taken into account when they were each fined £1 and 7/6 costs. They were told that they must 'get rid of one of the children' or they would be charged again. Should the couple apply to be licensed there was an opinion that it would not be issued. As the mothers of the children were in court listening to the verdict, one can presume that this matter was quickly solved.[15]

Sarah Cotton – 1919

In July 1919, elderly Sarah Cotton was found guilty of not registering herself as keeper of a nurse child. An illegitimate 3-month-old girl was found to have died for 'want of proper food and attention' at a coroner's inquest, where she said she would have taken the baby to a doctor earlier if it had been her own child. It seems surprising that she was not charged with manslaughter. She was sentenced to prison for one month.[16]

Chapter 6

Abandonment

Another way of getting rid of a nurse child was to abandon them. Many abandoned children were found with no way to connect them to the person who left them. However, in addition to the following, we must include the cases associated with Amelia Dyer: the abandonment of Bertie Palmer on Durdham Down;[1] the abandonment of Queenie Baker in Plymouth, which Arthur Palmer was found to be guilty of;[2] and the baby abandoned on a train at Newton Abbot by Polly and Arthur Palmer.[3]

Anne Cummings

The story starts with 25-year-old Mrs Anne Cummings, alias Finch, being indicted for abandoning and exposing a child under 2 years of age, Ellen Mary Cummings, whereby the life of such child was endangered, in September 1869. Anne Cummings was married to a Mr Finch who worked for Mr Patman, hairdresser of Knightsbridge, but had left her husband in 1868 and now lived as the wife of Charles Robert Cummings, a railway porter, lodging with Mrs Mary Eagle in Rectory Place, Fulham, London. The *West London Observer* described her as a very peculiar-looking woman.

At half past ten on the night of 5 July 1869, a boy named Henry Cleverly of 7 Britten St, Chelsea, saw a bundle in the doorway of 10 Gloucester Road that contained a female infant wrapped in a nightgown and a piece of old flannel. He took it to the police station from where the child went to Kensington workhouse. There it was attended to by Mrs Weatherstead, who said it appeared to be drugged with some narcotic as it slept for upwards of a week and during this time if she wanted to feed it she needed to shake it violently in order to rouse it from the stupor. The child was in a very dirty condition, very thin, presenting the appearance of having been starved for want of proper food and with wounds from thrush that had not been properly attended to.

After some enquiries, suspicion fell on Anne Cummings. Though she had not appeared to have been pregnant, she had shown Mrs Eagle a baby on 22 February, saying it had been born during the night. Mrs Eagle did not think the baby newborn as Cummings did not appear to suckle it and she thought it had been farmed due to other suspicious circumstances. Letters were found at the post office that were in Cummings's handwriting, negotiating with women to take their babies and ask no questions.

Anne Cummings said she had been confined with a child but that the baby in the workhouse was not hers as that one had been adopted by a lady in Kent, a Mrs Baker living in Waterloo Road, for whom she had written many letters.

Sergeant Troughton said the prisoner was in the habit of visiting an address in Coldharbour Lane, Camberwell (this is the address of midwife Mary Ann Hall), the occupant of which advertised weekly. The adverts offered furnished apartments for a lady, quiet and private, with an experienced nurse. He said five children had been found in the neighbourhood of Parsons Green since April, within a short distance from where the prisoner lived, and twelve in Kensington since January and several in Hammersmith and Chelsea.

When giving evidence at the trial, Charles Robert Cummings said he was not married to the prisoner but had been living with her for nine months and she had had a child in April – note this is not the same date as that given by Mrs Eagle in her testimony. He said the child had remained with them for about two months and he had seen it daily. It was sent away on 6 July. To the best of his knowledge, it was not the child the police had shown him and, if it was, it had much changed. He believed it had gone to a Mrs Baker in Kent and had not seen the child since. The prisoner had told him on 12 July she was getting another child for Mrs Baker.

There was some discussion about whether the prisoner had been delivered of a child on a Saturday night in April. Rather bizarrely, the landlady said she had seen the prisoner in bed with the baby by an open window, eating roast lamb, cauliflower and vegetables. Charles Cummings said she had not sat by an open window eating lamb and vegetables. Quite why this proved or disproved whether the woman had given birth or not is beyond me.

In summing up for prosecution, Mr Langford said Mr Cummings was living on the earnings of someone with a more nefarious character than a prostitute and his evidence was not to be trusted. Also, there was no

Mrs Baker – whose address was a post office in Waterloo Road – as there had been plenty of time to find her and she had not been found. He said that on 12 July – only seven days after the pretended taking of Cummings's child – she was negotiating to take another for £8 for the rest of its life. There was also a letter dated 12 June offering to meet at Bishop's Road railway station, ending with 'no questions asked'.

After the judge, Mr Payne, summed up the evidence, the jury took an hour to come to a guilty verdict. When sentencing, Mr Payne repeated Sergeant Troughton's evidence and said the number of infants deserted in the previous months was unprecedented for that area and that Cummings had been residing in locality at the time – two of those had died, a verdict of wilful murder having been returned at the coroner's inquests due to one dying from injuries received when it was thrown into an area (basement) and the other due to the child having died from exposure. In light of the number of children found in the area, an example should be made. Had it not been for the boy, Cleverly, finding this child it, too, might have died, and Mr Payne would be happy to have ordered a reward had it been in his power to do so. He sentenced Anne Cummings to five years' penal servitude.

The newspaper stated that the prisoner seemed indifferent to the sentence and skipped gaily from the dock down the steps to the cells below.[4]

Relationship Between Anne Cummings and Mary Ann Hall

After her imprisonment, Anne Cummings made a statement to the police with regard to her connection with midwife Mary Ann Hall. She says they met in April or May 1868 after Cummings had answered an advertisement for someone to nurse a child and, although she had not looked after this particular infant due to it looking unhealthy, they had kept in contact with each other.

Cummings said that Hall advertised in newspapers all over England both for homes for infants and apartments where ladies could be confined, paying as much as £100 over six months in advertisement fees. Mrs Hall had many allies in the neighbourhood: should a child die while at Mrs Hall's establishment, she was assured of receiving a certificate stating it was stillborn from the local medical attendant even if the infant were 3 weeks old and the local chemist, Aston, would supply laudanum and Syrup of Poppies, providing her name was mentioned.

Cummings alluded to other things about Hall: that she used the name Mrs Jones, and she thought abortions may have been carried out on the premises.

When premiums were paid, Mrs Hall accepted between £30 and £50, while she would give no more than £10 when passing the child on to another. These transactions often took place at railway stations and Cummings had taken babies to be given to other women on Hall's direction. In one case, Cummings had seen Hall dosing the baby with Syrup of Poppies before sending it away with her.

Another task Cummings carried out for Hall was to write letters and she said she recognised the name Mrs Waters but had no recollection of where she had encountered the name.[5] Margaret Waters was the first baby farmer to be hanged for murder and will be dealt with elsewhere in this book.

Richard and Louisa Brindley

The first we hear of Richard Joseph Brindley, 33, and his wife, Louisa, 25, is in Birkenhead in August 1896 when they were charged with abandoning a boy in Liverpool at the start of July. Detective Inspector Pearson from Chester had visited the couple in their home at New Ferry to make enquiries about a child they had been caring for whilst they lived at Penkridge, Staffordshire. Mrs Brindley said they had left Penkridge on the first day of July and had travelled to Liverpool. As they had been tired, they had given the child to a girl to hold in order to look around the shops and when she had returned, the girl and child had disappeared. However, gardener and groom Mr Brindley had a different story; he said they had given the child to a woman to nurse some weeks before they had left Penkridge.

In the house the police found all the evidence of a baby farm: letters relating to children, one of them stating that the Brindleys had agreed to adopt a child for £6, and one stating that a passenger named L. Clarke had left for America by ship on 22 June, a number of feeding bottles, two bearing the name of a chemist from Chester, a large box of good-quality children's clothing and linen, including two canary-coloured capes, and a copy of an advertisement: 'Adoption – beautiful country home for infant; no children; genuine love. – address and references; state the premium.'

While the police attempted to trace the children mentioned in the letters (a difficult job as many of the addresses had been removed), the Brindleys were remanded in custody.

It appears that on the night of 1 July 1896, a child was found abandoned in a doorway of School Lane, Liverpool. It was taken by the police to the Brownlow Hill workhouse, where it died soon after from paralysis, the death being classed as from natural causes at the inquest as there was no evidence that its cause had been exposure.

The police managed to locate a Mrs Dawson of Beaconsfield Street, Chester, who said she had rented rooms to a Mrs Elizabeth Louie Clarke. When Mrs Dawson had first met Mrs Clarke, the latter had been close to confinement and had returned to live in the rented rooms after the birth of a little girl, who, although healthy, had received a disabling injury to her arm during birth. Mrs Clarke had made arrangements for the little girl to be cared for by a Mrs Evans for a year. While staying in Mrs Dawson's rooms, Mrs Clarke was seen to have good-quality clothes and jewellery and some canary-coloured capes, two of which were for the child, one having been made by Mrs Dawson. After a visit to her solicitor, Mrs Clarke left for America to join her actor husband, who had refused to send her more money unless she joined him. Mrs Dawson later identified the canary-coloured capes found in the Brindleys' house and the baby's body as that of Mrs Clarke's baby, Alice Maud May Clarke.

On 24 August, Mr and Mrs Brindley were discharged from the Liverpool case but immediately rearrested, and later charged, by the Staffordshire police in connection with the death of a child, seven-week-old Arthur Workmen at Penkridge, in January 1896.

In January, Elizabeth Ann Ryan, wife of a skin collector from Dudley, advertised for a respectable couple wishing to adopt a child. On 17 February, after some correspondence with Mr and Mrs Brindley, Mrs Ryan and her sister, Mary Workman, took Miss Workman's baby boy, seven-week-old Arthur Workman, to Penkridge and left him in Mr and Mrs Brindley's care along with his clothing and £9 and 10 shillings. The boy had not been seen since. On 17 August, Mrs Ryan saw the Brindleys in Birkenhead and, when asked about the boy, Mrs Brindley said he had been given to a doctor's wife in Snow Hill, Wolverhampton.

At Cannock Police Court, Miss Workman said, after she had identified some baby clothes as those belonging to Arthur, she had not wished to get rid of the baby but she was unable to afford to keep him as she only earned 3 shillings and sixpence a week and she thought he would have a better home with the Brindleys. Although she had not asked for references for them, she thought the couple were very respectable and their letters had been very nice. She had been told that she would be able to visit the child at any time but had not yet been able to do so.

The problem that the Staffordshire police faced was the lack of a body and, although the Brindleys were held in custody for a further week, no evidence could be found and the Brindleys were, once again, released, only to be rearrested by the Liverpool police and charged with the abandonment of baby Clarke.

On 30 October, the case of the abandonment of a child under the age of 2 continued against Richard Joseph Brindley and Louisa Brindley. It was argued that the charges against both should be dropped. In Mr Brindley's case, it was said there was no evidence against him other than his own statement of where the child was. In Mrs Brindley's case, she had been subjected to three hours of inquisitorial cross questioning before she made her own statement and that her story had been a probable one. The recorder did say that if this were a case of abandonment, it was the mildest he had ever heard as the baby had been warmly dressed and it was a warm summer's evening.

The jury had a short consultation and returned a verdict of not guilty in Mr Brindley's case but guilty in the case of his wife. Mrs Brindley was then sentenced to five months' hard labour.[6]

As an interesting follow-up to this story, a Joseph Brindley and his wife Louisa are shown on the 1911 census as living in Handley, Staffordshire with a 7-year-old 'visitor'.[7] Were the Brindleys still involved in baby farming?

Chapter 7

Children's Homes

During this period, many well-meaning ladies set up children's homes with the specific intention of caring for illegitimate babies. The results were mixed; sometimes they had the financial support of the well-to-do, while others were full of good intent but lacked expertise, or money, to ensure a successful outcome.

Fulham Model Baby Farm

In September and October 1871, newspaper articles appeared extoling the virtues of a 'model baby farm' in Fulham. It appears that Mrs Matilda Dampier set up the Sophia Nursery at North End Road, Fulham in May 1871. Set in spacious gardens, St John's House consisted of a day nursery on the ground floor and night-time nurseries on the floor above. Each child had their own cot. Both nurseries were fumigated on a daily basis and well ventilated. The kitchen and laundry were well run, and everything was as good as it could be.

It is possible that Mrs Dampier was, in fact, the unmarried daughter of a clergyman who had felt compassion for the mothers of illegitimate babies and set up this home to care for the children until they reached one year of age, when they were returned to their mothers.[1] The prevailing society view of unmarried mothers was to castigate them. Mrs Dampier appeared to understand the heartache caused to the women when babies are taken from their mothers. *The Era* newspaper suggested that this baby farm could avoid the suicides of mothers and the murders of young babies by giving support during the first year of the child's life.[2] One wonders if Matilda Dampier was the unmarried mother of Henry Damper, who was christened in Hampshire in 1867.[3]

Regardless of Matilda's motives, the home was struggling financially. The mothers were asked to contribute to the upkeep of their offspring but there was still not enough money coming in, so an appeal was put out in these newspapers for help not just financial aid but also baby clothes, toys, perambulators, etc.[4]

It does not appear that this paragon of childcare survived for long, as I can find no mention of it again.

MacKenzie

It appears that in 1871 the residents of Portobello, Scotland were enraged by strange stories that were going about the town that the police had found skeletons of children in the house. The previous year, it had been reported to police that a child had been starving for want of food in the home. Bearing in mind that the trial of Margaret Waters was taking place in London at this time, the authorities had investigated thoroughly. In light of all these stories, the chief constable for the county, Mr List, visited 27 Tower Street. His visit only added fuel to the rumours and a mob collected outside the house, hooting and shouting, and, as the excitement increased, stones were thrown at the windows. The residents of the house were in great danger. The police eventually disbursed the crowd and posted a policeman outside for the remainder of the night.

The two MacKenzie sisters had lived at the Tower Street address for seven years, during which time they had kept a boarding establishment for children, often having as many as ten children in their care for a sum of £25 per annum per child, although they sometimes took less. During their time in Portobello, three children had died whilst in their care and these had been correctly registered. At the time of Mr List's visit, eight children were in residence, the youngest being 21 months and the oldest 7 years of age. All the children looked well cared for and were tidily dressed and fairly well fed. All seemed to be cheerful while playing with their toys. Although Mr List compiled a report to be sent to the Procurator Fiscal, he could find no evidence to confirm the rumours.

When the sisters arrived at Burgh Courtroom to be examined, they stated that they received a small annuity; however, it was not enough to support them, so they had decided to supplement their income by providing boarding facilities for children. Some of the children they had raised were now at boarding school in Edinburgh. They provided character references from several well-known gentlemen. They thought the rumours had been started by a girl who had been dismissed from their service.

That afternoon, they left Portobello with the eight children in their care and closed up their house.[5]

Martha Merrington

Miss Martha Crauford Merrington was a lady of independent means who in 1871 resided with her parents.[6] Her father was deputy principal at the Bank of England but by 1880 she was living with her unmarried sister in South Kensington. She was at the forefront of the Victorian women's movement to be elected to public posts. A successful campaign to get Martha Merrington elected to the Kensington Board of Guardians was run in 1875, making her the first woman to sit on a Poor Law Board. Guardians were elected on a yearly basis. However, four years later she was disqualified due to a ratepayer taking legal action against her candidacy due to her having moved to a new house on the day of the election; she therefore did not meet the residency requirement.[7]

She became the manager of several Board Schools in Notting Hill during the 1870s.

By 1873, Miss Merrington appears to have opened a crèche in Edenham Street, Notting Hill, when the area was still a village. This was one of the first such nurseries in the country. At this time, she was aided by a Miss Thompson, who continued to live in Notting Hill, carrying out many philanthropic works, after the crèche had moved away.

It is not surprising, given Miss Merrington's focus on women's participation in the community, that the doctor to the Home was Dr Frances Elizabeth Hoggan, the second woman to qualify as a doctor in Europe – just three months prior to Elizabeth Garrett Anderson becoming a doctor in Britain.[8] However, Dr Hoggan rarely visited the Home as it was some distance away from her Mayfair home.

Miss Merrington's Home for Infants and Young Mothers in Notting Hill had been taking in young unmarried mothers after the birth of their offspring.

Alice Alexander was separated from her husband and working at the Elgin Hotel, Notting Hill in 1877 when she placed her 2-month-old daughter, Alice Maud, into Miss Merrington's Home, which was by now in St James

Road, Notting Hill. During the three weeks the child was at the Home, Miss Merrington again moved the home, this time to 37 Montpelier Row, Brompton. Mrs Alexander had agreed to pay 5 shillings a week for the baby's keep but had, as yet, paid nothing. However, she had visited the little girl once when she seemed to be quite well. Sadly, young Alice died, and an inquest was held at The Talbot Tavern, Montpelier Street, that had been attended by Police Inspector W. Marsh.

Alice Foley had been in charge of the Home, receiving 6 shillings a week for each of the six infants kept there. On hearing this, the jury stated that this Home was a baby farm, but the coroner pointed out that that was not their role here, but they were to enquire into the cause of death and decide if any negligence had taken place. Mrs Caroline Halpin said she assisted her daughter in the management of the Home, and they had only held the appointment for a few weeks.

At 9.00 pm the evening prior to the inquest into baby Alice's death, Miss Merrington presented herself to the local police station to ask where she should apply to in order to get the Home registered as a Nursery for Infants. She was given the address of the Metropolitan Board of Works, whereupon she said she would write at once and attend to it. She said the Home had been used as a nursery since before the passing of the 1872 Infant Life Protection Act and was partly supported by donations and partly by money paid by the parents of the children. It was open to inspection at any time.

Inspector Marsh's report was sent to the Acting Superintendent, who referred the case to the Metropolitan Board of Works as he believed the Home was in violation of the Act.

Despite this assurance by Miss Merrington, it appears it took her some time to register the Home, as the Home once again made the news with the death of an infant.

Susan Bates, domestic servant from Talbot Road, Bayswater gave birth to her son William Henry in Kensington Workhouse Infirmary in 1879 and was then taken to Miss Merrington's establishment. When she returned into service, she left young William at the Home and paid 12 shillings a month for his keep. Subsequently, Miss Merrington moved the Home to Bridge Street, Battersea where William, who had always been a delicate child, died on 12 July 1880 at the age of 1 year and 8 months.

The Home cared for up to twenty children from the ages of 6 months to 10 years old. Two nurses were in charge and Miss Merrington visited on a daily basis. Nurse Frances Bentley said William had been fed bread, milk, sago, beef tea, mutton broth, egg white and other things. William had been taken ill the day before his death with diarrhoea, but Nurse Bentley had not thought it to be serious.

Dr Kempster, medical officer of health for the area, had visited the Home many times and had seen the young boy. He was of the opinion that from their appearance the children were not being fed with appropriate food, although there was sufficient of it, or at proper times. When he carried out a post-mortem on young William, the boy weighed only nine and a half pounds and the food that had been eaten had not been absorbed. He thought the children were given too much farinaceous food and not enough meat broth. He thought that when he visited there had been no one in charge and no proper management. There had been too many deaths at the Home, and he had reported the matter to the Metropolitan Board. The Board representative, Mr Spencer, said they were seeking to have an extension added to the Infant Life Protection Act 1872 as it only covered children under 1 year of age and failed to cover institutions at all. Miss Merrington had just registered the Home under the said Act; this would mean the Home would be regularly inspected. He said he thought that fewer infants should be kept together.

Martha Merrington requested that she give evidence at the inquest. She said the parents of the children in the Home paid as much as they could afford, the rest was covered by subscriptions or out of her own pocket, and that she gained nothing financially from the Home. She said that during the past year thirty-eight children had arrived at the Home and of these thirteen had died. She did not consider this to be an unreasonable number as many of them had been ill or dying when admitted. She said she had been in sole charge of the Home but had now appointed a matron to take charge.

The jury decided that young William had died of atrophy but requested that the coroner should write to the Home Secretary stating the desirability of an extension to the Act.[9]

Mary Ann O'Neill

Sometimes children's homes were set up for the best of reasons by those who were not qualified to look after children. The starting up of the Institution of the Infant Jesus in Manchester was one such case. One wonders at the naivety of Mary Ann O'Neill and that of the vicar-general who sanctioned the escapade.

Mary Ann O'Neill had been a nun in a convent for twelve years before she left the sisterhood and set up a home for young children – the Institution of the Infant Jesus – at 69 Grosvenor St, Manchester with the sanction of the vicar-general of the diocese. However, she failed to register the home in accordance with the Infant Life Protection Act. Her only assistant was Mrs Catherine Riley, whose husband had gone to America, and Mrs Riley's daughter.

Miss O'Neill did not always spend her time at the Home and care for the infants was often left to Mrs Riley.

On a Tuesday in April 1873, Mrs Riley found 10-week-old Charles Rogers to be so unwell she was frightened to wash him, and she brought the plight of the tiny mite to the attention of Miss O'Neill. On seeing the child, O'Neill insisted the baby be washed and she fed it herself but refused to allow a doctor to be called.

On Wednesday, authorised visitor Rev. Father Quick came to the Home with another visitor and found the infant dead. Mrs Riley did not know what to do with the body and Miss O'Neill had not been at the home since the previous day and did not return until the Thursday morning. A medical man was called, and, on his advice, the coroner was informed.

Father Quick did not think the children in the Home were kept very clean or carefully attended to. He said he thought the task too much for so few women. Eleven infants or young children were in the Institution at the time, the eldest being 6 years old, in addition to the deceased. Police Inspector Meade stated that eight of these children had bad eyes, some being unable to open their eyes. One of the babies was so emaciated that he did not think it should live. Father Quick removed four of the children and returned them to their parents and three others were taken to the workhouse by the police; one of these had suffered a broken arm that had gone untreated for a week. The two older children were the offspring of Mrs Riley, and these were well fed. Later, conveniently, the Riley family went to America. Comments were made as to the appalling smell in the home and the fact that the windows were kept closed.

Mr C. O. Murphy, surgeon, carried out a post-mortem examination and declared that there was no reason for the child's death but want of nourishment as there had been no food in the baby's stomach and it did not seem that it had tasted any for ten days. He was told the Home had three quarts of milk delivered each morning and that this was a third of what he considered necessary for the number of children in the Institution.

Mrs Riley said the children had been fed three times a day.

The magistrates commented that Miss O'Neill was ignorant of the proper way to treat children and that the authorities that had encouraged the institution should have monitored it more carefully.[10]

At the Manchester Assizes, Mary Ann O'Neill was found guilty of manslaughter but, when passing sentence, the judge stated that he did not feel she had been motivated by gain or any other improper motive but by some idea of charity or religion. He commented that of all the people in the world, nuns were the least likely to know anything about nursing babies. Due to this, his sentence was very lenient – two months' imprisonment without hard labour. The judge in this case clearly felt some compassion for the ex-nun.[11]

Matilda Muncey

In 1890, Mrs Matilda Muncey, the widow of an architect, ran a lying-in home at Reporton Road, Fulham, London in addition to a registered baby farm where she kept about thirty children.

Matilda Muncey first appears in the inquest into the death of Evalina Alice Marsh, daughter of Miss Sophia Marsh. Mrs Muncey was found by the inquest jury to be guilty of the manslaughter of baby Evalina due to neglecting the child and failing to give proper food while caring for the child, although the child had left Mrs Muncey's establishment the day before her death. Due to this verdict, she was put on trial, where two witnesses gave evidence to the effect that Mrs Muncey neglected the children in her charge by using dirty vessels and feeding bottles.

Muncey was also charged with causing the deaths of the child belonging to Mary Jane Titchner and the child of a woman named Coleman.

Another witness, Ellen Fuller, had taken a child that eventually died from Mrs Muncey, along with a bottle of milk to give to the child. Mrs Fuller had not given the milk to the ravenous child as it smelled badly and was curdled. The child had also had a suppurating wound on its navel. The doctor that was called said the child had been neglected.

Jane Mead, a monthly nurse who lived at the Reporton Road address, remembered the Marsh baby as a fine child until she was about 10 days old, when she became emaciated. Mrs Mead also spoke of a baby named Sidney Collins, although he had initially been called Coleman. This child had left the home but had been returned later. At that time the boy had been well, but the mother left for Australia, paying £20 for Mrs Muncey to adopt the baby. The boy died a week or two later. This boy was not placed on Mrs Muncey's register and when its death was registered it was said to be the child of a lodger who was actually Jane Mead, the monthly nurse.

Sophia Marsh stated in her evidence that she had seen Mrs Muncey habitually drunk and treated the children in her care badly. When questioned as to why she then left her own child with Mrs Muncey, she replied she had told the prisoner that she would take her baby away if it were not well looked after. Residents of the lying-in home were not allowed to use their own doctors but only Dr Davis or Dr Thomas (there seems to be some indication that Dr Thomas was not qualified, as only Dr Davis signed any certificates needed). Mrs Muncey had also tried to persuade Miss Marsh to register the death of the Coleman baby as her own, but she had refused. The post-mortem carried out on baby Evalina showed no food in her stomach and it was suggestive of a lack of proper feeding in the first few days of life.

Mr Samuel Babey, inspector under the Infant Life Protection Act, said that Mrs Muncey had started baby farming in 1882 at Walham Green and had later moved to Fulham. There had been an occasion when Mrs Muncey had not been paid for the care of children under her control and she had had to allow the four children in her care to be taken to the workhouse. Since then, she had had thirty-six children on the register, twelve of whom had died. He had not been able to find any child named either Coleman or Collins on the register, making it a 'secret child' and, therefore, an infringement of the Act. Mr Babey stated he had no jurisdiction over confinements.

The register of children cared for at the baby farm would be available as evidence and Mr Babey claimed it would show that the deaths of the children in Mrs Muncey's care were not the result of accidental death but of habitual neglect.

In the event, Mrs Muncey was found not guilty of manslaughter but was tried for not registering the Coleman child correctly or giving information of its death to the coroner. Mrs Muncey was found guilty of both these offences and was fined £5 and 5 guineas costs or one month imprisonment for the first offence, but the offence of withholding information from the coroner was considered more serious and she was sentenced to one month with hard labour. Jane Mead had also been convicted of giving false information.[12]

It seems that this conviction may have failed to stop Matilda Muncey from continuing to run her lying-in home as the following year, 1891, the census sees her with a female lodger and Jane Mead is visiting! We can only hope Mr Babey kept an eye on the activities of Mrs Muncey.[13]

Chapter 8

Fraud

Occasionally cases of fraud appear in relation to baby farming.

Mary Ann Hall

The case of Mary Ann Hall is inextricably linked to that of Anne Cummings, who was found guilty of abandoning a child in 1869.

Mary Ann Hall was baptised in Chelsfield, Kent in 1821, daughter of labourer Peter Crafter and his wife Sarah.[1] On 22 May 1842, she married David Hall, a carpenter at the Parish Church in Plumstead, Kent, now part of Greater London.[2]

Stout Mary Ann lived at 6 Chapel Place, Coldharbour Lane, Camberwell, London with her small husband, David, since 1864; prior to that they had lived a short distance away at 4 Denmark Road, Camberwell. Mary Ann had been a cook in a private house and David had been a ship's carpenter. Both were heavy drinkers. Before her arrest, the house had been cause for concern in the neighbourhood and police had been watching the place for some time. It had been noticed that since the arrest of Margaret Waters, David Hall had been observed keeping watch from a window. It was thought that some 'tidying up' had taken place both in the house and garden to remove any evidence that could incriminate them.

The next-door neighbour, Mrs Warren, had told police she had seen a great number of pregnant women entering number 6 and had heard through the wall their groans as they gave birth but, although she had smelled strange smells of burning or boiling, she had never heard a child's cry or seen a baby leave the house. Mr and Mrs Tennant, neighbours on the other side of number 6, confirmed Mrs Warren's statement but added they had seen a child being carried head downwards in the garden and two small coffins carried out during the night. They also saw a hunchbacked woman taking parcels from the house after each confinement and Mr Hall washing clothes and feeding the cats with lumps taken from the clothes.

Various servants of the Halls were questioned by the police. All remembered women coming to be confined at the house. Some told of babies being taken to the Foundling Hospital, being stillborn and being taken by the local undertaker. One, Mary Ann Goddard, told of a baby being taken to be given to a woman whose husband would be told the child was his and that Mrs Hall had received a number of sovereigns for this. Another servant told of being threatened with an axe by Mrs Hall. Susan Young told of a woman coming and taking babies from the house, hidden in her cloak. Mrs Hall's niece had worked in the house, and she said she recognised the name of Mrs Waters as someone who took babies from Mrs Hall. This was confirmed by the next servant, Matilda Barrett. Miss Barrett also said she had seen a baby being disposed of in a hole in the garden. This area was excavated by the police who found cinders, lime and some fatty earth that was covered with small maggots. From these statements, the police estimated that forty-six women had given birth at the house yet only eight births had been registered from there, Mrs Hall being the informant of just one.

The police then went about trying to trace as many of the women who were confined at Chapel Place as they could. Many of them said they had paid Mrs Hall money for attendance at the birth of their children and large sums in addition to have Mrs Hall find homes for their offspring. Some were told they would be able to have access to the babies but, in the event of them asking for contact, none was ever given; often the woman would be told her child had died but details would never be passed as to where the child was buried. One, a Miss Hill, told that two pawn tickets she had sewn into her stays had disappeared while she was at Chapel Place. One of these had been for silver spoons and forks and the other for a gold watch and two gold bracelets. Mrs Hall had denied ever seeing them, but Mr Hall was taken into custody on an unrelated charge and a pawn ticket for two gold bracelets was found on him. When recovered from the pawnbroker, Miss Hill identified these as hers and the silver items were found in a box in the Halls' house. Miss Hill refused to press charges and she was given the items by Mr Hall. One woman spoke of an unidentified female coming to the house and taking infants away. Two of the women had registered the births of their babies and these were taken to be nursed; however, neither lived long, their deaths were registered, and their places of burial were known. All these unmarried women were known as 'Mrs' while they were at Chapel

Place and Mrs Hall was very particular that secrecy was observed and that the servants had no knowledge of the working of this business.

The police then tried to locate where the babies born at Chapel Place ended up. The earliest that could be traced was in 1866 when Jane Morse of York House Lane, London Road, Gloucester answered an advertisement placed in the *Daily Telegraph*. Morse later visited Hall in Camberwell and took two children, a boy of about 15 months and a girl aged 4 weeks, for a premium of £7 each. The boy died about six months later, but the girl was still alive when the police contacted Mrs Morse. In March 1868, this same baby farmer received another baby girl of 5 days old after payment of a premium of £10. This baby died five months later. The County Coroner stated that both of these children had been attended by a medical man prior to their deaths.

In 1867, Mrs Hall's sister Elizabeth Crafter of Greenstead Green, Kent (now part of Orpington) took a little girl known as Amelia Vine for 8 shillings a week. Amelia lived for 9 months. In 1868, another girl was sent to Mrs Crafter. The 2-week-old baby died five weeks later of diarrhoea and thrush. Both were attended by Dr Edmonds. One of the women interviewed who had been confined at Chapel Place in 1869 and had registered the birth of her baby said Mrs Hall had recommended Mrs Crafter to her to take the child when it was 2 weeks old. The infant lived for three weeks after leaving its mother, it was attended by the doctor and had been buried in Farnborough Churchyard.

One infant girl was taken by the man who did Mrs Hall's mangling, Mr Allen, and his wife. The child had lived 18 months and had been attended by Mrs Hall's own doctor, Dr Puckle of Denmark Hill. Mr Allen said he and his wife had often seen Mrs Hall going in the direction of Margaret Waters's house, which was close to them, but not since Waters had been apprehended.

Greenstead Green appears to have had more than its fair share of baby farmers, as Mary Ann Hall used two other women in the area in addition to her sister. Widow Mary Spencer took a 2-week-old boy in October 1869 for 6 shillings a week until Mrs Hall took the child away, saying that the mother was unable to keep up the payments and the child was to be sent to its grandmother. In December the same year, Mary Spencer received a girl of 2 days old for 8 shillings a week that was to be paid by the baby's father, Mr Brooke of Friar's Court, Kemply, Gloucester. This child was still alive in November 1870. The other baby farmer from Greenstead Green was Mrs Ann Gregory, who had been paid 7 shillings a week for six years to care for a boy. The weekly fee had been paid regularly by his father, Mr George Albert Turley, a draper from Worcester.

Mary Ann Hall also kept two boys herself, 6 and 7 years old. The mothers of these two boys were traced: Harry was the illegitimate son of a woman named Bragg who kept a linen draper's shop in Lever St, St Luke's. Tommy's mother was a widow, Martha Wheeler, of Kennington Road, who gave birth to the boy several years after the death of her husband.

These were the only children that could be traced out of the estimated forty-six births at Chapel Place.

In attempting to find traces of the other babies, the police dug in the garden of number 6. The boy, Tommy, had told police that David Hall had taken babies away and put them in a hole near the fowl house, which he pointed out to them. The police found the hole and five others all about twenty feet away from the house, hidden from the view of neighbouring houses by a high fence. The holes varied in size from three foot to five foot deep and four and a half foot long and each contained cinders, ashes, lime and wet slimy earth that crawled with maggots. The flagstones in the passage were removed and the closet was emptied but no remains were found there.

During the search of Mrs Hall's house, Sergeant Relf found a list of baby clothes written in the handwriting of Sarah Ellis, sister of Margaret Waters, the first woman to be hanged for murder after baby farming, who was at this time serving an eighteen-month prison sentence with hard labour at Wandsworth Prison for her part in Mrs Waters's business. On interviewing Ellis in prison, Sergeant Relf discovered that Waters and Hall had had dealings with each other, and arrangements had been made for Hall to meet Waters in order to hand over a baby and £5 but that this transaction had not taken place due to Waters being apprehended by the police. This, added to the evidence given by Mr and Mrs Allen (a recipient of one of the babies from Mrs Hall's establishment), convinced Sergeant Relf that Hall and Waters were well aware of each other's business and that this would have accounted for where some of the infants had gone.[3]

Sergeant Relf also interviewed Anne Cummings and much of the result of this has been related previously; however, she also stated she had taken infants in a drugged condition from Hall and delivered them to various women at different railway stations and other places. Relf realised that Cummings's description matched that of the woman mentioned by one of Hall's servants as the woman who came to Chapel Place and took babies away. At this point, Relf tied the two investigations together and managed to ascertain the dates when some of the babies were taken from Hall's house and found they equated with the dates when babies were found abandoned in areas of west London:

- Amelia Woodford and boy found alive in Kensington on 31 March 1869.
- Woman from Colchester and boy found alive in Fulham on 2 April 1869.
- Woman called Mrs Hall's niece and boy found alive in Kensington on 11 May 1869.
- Mrs James and Mrs Henry and two girls found alive in Fulham on 14 May 1869 (although Relf was unable to say which of these baby girls belonged to which woman).
- Mrs Shaw and girl found alive in Kensington on 4 June 1869.
- Mrs White and girl found alive in Kensington on 22 July 1869.

Relf lists the other instances of abandoned babies in Fulham and Kensington, although he was unable to locate the mothers of these: three boys in Fulham on 10 April, 16 and 22 July, the latter being found dead due to exposure. Four girls and a boy in Kensington on 1 and 18 April, 2, 6 and 30 July, the last being the boy Cummings was convicted of abandoning and the girl on the 6th being the unfortunate baby that was thrown into the area.

Relf concludes by commenting that he is convinced that this baby trafficking is where the infants born at Mary Hall's establishment ended up and that Hall had made a good living from the trade as bonds to the value of £800 had been found in the house. He felt that she should be convicted of accessory before murder but in order for this to happen, the principal witness against her (Cummings) would need to confess to murder, which was unlikely. He asked that it be taken into consideration that all such houses should be watched, and visitors followed in order to stop the trade of baby farming.

Mary Ann Hall was remanded in custody for wilful murder of an infant. Anne Cummings was interviewed by the police, and she said that Hall had duped her into committing crime and, as Relf had feared, it was only the fear of being prosecuted for a higher offence than the one she had been convicted of that stopped her from saying more. Needless to say, Hall was released, and the prosecution was abandoned.

An interesting aside shows that letters were found at Mrs Hall's address coming from a Mary Smith of Totterdown. This is believed to be an alias of Amelia Dyer, who was convicted in 1896 of the murder of two infants and was to become, probably, the most notorious baby farmer of all.[4]

The Trial of Mary Ann Hall

Given the above evidence, there can be little doubt that Mary Ann Hall was deeply involved with the trade of baby farming, so it is surprising to discover that she was tried for fraud! What is clear from evidence given at her trial is that she had now acquired a reputation locally as someone not to be trusted and, as we have seen above, the police had shown great interest in her.

Surveyor George James Loe's wife, Emma, died in the summer of 1868 and soon after, Annie Augusta, a woman he had provided a house for in Font Street, Kennington for some time, came to live with him. Although they were not married, she went by the name of Mrs Loe.

In November of the same year, George registered the birth of a daughter, Mary Laura. He registered his name as George James Loe Harper and the girl's mother as Annie Augusta Harper, formerly Bennett. He later explained that he was not called Harper but used the name as Annie had requested. He had not known Annie's surname, but she had called herself Mrs Bennett when he first knew her. Annie had been attended during the birth by a nurse, Mary Ann Hall, who was going by the name of Mrs Jones at this time. Sadly, the child died in April 1870 and two months later Annie announced again that she was 'with child'. When George saw Mary Hall in his house some days prior to this birth, he was now aware of her reputation and ordered her to leave the house, accusing her of 'bringing the previous child to my house' – George had clearly heard of Hall's reputation and suspected the baby girl, Mary Laura, had not been his child. Hall became quite violent and, using bad language, threatened George for suggesting such a thing. George was quite frightened by this.

On 22 October, George went to Brighton on business but returned earlier than expected due to having received a telegram.

George had paid for a nurse, Mrs Collins, to attend Annie. Mrs Collins had seen Annie in the weeks before the birth but had not seen her without her clothes on. When Mrs Collins arrived at the house to assist with the confinement, she was sent away by Mrs Hall, who said it was too early, so she went downstairs, and half an hour later hot water was called for. When Mrs Collins took it up the baby, a girl, had arrived. She was asked to wash the child, but she did not think the child appeared to be newborn or unwashed. She was also concerned that the child didn't cry but appeared to be in a stupor. George had wanted the best for his 'wife' and had also arranged for a doctor to attend her. Dr Farr had also seen 'Mrs Loe' after the birth of her first child. This time, although she seemed too weak to speak at first and he had been shown the afterbirth, he did not think she had the appearance of a woman who had just given birth. After Mrs Hall left, Dr Farr had a serious talk with Annie and told her that the presence of 'that woman' had given him strong suspicions and he didn't believe she had just given birth. He had wished to examine Annie but, although she allowed a breast examination, she would not allow anything further.

George returned to the house at 7 o'clock that evening after Hall had left, but when she returned in the morning, George confronted her before she could enter the house. He accused her of bringing the child into his house the previous day. Hall turned tail and ran down the road followed by George. George continued to chase after Hall, stopping her going on a train before following her onto an omnibus and finally in a cab chase (the words 'follow that taxi' come to mind) until he came across a policeman who arrested her. He then returned to his house to find Annie gone and the baby in the care of Mrs Collins. George stated at the trial he had not seen or heard from Annie since.

Charlotte Farrant, a married relative of Hall, gave evidence saying that the child was her legitimate daughter and Mary Ann Hall had suggested she give the baby up for adoption due to Farrant's ill health. Dr Isaac Shortland Shillingford had been present at Farrant's home shortly after the baby had been born on 22 October. A cab man, William Adams, testified that he had transported Hall from Farrant's address to Loe's home on 22 October, although he had not seen any infant.

The baby girl was taken back by Mrs Farrant.

Mary Ann Hall was convicted of fraud on 12 December 1870 and sentenced to two years' imprisonment and fined £100.[5]

During the trial, evidence was given by Mr Loe's parlour maid, Caroline Savill. There is nothing to indicate that this is the same Caroline Savill that had been named as a baby farmer in a coroner's inquest at Bow earlier in the year, but it does seem quite a coincidence.[6]

As an interesting aside, the 1871 census for Brighton shows a surveyor, George Loe, living with his much younger wife, Annie.[7] Do we presume George once more succumbed to the delights of Annie Augusta?

After the Trial and Conviction of Mary Ann Hall

The police made an inventory of possessions found at the home of Mary Ann Hall. They found various bonds totalling £608 14 shillings and ninepence, a vast sum of money for the time, in addition to a variety of other items. Clearly there was enough money to pay her fine of £100.

Normally one would expect this to be the end of the story, but there was a scramble to take possession of Mary Ann's assets. In early 1871, Police Inspector Daw visited her in Wandsworth Prison, where Hall stated that she had been lawfully married to David Hall for the previous thirty years but that she wanted her bonds, papers, house and body linen to be given to her sister Ann Gregory, not her other sister Eliza Streek, after the £100 had been deducted to pay her fine. Daw also visited David Hall and he objected to anyone taking possession of these items as he was Mary Ann's husband but wished that the fine be paid. It appears that all the possessions were handed over to David Hall before the fine was paid. In January 1873, the police tried to recover the £100 from David Hall but discovered he had cashed in all the stock as it had been invested in joint names, and he now worked as an itinerant saw setter. He was last seen in Camberwell dressed in rags and tatters and it was thought all the money had been spent in the company of 'fast women and loose living'! The fine was never paid.[8]

It would be expected that on her release from prison Mary Ann Hall would disappear. We have to remember that it was very easy to change identities – just move to another area and call yourself something else – so it is surprising to find a midwife, Mary Ann Hall, appearing in court in Manchester in September 1890. The charge was 'Concealing the birth of

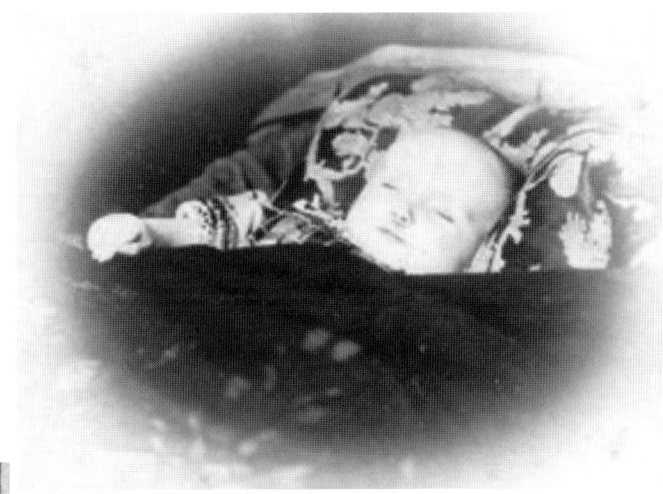

'Sleeping' Baby. (*With permission from Neil R. Storey*)

A coroner's inquest, 1901. (*George R. Sims, ed.,* Living London, *Cassell and Company Ltd, 1902*)

Miss Burdett Coutts Lodging House, Colombia Square.

Buckingham Street, Wolverton in 1910/11. (*With permission from Jacqueline Nott*)

Eva Muriel Grundy with husband and first child. (*With permission of the Hewines family*)

Eva (middle right) in 1962 with members of her family and her 'Carter family'. (*With permission of the Hewines family*)

Crowds outside a coroner's court, 1901. (*Visitvictorianengland.blogspot.com*)

Benjamin Waugh. (A Pocket History of the NSPCC)

Advertisement for baby food.

Illustration of the Tranmere baby farmers, John and Catherine Barnes (The Illustrated Police News, *11 October 1879*)

Torquay, 1860.

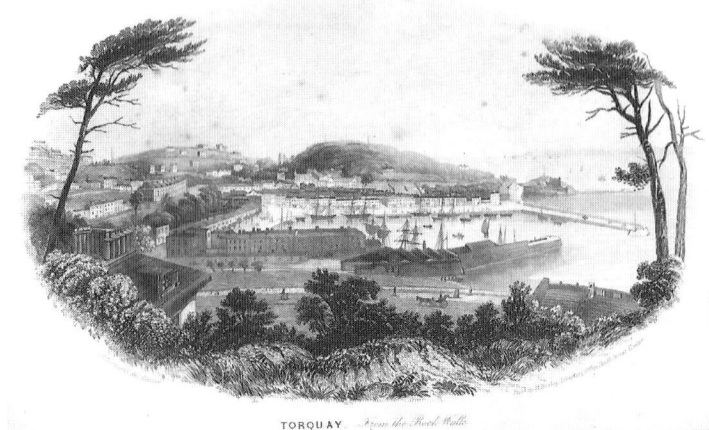

Imperial Hotel, opened 1863.

Charlotte Winsor's cottage (Life and Trial of the Child Murderess, Charlotte Winsor, Office of the Illustrated Police News, *1866*)

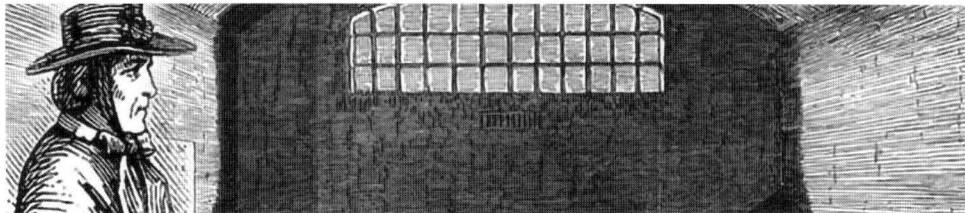

Charlotte Winsor in prison. (Illustrated Police News, *10 August 1867*)

Illustration of the execution of Margaret Waters from the *Illustrated Police News*.

Sophia Martha Todd in prison uniform. (*The National Archives*)

Amelia Dyer. (*With permission from the Thames Valley Police Museum*)

The Refuge for Female Convicts, Fulham, in 1858. (Illustrated London News)

Willie Thornton. (Lloyd's Weekly Newspaper, *19 April 1896*)

Site of the first parcel containing Helena Fry's body. (Lloyd's Weekly Newspaper, *19 April 1896*)

Label from parcel containing body of Helena Fry. (*With permission from the Thames Valley Police Museum*)

The Clappers Bridge, 1896. (Lloyd's Weekly Newspaper, *19 April 1896*)

The Clappers Bridge, 2014.

A fisherman's bend knot

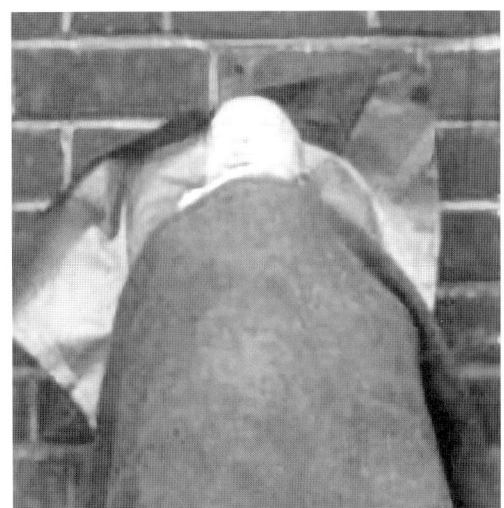

Body of Doris Marmon. (*With permission from the Thames Valley Police Museum*)

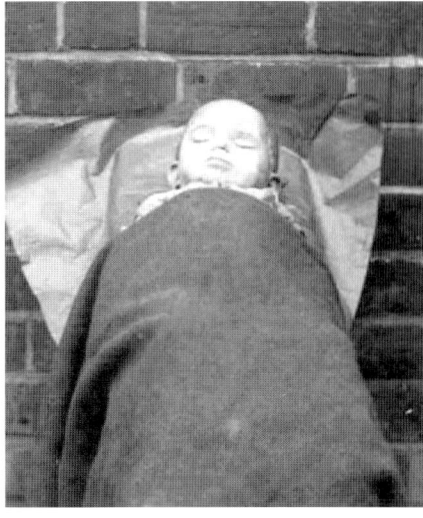

Body of Harry Simmonds. (*With permission from the Thames Valley Police Museum*)

Claymore House. (Penny Illustrated News, *24 January 1903*)

Danbury Street. (Penny Illustrated News, *24 January 1903*)

Sergeant James, Chief Inspector Tewsley and Detective Inspector Anderson and the carpet bag. (*With permission from the Thames Valley Police Museum*)

Amelia Sach and Annie Walters in court. (Penny Illustrated News, *24 January 1903*)

a child'. It appears this Mary Ann Hall was seen throwing a parcel into the canal that was found to contain the decomposing body of a baby girl. Hall was apprehended and police searched her home to find many drugs, chemicals and buckets of lime. The cellar had a sickening stench and a portmanteau contained bloody marks and the smell of decomposition. The flagstone floor was taken up but found to be set on firm earth that had not been disturbed. A post-mortem was carried out on the infant, but the cause of death could not be ascertained. Hall declared she had nothing to do with the parcel and the jury returned a verdict of 'found dead' and no charges were pursued against Hall.[9]

Was this the same Mary Ann Hall?

Joseph and Annie Roadhouse

Clerk Joseph Roadhouse, 28, and his wife, Annie, 24, appeared at the Old Bailey in London on 4 May 1891 on a charge of deception and fraud. Both pleaded guilty to the charges brought against them and were sentenced to eighteen months' and twelve months' hard labour, respectively. Reading this stark account doesn't suggest a connection to baby farming but the Roadhouses were fully engaged in the business of 'sweating' babies – taking babies and passing them on to others while making a profit from the transactions.

In a statement to Detective Chief Inspector Abbeline, Annie said she had advertised for a child to adopt. They thought it better to give an address in Birmingham rather than their own address in Oseney Crescent, Kentish Town in order to stop being bothered by the natural mother of the child. The advertisement was answered by a woman named Colbatch and Mrs Roadhouse signed to adopt and took the child. However, when she got the baby home, her husband didn't take to it, and she decided to advertise for someone to take it. This advertisement was answered by a Mrs Heeling and the child was handed over to her. This all seems quite straightforward but all is not quite as it seems, and the following case is reminiscent of that of Mary Ann Hall in 1870.

Apparently, Mr Heeling, a ship's labourer at Victoria Docks, was under the impression he was the father of the child!

The court heard that not only had Mr and Mrs Roadhouse obtained money by false pretences but that they had obtained children under false pretences by claiming to want to adopt children and bring them up as their own. They had put advertisements into a variety of newspapers giving addresses of shops where letters could be sent for a fee. Having received replies to these advertisements, letters were exchanged, and arrangements made for children to be given into the care of the Roadhouses with the payment of a premium and a bundle of clothing. It was said in these letters that Mr Roadhouse had a responsible position in either Birmingham or Preston. After the child had been exchanged, the mother would sometimes get a letter saying the child was doing well, although on one occasion it was said the child had sickened and died.

Advertisements were also placed asking for other persons to adopt children. Mrs Roadhouse admitted that she would hand over the children without asking what would become of it. Suspicions about the fate of the children should no one come forward to take them were impossible to say. It was observed that the whereabouts of children that had passed through the hands of the couple should be found as several children had been found abandoned in the streets.

After their arrest, a book had been found in their home with upward one hundred names and addresses. It was thought these were the names of women who had given children to the prisoners.

It was said that Mr and Mrs Roadhouse had lived at the same address for eighteen months but that no child had ever been seen there. Clearly a large sum of money was being made through these fraudulent means.[10]

Francis Ruth Naomi Measdale/May Duckham

A strange case was brought against 25-year-old Francis Ruth Naomi Measdale, otherwise known as May Duckham, by Miss Emily Ford for obtaining £20 by false pretences in July 1900.

Miss Ford had been working as a house servant to solicitor Mr J. C. Ainley and his wife, Mary, for almost eighteen months. When she started working for Mr Ainley, her baby was already being cared for by the kindly Mrs Copeland for 5 shillings a week. However, this only left Emily with tuppence a week from her wages when she noticed an advertisement in a newspaper from a person wishing to adopt a child. She arranged to meet the advertiser, Mrs May Duckham, who told her she was a nurse and the wife of a doctor living in Deal, Kent. This seemed like the perfect solution to Emily's problem, and a meeting was arranged. Mrs Copeland was less keen on giving up the young child as she had a feeling that Mrs Duckham might not be all she seemed. By this time, it was too late for Mrs Duckham to return to London and Mr Ainley offered to allow her to stay at his house for the night.

Mr Ainley must have had a high regard for Miss Ford as he had offered to loan her the £20 premium on condition that the sum be paid back weekly from Emily's wages, and, the following morning, he gave £20 in a mixture of cash and a cheque to Mrs Duckham. Emily accompanied Mrs Duckham and the infant to the train station. Inexplicably, Mrs Duckham didn't catch the train to London but took a train to Leeds, returning the following day in order to cash the cheque. It was in consequence of this that the police were called.

Mrs Duckham was traced to Deal in Kent where she was attempting to find a woman to take care of the child for a few days. It is thought that had the police not arrived on the scene the transaction would have taken place and Mrs Duckham would have disappeared, never to return.

Investigations took place and it was found that Measdale had been advertising for children to adopt for several years. The man she had been cohabiting with, Alfred Duckham, was not a doctor as she had claimed but had been imprisoned by Wakefield magistrates for two months for embezzlement.

It was found that Measdale had 'adopted' nine children for sums varying between a little over £2 to Miss Ford's £20. Four of these had died within weeks of going into her care. One girl had been adopted by a nurse, Mrs Simmons, in Chatham after Mrs Simmons had discovered Measdale in the process of injecting the child with chloroform. One had been sent to a licensed baby farm run by Laura Horwood in Tooting, London for 5 shillings a week, but was now £2 in arrears. One had been left with Annie Burns for a weekly fee of 5 shillings; however, after keeping the baby for three weeks, payment never materialised, and the child was taken to Leeds workhouse. One was sent to Southport, and one was with a Miss Ruth Young in Leeds. Clearly Measdale had no intention of keeping any of the children left in her care.

Measdale claimed that the man she had been living with had influenced her into taking these children while he 'loafed around', living on her ill-gotten gains.

The case against Measdale seems to have been brought by Miss Ford, not the police, and this caused some discussion to take place in the magistrate's court as it was suggested that, as it had been Mr Ainley who had paid Measdale, it should have been him that brought the prosecution. It was decided that Miss Ford was the proper person to bring the prosecution as she was paying Mr Ainley back and, indeed, had already started to return his money.[11]

The case was committed for trial at the West Riding quarter sessions where, after pleading guilty to obtaining money in connection with an alleged baby farming case, Duckham/Measdale was imprisoned for nine months.[12] Given the number of children that had been through her hands, I'm surprised she got off so lightly.

Chapter 9

Cruelty

Many of the cases found contain cruelty issues but usually these are dealt with in other ways. The cases of cruelty brought to court increased after the formation of the NSPCC.

NSPCC

Cruelty to children was rife in Victorian Britain. In 1881, the Reverend George Staite wrote in a letter to the *Liverpool Mercury*: 'whilst we have a Society for the Prevention of Cruelty to Animals, can we not do something to prevent cruelty to children?' However, the British public and government were reluctant to interfere in the private lives of its citizens. Lord Shaftesbury replied to Staite: 'The evils you state are enormous and indisputable, but they are of so private, internal and domestic a nature as to be beyond the reach of legislation.'

In the United States of America in 1875, just such a society had been started with the setting up of the New York Society for the Prevention of Cruelty to Children. Liverpool banker Thomas Agnew saw the work done by this society whilst he was in New York and, in 1883, he started the Liverpool Society for the Prevention of Cruelty to Children, along with liberal MP Samuel Smith.

In July 1884, the London Society for the Prevention of Cruelty to Children was established with Lord Shaftesbury as its president and the Reverends Benjamin Waugh and Edward Rudolf as its honorary secretaries. By 1889, this Society had thirty-two branches throughout England, Wales and Scotland, each supporting an inspector to investigate instances of child abuse.

At the London Society's AGM in 1889, it changed its name to the National Society for the Prevention of Cruelty to Children, making Queen Victoria a Patron and Rev. Waugh its director.

In 1889, the first Act of Parliament, the Children's Charter, passed into law. Police could now raise a warrant to search premises where it was thought a child could be in danger and arrest anyone found to be ill-treating a child. The NSPCC had spent five years lobbying parliament to implement such a law.

In 1895, the Society received its Royal Charter. It now had 163 inspectors.[1]

By the 1890s, the NSPCC became increasingly involved in cases of baby farming and the following stories deal with some of these cases.

Martha Ann Seville/Denton – Baby Farmer and Bigamist

Thirty-eight-year-old Martha Ann Denton was married to a baker, George Hagues Denton, in Chester when she eloped with the lodger, a man named Ferguson. This relationship didn't last, and Martha is later found at 20 Seaview, New Ferry, bigamously married to shoemaker, Joseph Seville, and working as a baby farmer. Initially both Martha and Joseph were charged with wilfully neglecting 15-month-old Maggie Clarke.

During the years they had lived at Seaview, they had had three children in their care that had died. Of these, one had died in April 1877 and another in March 1878 and inquests had been held in both these cases. Despite the prisoners being censured for their neglect of the children, the jury gave the verdicts of 'natural causes'. No inquest had been held on the third child's death.

The police were now interested in the couple; having reason to believe they were keeping a baby farm, they were collecting evidence against them. In November 1879, the relieving officer for the Wirral Guardians, Mr Hawkes, asked for a warrant to apprehend the prisoners and on entered the filthy home the police found three children, 8-year-old Leonora, who had been 'farmed' for a weekly payment, a 5- or 6-month-old baby that the prisoners claimed was their own. Both of these children appeared to be in a healthy state but the third child, 15-month-old Margaret (Maggie) Clarke, who had been given to them by a young woman, a domestic servant, from Toxteth Park after the Sevilles had answered an advertisement in the *Mercury* newspaper, was extremely emaciated. Maggie's mother had agreed to pay £5 and had initially paid £2 and subsequently 6 shillings but the Sevilles had not received any more. On searching the house, the police had found several letters referring to babies and a note that simply said, 'I will send more money in a fortnight.' Was this from Maggie's mother? On being taken into custody, Martha stated that it was a pity they couldn't find the mother and make her suffer! All three children were taken to Clatterbridge Workhouse.

Dr William Main had visited the home and had seen young Maggie in a wretched emaciated condition with diseased bowels that he believed was caused by improper feeding and with the appearance of a 9-month-old. He thought the child was about to die. All three children were taken to the workhouse, where young Maggie was found to weigh just 8 lb 2 oz. While at the workhouse, the baby was fed the best food and seemed to gain weight but ultimately could not rally enough and died over a week later.

Despite young Maggie's death, the medical evidence of the cause was not conclusive and so Mrs Denton/Seville could not be charged with manslaughter, but was tried for cruelty and bigamy, whilst Mr Seville was released. It was not possible to bring the charge of avoiding the provisions of the Infant Life Protection Act as the Sevilles had not kept more than one child at a time, it having been found that the two other children found in the house were, in fact, the Sevilles' natural children.

Rose McCourt, who lodged with the prisoners, said the child had been fed correctly with condensed milk, bread, biscuits, toast and fat bacon. She said that Maggie had slept with Martha but had been in a poor condition when she had arrived from her mother. To contradict this, Mrs Rebecca Moran, who had lodged at the house, stated that the child had been plump and healthy when it had first arrived. It was also stated that at first the baby was fed condensed milk but later only skimmed milk twice a day, morning and night, and at other times only had a dry bottle to suck.

Evidence was given of the condition young Maggie was found in. In addition to the emaciation there was an offensive odour and indications of rickets and bronchitis. At the inquest a verdict of death by natural causes was made.[2]

When Mrs Seville/Denton appeared before Mr Justice Grove at Chester Assizes, she pleaded guilty to the charge of bigamy. The judge stated he was surprised she had not been charged with manslaughter but found guilty of cruelty and was unable to give a sentence that was harsher for this offence, but that the old law was drawn up at a time when such serious offences were not contemplated. For bigamy she was sentenced to six months' hard labour and for cruelty twelve months' imprisonment. The sentences were to run concurrently, so she would serve six months' hard labour and six months' imprisonment without hard labour.³ It would appear that this woman got off lightly.

McIntosh

This case shows just how devious some baby farmers could be. In November 1880, Edinburgh police uncovered a baby farmer by the name of Mrs Barbara McIntosh (although there appears to be some suggestion that her name may have been Barbara Gray) from High Street, Portobello. It appears that she had an ongoing advertisement in newspapers offering to adopt children that was worded to allow the reader to think she had experience in bringing up children. Most of the children handed to her were healthy illegitimate babies who came with a premium of between £10 and £25. The children would be kept for several weeks until they were in a weak, emaciated condition when they were farmed out to someone else with a weekly fee. These children died within the month. The real trick to this was to ensure the women who received the sickly babies resided in different parishes, thereby the connection between the children was avoided, similar to the ruse used by Amelia Dyer the previous year.[4] Medical reports on the children all showed they had died from malnutrition produced either by drugging them or by lack of nourishment, and none of the medical men involved knew of more than one case.[5]

The comment that the children had been drugged suggests the use of one of the opiate-based medicines being used to quieten the babies, which led to the children not asking to be fed. This is the same method used by many baby farmers, as shown in the case of Margaret Waters in 1870.[6]

Given how cautious Mrs McIntosh was, it is surprising she was apprehended, but it came about by her receiving in July 1880, from a woman who had come into Edinburgh from the country in order to be confined at the Edinburgh Maternity Hospital, a healthy child for adoption with a premium. This same child later arrived at South Leith Poorhouse in an emaciated condition, where it died soon after.[7]

Mrs McIntosh was charged with culpable homicide or, alternatively, culpable, and wilfully neglecting children of a tender age, in consequence of which they died. Four cases were cited in this charge, although the authorities believed that seven children had passed through her hands in this way. In the event, Mrs McIntosh pleaded guilty to the lesser charge and she was sentenced to fifteen months' imprisonment, which seems a very light punishment for such a crime.[8]

Ann Crabb

As we saw in the case of Charlotte Winser, there are occasions when a child's mother and a baby farmer appear to collude in the death of the child. Just such a case occurred in 1890 when, on 13 November 1890, 8-month-old Sidney Arthur Parris was found dead beside his mother, Elizabeth Julia Parris, at Little South-sea Street, Portsmouth. Twenty-nine-year-old Mrs Parris was a widow and the child's father was said to be a corporal in the York Regiment. The midwife who delivered the baby said he had been 'as fine a baby as she had ever saw'. Parris had obtained a position as a collar ironer averaging 16 shillings a week in wages and had paid 56-year-old Ann Crabb, with whom she lodged, 2 shillings and sixpence a week to look after the boy while she was at work. Mrs Crabb also had other children under her care who were better cared for than the deceased.

The plight of young Sidney was brought to the notice of the NSPCC by a Mrs Hunt, saying that the boy was treated 'like a convict and would die', so when death occurred Mrs Parris and Mrs Crabb were charged with manslaughter.

At their trial, several witnesses were called to testify that the child was underfed and left alone for long periods of time while Mrs Crabb visited public houses. Crabb had been seen shaking the child and saying, 'the little _____ being too strong to die'. Both women had been warned by neighbours that the boy was ill-treated, and Mrs Parris had first said the neighbours were 'interfering' but had later said she would deal with the problem. She had been advised to call for a doctor to see the baby.

When the body had been examined by Dr Pearce, it was found to be emaciated, with a stomach that was almost empty of food, and to weigh just seven pounds and that the boy had been neglected over the course of several months. He pronounced that death had been caused by improper and scanty food.

The judge blamed the mother for leaving the child in the care of such a woman as Mrs Crabb, who left the boy alone for a long time. Both women were found guilty but of different charges; the mother of gross neglect and Mrs Crabb of criminal neglect. Gross neglect was not a criminal charge and, although she was morally responsible, she was acquitted while Mrs Crabb was sentenced to six months' imprisonment.[9]

Ida Mitchell

When George Laiter, an officer from the NSPCC, visited the home of Ida Charlotte Mitchell, 31, at Murray's Buildings, Vauxhall on 1 December 1890, he found two children, 5-year-old Maud Morrell and a 12-month-old boy, in a filthy state, hungry and cold. Young Maud was in such a poor state she couldn't stand and was later found to weigh just 20 lb 12 oz when her weight should have been nearer 33 lb. Mr Laiter found clothes for the children and took them to Dr Butler, where they ate ravenously, and it was thought they had been starved and neglected for a long time.

Ida Mitchell was charged with neglecting the children with intent to cause injury. Giving evidence in her defence, Emma Davis said she had handed an illegitimate baby boy over to Mitchell in December 1889 and had seen him since and thought him well cared for. She also knew that Mitchell had received £20 for a child that had since died. Despite this evidence, Mitchell was found guilty and sentenced to twelve months' imprisonment.

The jury complimented the NSPCC on bringing the case and awarded the Society a sum of money.[10]

Alice Reeves

Officers from the National Society for the Prevention of Cruelty to Children were carrying out surveillance on the home of 40-year-old Alice Reeves, alias May Jackson, Smith and Clare, in Eastlake Road, Coldharbour Lane, Brixton, London. This address was within 200 yards of the Gordon Grove home of Margaret Waters, who had been hanged twenty years earlier.

When the house was entered on 30 December 1890, eight children were found in various states of emaciation. The house was filthy, and the stench was overpowering. Over the next few days, David Patten, officer of the NSPCC, visited several times. An attending doctor ordered that food be given to the children and they all ate ravenously. One child, Stephen Simmons, was in a particularly desperate condition on 1 January 1891 and when Mrs Reeves saw how serious her situation was, she suggested the child be taken to the Harpur Street Shelter belonging to the NSPCC to receive the best care. The other six children were taken there the following day after Mrs Reeves was arrested and charged with the wilful neglect of the children. Two of these children, who were plump and healthy, were said to be the offspring of Mrs Reeves's daughters. It appeared that the children were principally taken care of by a boy of about 13 or 14.

The house was searched and ninety pawn tickets relating to items of children's clothing were found. Mrs Reeves had been advertising for children using several aliases and it was found that four children had died whilst in her care.

Attempts were made to trace the parents of the children and the mother of a boy, named Stephen Simmonds, who was in the most pitiable state and later died, was said to be Emily Simmonds, a lady's maid, who had been paying a weekly sum for his care and had, in addition, paid for medical treatment for him, although there was no evidence that he had ever received any such treatment. At little Stephen's post-mortem, it was found that he had died of inflammation of the lungs following starvation and neglect. The jury at his inquest decided that Mrs Reeves should be charged with manslaughter.

Louis De Clare, aged 13 months, also died after being removed from Eastlake Road. It was said that this child had been well nourished but had contracted measles. His inquest decided he had died of natural causes.

The parents of Albert Reeves, 1 year and 9 months, had been found and they had paid £20 for the boy to be taken in the charge of by Mrs Reeves. This boy also died after being taken from Mrs Reeves and the jury at his inquest found a verdict of manslaughter against Mrs Reeves after being told the child had died of starvation.

On 9 March 1891, Alice Reeves appeared at the Old Bailey charged with the manslaughter of Stephen Simmons.

Stephen's mother, Emily Simmons, had given birth to the illegitimate baby in July 1889 and had taken care of the boy until he was 14 months old when she took him to Eastlake Road and into the care of Alice Reeves. In December, Emily's sister, Ellen, wrote to Mrs Reeves saying she would visit on 17 December and, as a result of the reply she had received informing her the child was very ill, she visited on the day before she had intended.

What she saw was a boy who was very thin and in a bad condition, suffering from diarrhoea and fits. Mrs Reeves said this had been caused by teething and had been attended by two doctors. Ellen paid several weeks' fees of 6 shillings a week and 2 shillings postage to allow letters to be sent informing of the child's progress. The following day, Ellen received a letter from Reeves saying the boy was a little better and asking for more money to buy expensive food. The kind aunt sent £1 and 15 shillings. On 27 December, Ellen visited again and thought the child continued to be very unwell. Three days later, another letter arrived asking for yet more money (15 shillings) and Ellen sent £1. On 3 January, Ellen was informed that Stephen had been removed from Eastlake Road and, after visiting the house, she saw the boy at the NSPCC's Shelter. Five days later, she identified the body of young Stephen.

Surgeon Patrick George Simpson attended the Reeves household on 10 December, having been called in to see Stephen. He was informed that the baby was Alice's child and that Alice had been away, leaving her daughter in charge of the boy. Three children were seen by Mr Simpson, and he was told that all had been delicate from birth. He wanted to examine Stephen, whose face was thin, dirty and emaciated, but found him wrapped in filthy clothing covered in vomit and diarrhoea. He told Mrs Reeves to wash the child and that he would send medicine for the diarrhoea and would return the following day to carry out a thorough examination. Over the next few days, he continued to visit and prescribe medicine for the boy and on one occasion was asked to look at another child who was in a similar condition to Stephen. He also saw a 3-year-old girl called Nellie who was said to be having fits. Despite continually telling Mrs Reeves the importance of keeping the children clean, they were often in a filthy condition. Mr Simpson told her in strong terms that she was not taking proper care of the children. Eventually Mrs Reeves was told that Stephen should be taken to the hospital immediately and he would write a letter for the hospital. Mr Simpson had the letter returned unopened with a note saying the child's grandmother had refused permission for Stephen to attend the hospital. Mr Simpson said he could no longer take responsibility for the child if it was not taken to the hospital and the police were informed. On 6 January, Stephen was in the Harpur Street Shelter suffering from pneumonia and two days later he died, the cause of death being pneumonia exacerbated by emaciation due to lack of food or improper feeding.

Surgeon Frank Reid stated that there were several children taken from the house: 13-month-old Lewis; 2 year, 9-month-old Nellie, 1 year, 8-month-old Albert and 1 year, 3-month-old Alice Major. Of these, Alice was returned to her parents and the other three had died.

Alice Reeves was found guilty of the manslaughter of Stephen Simmons and sentenced to ten years' hard labour.

Although there were charges of manslaughter against Alice Reeves with regard to the deaths of the other three children, no evidence was offered.[11]

Abi Joan Barton

Abi Barton advertised 'a happy home for children' under the name of Mrs George, Home Farm, Allnutt's Estate, Epping; however, when an inspector of the Society for the Prevention of Cruelty to Children visited the house in January 1891, he found the home was far from happy. A person from the neighbourhood had alerted the Society to the house, which was two houses joined together. He found the place was filthy, with very little furniture. The house smelled offensively, and the straw and flock beds were in a dreadful state. Eighteen children between the ages of 2½ and 11 years old were found to be living in the house. All of them were dirty and some were suffering from bronchitis and ringworm, and all were insufficiently clothed and crawling with vermin. A medical officer stated that the house was unfit for children and was likely to result in bronchitis or pneumonia. Before Christmas, several children had been removed as there had been twenty-five in residence. Prior to moving to Epping, Mrs Barton had lived in Loughton, Essex, where she had been taking in children under 1 year old for a premium. When two of these children had died, inquests had been held but no criminal proceedings had taken place but, shortly afterwards, she had been fined £3 for not being registered under the Infant Life Protection Act.

After the visit from the Society, Mrs Barton was summoned under Section 1 of the 1889 Act to appear at Epping petty sessions charged with wilfully neglecting the children in her care. After hearing the evidence, the bench decided that the neglect was not wilful and adjourned the case *Sine Die* (with no date for resumption). She was told that if the house were kept clean and the children's health improved, there would be no further action taken but that a careful watch should be kept.[12]

Elizabeth Bailey

On 11 October 1894, Police Sergeant King saw widow Elizabeth Bailey sitting by the sea with a baby on her lap. The boy, 4-month-old Alfred Ernest Lacey, was covered in sores, which Mrs Bailey said were caused by the life the mother led – could this be syphilis? – and he was nothing but skin and bone, his skin hanging loose over his body and his hair worn away at the back of his head by being left lying down too long. Mrs Bailey said the child was just getting over bronchitis.

Two days later, Sergeant King visited Mrs Bailey's home at the appropriately named Dark Alley, Gosport. This time the boy was cleaner and wearing new clothes but physically no better. He was feeding from a dirty pickling bottle with a tube that was corroded and thick with stale milk. There were four other children in the house that were Bailey's own children.

Elizabeth Bailey was summoned to Gosport petty sessions by Mr Barker of the NSPCC for neglecting baby Alfred and causing him unnecessary suffering.

It was stated that Bailey neglected the baby chiefly when she was drunk.

Frances Lacey, the boy's mother, placed the baby to be nursed by Bailey when he was 7 weeks old for 4 shillings a week and, at that point, he had been healthy and in good condition. She had visited the baby regularly and had found him neglected so had taken him back to her home in White's Row, Portsea (interestingly this would have been around the same time as the NSPCC had taken an interest in the case and one wonders how much care Miss Lacey would have had for her little boy without the authorities' involvement).

Mr Barker of the NSPCC had also visited the house on 13 October and found that the baby was in a clean cot but that this was the only clean place in the house and that there was no accommodation provided for the other four children, all of whom were badly clothed. It appears Mrs Bailey had made some attempt at improving the lot of baby Alfred after her meeting with Sergeant King two days previously. Mr Barker said the child had been much neglected but was now showing an improvement; however, when the boy was produced in court it was evident he was still showing a sickening appearance.

Mrs Bailey assured the court that she loved the child too much to neglect him, but this was not believed by the magistrates, who found her guilty and sentenced her to six weeks' imprisonment with hard labour.[13]

Emma Betts

In 1895, Loughborough Police Court saw a case brought by the NSPCC of cruelty against Emma Betts, a married woman from Sileby, Leicestershire. Mrs Betts had four children living with her: 17-year-old Edith Gamble, 7-year-olds Arthur Taylor and Douglas Wright, and an unnamed baby boy. All four had been placed with Betts for a weekly fee and the older children had lived with Mr and Mrs Betts for some time, as can be seen on the 1891 census return.

Emma Betts was said to be a heavy drinker and the baby was left in the house while she went drinking. Young Edith went out to work so was unable to assist with the care of the baby.

On 27 August 1895, PC Pegg went to the house at 10.30 pm, found the door undone and had found Mrs Betts lying across the hearth in a drunken state. When he eventually managed to arouse the woman, he said he wanted to see the baby, whereon Mrs Betts refused to allow him to look over the house and blew the lamp out in order to stop him. When he relit the lamp, Mrs Betts then proceeded to pick up some tongs and struck the lamp, which was in PC Pegg's hand, breaking the glass. When PC Pegg eventually managed to see the baby, the child was asleep in a bed with one of the older boys. He found that the baby's left eye was completely closed, and the left side of the face was covered in bruises.

A day or two later, PC Pegg visited the house again, this time accompanied by Inspector Collard of the NSPCC, when they were told by Mrs Betts that the injuries to the baby, whose name she could not remember, had been caused by her having dropped the child on the day of the flower show. The baby was dirty and there were sores on the back of his head and the back of his ears were raw. Mrs Betts received 3 shillings and sixpence per week to care for this child.

Throughout the trial, Mrs Betts caused so much fuss and interruption to the proceedings that she was removed from the court. When it was suggested that the case should be adjourned for a week, Inspector Collard and PC Pegg said that the woman was always like that, so the case continued, and she was brought back.

Evidence was given by a Mr Walker, who lived in the same court, that Mrs Betts spent most of her time in the public house, leaving the baby alone, and she had been very drunk on the day of the flower show.

Dr Garvin stated that the baby was underweight, and its health was run down.

The magistrates came to the verdict that Emma Betts was guilty of cruelty to the boy and sentenced her to three months' hard labour.[14]

Joseph and Agnes Bailey

In 1895, John Ottley of the NSPCC received a complaint about Joseph (36) and Agnes Broadhurst Bailey (38) of Upper Knowle, Somerset who had recently moved from Cumberland Road, Bristol. On the afternoon of 7 February, he visited their home at Shaftesbury House in the company of Police Sergeant Windmill, where he was told by the Baileys that they had three babies in their care. He was met by Mr Bailey, who was holding baby Dorothy Marshall (Akehurst) in his arms. According to the Baileys, Dorothy had been with them for three weeks and had come from London for the payment of 6 shillings a week. Mrs Bailey was also holding a young child, 4-month-old Henry Ernest Bill, who had come from Sidcup, Kent a month before with £8. Henry looked unwell. Mrs Bailey then went upstairs and returned with another child, 9-month-old Cyril Joseph Bailey, who they had adopted.

Mr Ottley asked to see the children's sleeping arrangements. Mr Bailey said it was untidy and Mrs Bailey said that he should come another day. Nevertheless, Mr Ottley went upstairs where he found a cot and a bed in one room; in another he found baby Henry lying on a bed. When he returned to the landing, he saw Mrs Bailey closing a door to another room. When asked what was inside, Mrs Bailey replied that it was a lumber room and was empty, and, sure enough, when Mr Ottley entered, he found an empty room. However, there was a door at the far end and, on entering this room, he found three more babies; two were on the floor while the third was being held by a boy of about 12 years of age named Bertie who had come from Bristol. These three were identified as: Mary Winston, 12 or 13 months old, who had been brought to the Baileys the previous June for £10; 8-month-old Sidney Bruce from London who had been there for two months for £6; and 7-month-old Ernest Thompson from Bath who had been there for six weeks but had not come with any money. While the rooms were warm, with fires lit, none of the children were properly dressed and the beds were unclean.

The Baileys were indicted for keeping five children under the age of 1 for the purposes of nursing or maintaining apart from their parents.

When giving evidence against them, Dorothy's mother, widow Elizabeth Akehurst, said she had wished to make provision for her daughter and had advertised in a newspaper under the name Marshall. This had been answered by Mrs Bailey, who had wanted to adopt the baby 'as her own' and after some thought Mrs Akehurst had arranged to visit the Baileys at Shaftesbury House on 6 February. Being satisfied with what she saw and believing there were no other children in the house, she left a healthy 10-week-old Dorothy and £15 in gold with them. Within two weeks, Dorothy had died. However, at the inquest into Dorothy's death, Dr Logan said the child appeared to be well nourished with no visible signs of neglect but had died of asphyxiation due to a congestion of the lungs.

A similar story was told by Anne Bill of Sidcup, Kent. She, too, had had an advertisement answered by Mrs Bailey and had visited Shaftesbury House. She saw no other children and left healthy baby Henry and £6; again, the child had died within two weeks.

Sixteen-year-old Ada Jane Dix had worked for the Baileys and stated that if the babies drank their milk too fast, Mrs Bailey would smack them, and she had witnessed Mr Bailey hitting one with a slipper several times a day, although the others were never harmed in this way. She also said that the supply of milk and condensed milk had once run out and she had been going to pawn her own skirts and some of Mrs Bailey's things in order to buy more milk.

For two days from 14 February, Mrs Bailey's sister, Mrs Mary Nash, looked after five children at Shaftesbury House. She stated that there was plenty of everything, food and clothing, and that when Dr Logan had examined the children to ascertain if they were fit to enter the workhouse, all were except Dorothy, who was poorly and died during this period.

Both Mr and Mrs Bailey maintained they had cared for the children well and that the illness of the two children who had died was due to them travelling during the cold weather and that they had caught chills. They had not realised they needed to register under the Infant Life Protection Act. Mrs Bailey stated that she had no need for the money associated with nursing the children as she had money of her own and had invested in freehold worth £1,000 in Salisbury, even showing a photograph of the property.

The chairman pointed out to the jury that ignorance was not an excuse. The jury found the couple guilty, and they were each sentenced to four months' hard labour. No evidence was offered for two other indictments against them.[15]

As an amusing footnote to this story, the four babies who were taken to Bourton workhouse were not labelled with any form of identification and, it appears, they got muddled up. The master of the workhouse sent to Bristol for the little boy who had lived at Shaftesbury House. The boy did a sterling job of identification, and all the babies' clothes were labelled with the correct names and the children had coloured ribbons attached so that no more confusion could take place. This was considered necessary as there was now, according to the *Bristol Mercury and Daily Post* of 28 March 1895, 'no fear of any complications arising in the future over the ownership – we will not venture to say paternity – of any of the babies.'[16]

Eva Marshall

In 1899, 1 Circular Road, Tottenham was the house of unlicensed baby farmer Eva Marshall. She was taken to court by the NSPCC for receiving five illegitimate children for fees totalling 12 shillings and sixpence a week. She was also charged with neglecting the children, Louis Foley, 10 years, Florence Palmer, 3½ years, May Howell, 3½ years, Edward Bashford, 2½ years, and Blanche Harding, 6 months. They were so dirty and neglected that two of them were taken to the workhouse, where one of them later died. This child had been received from Mrs Packer, who had appeared in the coroner's court just weeks earlier after several children in her care had died. In addition to these five children, there were also three children that belonged to Marshall, one of whom was old enough to go out to work.

Mrs Marshall claimed ignorance of the law regarding registration, but said she was not cruel.

She was found guilty of both counts and fined 40 shillings and costs, or one month's imprisonment on the first, and 60 shillings and costs, or one month's imprisonment on the second.[17]

Annie and Thomas Pavitt

In September 1899, Mr Akehurst, inspector of the NSPCC, received an anonymous letter that sent him to 8 Albion Road, Eastbourne, where he met Annie Pavitt, 42, and her stout, white-haired, insurance agent husband, Thomas, 51. Despite not being registered under the Infant Life Protection Act, when asked if she had a nurse child, she showed him a thin, emaciated child, Ivy May Pengelly, weighing half the normal weight for a child of 8 months old, lying on a low couch in a back room. Mrs Pavitt said the girl's condition was due to sickness and diarrhoea that the child had had for six weeks but was getting better as it no longer had diarrhoea. Mr Akehurst inspected Ivy and found her to be dirty and flea-bitten. She had been fed on a mixture of one-third cow's milk and two-thirds water. Mrs Pavitt had called Dr Wheeler Taylor to see her and had followed his instructions. Dr Wheeler Taylor was called and, after taking his advice and against Mrs Pavitt's wishes, Mr Akehurst applied to a magistrate to order the removal of the little girl from the Pavitts' care to the workhouse. Ivy died in the workhouse ten days later. The doctor felt unable to complete a death certificate and an inquest took place.

During the inquest, Mr Akehurst gave evidence about the condition of the house. He said the child slept in a cot next to the bed where the couple slept, which was dirty and smelled very strongly. The coroner suggested that some people of this rank were not always very clean, but Mr Akehurst said that the child had no means of moving from where it had been placed and that it was very dirty indeed. He also said there was little food in the house. He had seen a tin of Neaves Food with a little in the bottom of the tin. Ivy had not been fed this but had been fed milk. Mr Akehurst had seen milk in the house and there was untainted milk in a clean bottle.

The Pavitts were charged with neglect of the three children that were in their care. During the trial, which took place at the magistrates' court, it transpired that the Pavitts had advertised in a newspaper for children either to adopt for a deposit of £10 or for the payment of a weekly sum. Mr Pavitt was an insurance agent and had insured all the children. Had Ivy's insurance policy paid out on her death, the Pavitts would have been paid 30 shillings.

Emma Pengelly, Ivy's mother, gave evidence saying she had answered an advertisement and had given 2-month-old Ivy to a Mrs Smith, who she identified in court as being Mrs Pavitt. 'Mrs Smith' had visited Miss Pengelly's mother's house, bringing an agreement with her signed as William Smith and Ella Smith, and said she would like the baby christened as Smith and that she would clothe and educate her. Baby Ivy was healthy, although she had been fed Nestle's Milk but had been upset by it and the doctor had recommended she be fed pearl barley, when taken by 'Mrs Smith' to Brighton Station. Miss Pengelly then received several letters saying the baby was well until she was told, six weeks earlier, that Ivy was unwell with diarrhoea and sickness. Miss Pengelly had had letters from the vaccination officer telling her that no one by the name of Smith lived at 8 Albion Road, Eastbourne. She had believed that her baby was being looked after by a couple who were in a better situation than appeared to be the case and she had received very nice letters from 'Mrs Smith'.

When giving evidence, Dr Wheeler Taylor said he had frequently visited the Pavitt house to see Ivy and believed she was being fed improper food. He had recommended cow's milk and barley water and had sent the woman who nursed his own child to Mrs Pavitt to show her how to make the food using Robinson's Prepared Barley, but he did not believe Mrs Pavitt was following his advice. He thought that Ivy had been improperly fed or starved as the child was getting worse. When he visited the house, the milk he saw was fresh and wholesome and Mrs Pavitt appeared to be fond of the child, cuddling her and saying kind words to her.

Dr James Adams carried out the post-mortem on Ivy and found there to be no sign of disease but a complete absence of any fat on her body. He concluded she had died of slow starvation.

In her defence, Mrs Pavitt said she did all she could for Ivy. She said she tried to give her beef tea, bath biscuits and a few drops of brandy in addition to the milk and barley water.

Mr Pavitt, while backing up his wife's claims about the feeding of Ivy, even saying that everyone including the cat was well fed in his house, then said he had nothing to do with the adoption or child rearing and was at work most of the time. Despite this, letters written to Mrs Glen in his handwriting were produced. He also said he had only insured the children in order to achieve his weekly total. However, he appears to have written that 'Mr and Mrs Vincent' were very respectable.

The other two children in the Pavitts' care were 11-month-old Norah Glen and 10-month-old Arthur Woodford, both of whom were vastly underweight when found. Norah's mother had written to a 'Mrs Vincent' in answer to an advertisement. Norah had been taken for £1 a week until £12 had been paid. When Norah was taken to the workhouse, she had no hair on the back of her head, which indicated she had been left lying on her back for much of the time. Arthur's mother was illiterate, and letters had been written on her behalf by a Mrs Ellen Foster to a 'Mrs Pratt'.

A young woman named Jane Shepherd said she had given her child to Mrs Pavitt to nurse but when she visited, she had seen the sores on Norah's head and had taken her own very thin child away. Since leaving, her child had put on weight.

When the Pavitts first moved to Eastbourne, they had rented rooms in the house of Mrs Esther Smith in Havelock Road and Mrs Smith said Mrs Pavitt had told her that if a doctor were called to see a child within six weeks of its death, an inquest would not be called.

Evidence was given that Mrs Pavitt had been sentenced to two months' hard labour in Loughton in 1896 after abandoning a child with broken arms.

The chairman said that it was detrimental to society to allow people to advertise under false names for the adoption of children. Both were found guilty and sentenced to six months' imprisonment with hard labour.[18]

Amy Douglas

Widow Amy Louisa McNeil Douglas, 28, was a lucky woman. The judge, when passing sentence in 1899, stated that 'there were many points in the prisoner's case that almost made it appear she was a murderess' and that she was 'utterly indifferent to human life'; nevertheless, she was found guilty of manslaughter and sentenced to five years' penal servitude.

Ellen Roberts, inspector, under the Life Protection Act, for West Ham, visited Amy Douglas at 19 Cromer Road, Walthamstow, and found Amy Douglas and seven children, one of whom was dead. Douglas was not registered under the Act and Mrs Roberts assisted Douglas to complete the required forms. Although the parlour was clean, there was little furniture, and the mattresses and bedding were filthy. Over the course of a month, Mrs Roberts visited several times and found some improvement in the conditions, but no more furniture, the babies sleeping in straw-filled boxes. On her last visit, she was informed that Douglas was moving to Chingford, whereupon Mrs Roberts informed the Board of Guardians at Chingford.

When in Chingford, Douglas registered under the Infant Life Protection Act, and when visited by inspector Samuel Wilks on 15 June, he found six children: 7-year-old Catherine; 7-month-old Cyril; 9-month-old Herbert (these three said to be Douglas's own children); 4-month-old Winifred Emma Keen; 3-month-old William James McDonald; and 3-month-old Evelyn Constance Hodson. All the nurse children appeared to be emaciated and unwell, so Dr Priddie was called to attend the children. By 21 July, only Winifred looked a little better. In response to Mr Wilks receiving a telegram, he visited again on 10 August, only to find the youngest two babies dead and Winifred still emaciated. She was taken to Epping Infirmary, where she was found to weigh just 10 lb 8 oz.

Dr Priddie carried out the post-mortem examination on Evelyn Hodson and concluded that the baby had died of improper and insufficient feeding over a number of weeks. Dr Francis Beresford performed the post-mortem on William McDonald and came to the same conclusion as Dr Priddie. William, too, had died of improper and insufficient feeding over a number of weeks.

By 11 August, Winifred Keen was also dead, and the post-mortem came to the same conclusion as to the cause of death as the other two.

It later transpired that neither Cyril or Herbert were Douglas's own children but nurse children for whom she had received £12 and £6 in premiums.[19]

The prosecution case was that she had wilfully neglected and starved the children in her care with the result that the deaths had occurred. Douglas, who defended herself, denied she had starved them but said she was inexperienced in caring for children and hadn't realised they were so ill. A fourth child had been in her care but had been unaccounted for at the time of her arrest. When asked about this child, she claimed the child had died suddenly while she had been away from the house. She had then put the baby in a bag and had left it close to some stables. The police investigated this claim and found that a child's body had been found in a bag in the street and an inquest had been held that showed no evidence that the baby had come to a violent end.

Quite why Douglas was not charged with murder is unclear, but she certainly escaped the hangman, although she was taken from the dock in tears, perhaps not realising just how fortunate she was.[20]

George and Sarah Snelling

The NSPCC brought a prosecution against George and Sarah Snelling of Gladstone Terrace, Battersea Park Road, Wandsworth in May 1899 after finding six children aged between 9 months and 12 years of age living in appallingly dirty conditions. All but the eldest had been kept in a filthy and verminous condition. The eldest boy had been found to have a good singing voice and Sarah had been taking him around the local public houses to sing in concerts for 7 shillings a night. This income was in addition to the 30 to 34 shillings a week that she received for the care of the children.

Sarah was found guilty of neglect and sentenced to six months' imprisonment while George was thought to be less culpable but had failed to stop such cruelty and was sentenced to one month's hard labour.[21]

Holliday and Leonard

Sixty-eight-year-old Sarah Leonard had only lived with her three daughters, Annie, 39, Lily, 36, Rose, 31 and Lily's husband, George Holliday, 30, at 138 Grosvenor Road, Bristol a week when Inspector Ottley of the Society for the Prevention of Cruelty to Children called on 18 July 1899. Despite hearing people moving around inside, no one answered his knock. Fearing the worst, Inspector Ottley returned twice the following day but still there was no reply. On 22 July he returned, this time accompanied by the police, a doctor, and a search warrant. Inside he found four children: Sarah Elizabeth Holliday, daughter of Lily and George, Maggie Kidwell, 2, Claud Kilminster, 8 months, and Ernest Leonard Northam, 7 months. All the children were covered in dirt and some of them were so sore and raw that they were bleeding. The whole house was filthy, and the stench was almost overwhelming; pigeons had been kept in the house and two dead birds were found. Some laughter was elicited in court when Mrs Leonard joked that she would have cooked them, had she known the visitors had been coming, only to have Ottley reply that the pigeons would not have needed cooking were they left any longer. Dr Walker certified for the removal of three of the children to the workhouse, where Claud later died of an abnormality of his heart.

A vast quantity of papers was found in the house, including fifteen or twenty insurance forms and two documents, signed by Annie Leonard, showing payments of £40 and £20 had been made in respect of two children. This was used to prove that children were being taken to 'farm'. All the adults living in the house were charged with ill-treating and neglecting the four children.

George Holliday worked at Bristol docks and claimed that while he was living with his mother-in-law, he had nothing to do with the children. The court accepted this plea and the charges against him were dropped. George's wife, Lily, also claimed to be out working all day, and so took no part in childcare. Charges were dropped in her case, although it was said that she had had a narrow escape as she must have been aware of what was going on. The other three defendants denied neglecting the children, claiming that the house had been left in the filthy state by previous tenants. However, they were found guilty of gross neglect and sentenced to three months' hard labour, with Sarah being 'placed in the first division due to her age and state of health'.[22]

Chapter 10

Manslaughter

As shown in the chapter about cruelty, there are some cases where baby farmers were found guilty of the manslaughter of children in their care. In some of these cases it seems inconceivable that they were not charged with murder and sentenced to death. While they probably felt aggrieved at being incarcerated for their crimes, they should be pleased they got away with their lives.

Cecilia Baker

Occasionally we find a case where the baby farmer is found not guilty of manslaughter and the case against Cecilia Baker is one such case. This case is indicative of the appalling conditions so many lived in during this period.

Seventeen-year-old Agnes Anderson gave birth to a baby girl, also called Agnes, in Holborn Workhouse in June 1871. Having nowhere to go when she left the workhouse in July, she roamed the streets for several days until she started lodging with a Mr and Mrs Bentley, paying 3 shillings a week to share their room. She then went out to earn her living 'the best way she could' – does this indicate that Miss Anderson was working as a prostitute?

Around this time, she gave the baby into Cecilia Baker's care for 8 shillings a week. Mrs Baker lived in a basement kitchen at 16 Colville Place, Charlotte Street, Marylebone. The kitchen was described at the inquest as 'damp and unhealthy, and totally unfit for the habitation of any human being. In this filthy hole lived seven human beings…' After failing to pay for three weeks, Anderson took the child from Baker and gave her to a Mrs Smith who took care of her for a week at the rate of 6 shillings and sixpence, but after finding Smith had pawned the child's clothes, she took the unfortunate infant back to Mrs Baker.

During this time, the baby's condition deteriorated and was taken in a wretched state by Anderson to the Middlesex Hospital and to a chemist and was told at both that the child was not receiving enough nourishment. Mrs Baker had been feeding the child on milk, gin and aniseed when it was fed at all, as Baker was often drunk and failed to feed the baby for long periods of time.

In addition to this poor care by Baker, Agnes Anderson would take the child out at night and tell passers-by that the baby was dead and ask for money to bury it. She would then get drunk and feed the child gin, oranges and oysters. The poor child got into a dreadful condition and was crawling with vermin.

Eventually the matter came to the notice of the magistrate. The child and her mother were sent to the House of Detention on 8 September and the child died on 12 September. Both Anderson and Baker were charged with manslaughter. Anderson accused Baker of feeding the child gin in order to make it sleep and said the baby was often asleep when she visited. Baker had told her that the child would thrive whilst it was asleep. Baker, on the other hand, accused Anderson of failing to pay the agreed 8 shillings a week and said she had refused to allow Anderson to take the baby out at night if she had arrived drunk.

Dr Saul said it was difficult to say what was the proper food for a baby and that some of the symptoms he had observed in the child could be normal signs of disease.

On hearing these facts, the judge directed the jury to find the prisoners not guilty of manslaughter.

It is difficult to see how this infant could have thrived given the conditions and care she was given and perhaps it shows the different mindset that was prevalent at this time. Perhaps at a later date this pair would have been charged with neglect.[1]

Augusta Gammage

When Putney gardener John Tidy's wife died, he needed someone to take care of his two children, a girl of 4 years, 9 months old and boy, John Henry, who was 2 years and 9 months old. A neighbour recommended needlewoman Augusta Gammage, who agreed to care for the children at the rate of 5 shillings a week and on 7 September 1874 he took the pair to live with Gammage. Mr Tidy was a caring father, visiting and taking vegetables, meat, milk and biscuits for the children in addition to the sum agreed. After one such visit, he noticed John had marks on his back, arm and face, as if he had been hit with a stick. Gammage initially said the child had fallen onto the fender but there was no fender and eventually agreed she had slapped the boy. Mr Tidy told her that should he see any marks on his children again he would prosecute her.

Gammage lodged in a room in the house of Mary Ann Luther who had warned Gammage that she had heard the slaps and consequent cries of the children and said she would call the police or the children's father should she hear it again. Gammage had told her the children were dirty and she had slapped them because of that.

Neighbour Eleanor Sadler overheard Gammage berating the little boy for being dirty and heard slaps that lasted for half an hour.

Clearly Mr Tidy was not happy with the care being given to the children as he gave notice on the 5 October that he would be taking the children away five days later. When he called at Gammage's house at 5 o'clock on 10 October, he was told that John was unwell in bed with a cold but otherwise the two children were getting on nicely.

At around 10 o'clock that night, Annie Cubtaner saw a woman, who was being followed by a little girl, throw a small child over her shoulder while shaking it and telling it to 'wake up, you little wretch'. Mrs Cubtaner watched as the woman went into Mr Tidy's front door and a minute later came out alone and returned towards Mrs Luther's cottage.

At 9.45 pm that same evening, Gammage appeared at Mr Tidy's house carrying John Henry. She said he had been taken worse, but she had not called a doctor. The child was put to bed in a helpless state, but his father was unable to see what the problem was due to the poor lighting. He called the girl from upstairs, and they examined little John and found a great number of marks on his face and arms before the unfortunate boy died. Mr Tidy sent for Dr William Shears.

Dr Shears found the boy's body, face, arms and legs to be covered in bruises and burns. During the post-mortem, it was revealed that the boy was undernourished with inflammation of the stomach and large intestine that corresponded with a bruise on the surface of the skin and a blood clot was discovered in the brain. He said that, apart from the injury to the brain, none of the other injuries would cause death on their own and that the brain injury may have been caused by a fall, but the bruises and burns could not have been caused by accident.

Mr Tidy said that his little girl had also had bruises and burns on her arms.

On 26 October 1874, Augusta Gammage was found guilty of the manslaughter of John Henry Tidy and sentenced to ten years' penal servitude.[2]

Betsy Binmore

The 1861 census shows Betsy Binmore to be living with her husband, Edward, an agricultural labourer who was 27 years her senior, and her year-old daughter, Sarah Jane.[3] In 1871, the census shows her to have started baby farming as she has two young babies, Ernest Fry, aged 2, and Frederick Almond, aged 5 months, visiting her home.[4]

In September 1874, Betsy registered the birth of Edith Ellen Holmes. Edith's mother is named on the certificate but not her father, so it would appear that Edith is illegitimate. Edith was born in Betsy's home; this may indicate that Betsy was working as a midwife – she certainly appears to be using her home for accouchements.

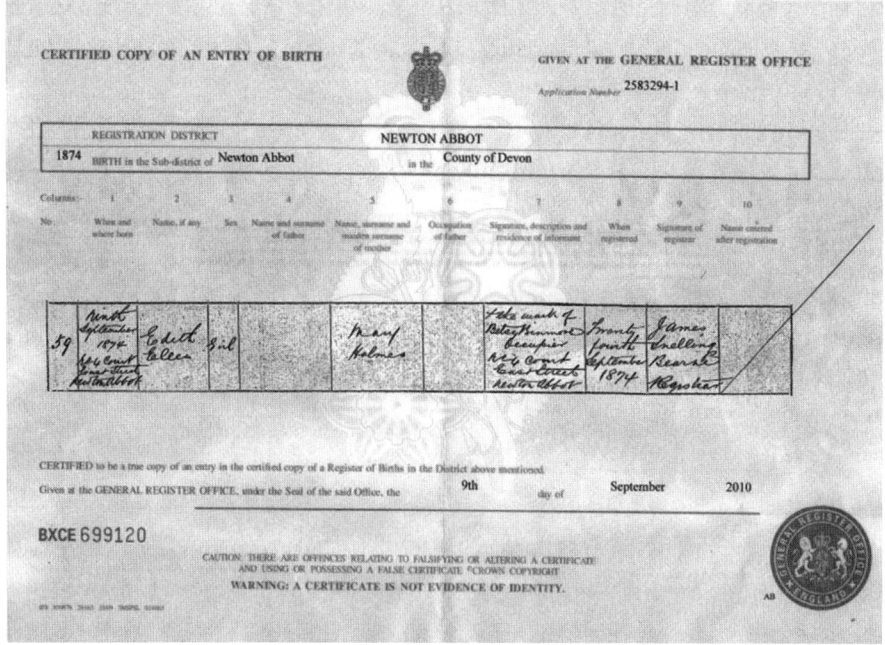

Birth certificate for Edith Ellen Holmes.

It is thought that Edith was one of the emaciated children found in the house after Betsy's arrest.

In January 1875, a coroner's jury found that Margaret Phillips, age 5 months, had been the victim of manslaughter; however, it was mentioned that three other babies had died while being cared for by Betsy Binmore, and she was sent to trial for murder by the magistrates.[5]

During her trial in March of that year, the child's unmarried mother, Mary Phillips, stated she had given birth in the Union Workhouse at Newton Abbot on 1 August 1874 and had stayed in the workhouse, feeding the baby, for two months and the baby had been healthy. She clearly did not wish to keep the child as she entrusted Margaret to mother of nine, Mrs Mary Hall, 'to keep'; however, she changed her mind about this as she took the baby from Mrs Hall after noticing that the baby had lost weight. She called at the chemist and got two powders for her. Margaret had not liked suckling from a bottle and had been a 'cross child'. She then went to stay for two weeks with Mrs Betsy Binmore, who was very kind to the baby. During this time, she fed the baby on bread and one pint of milk a day. When Miss Phillips left for Torquay, and later Bath, she left Margaret in Betsy's care for 2 shillings and sixpence a week, to be paid monthly. She stated the baby was then fed on milk and cornflour, but she did not know how much. Each week she received a letter detailing the baby's health and she had not been informed that the child was unwell.

The nurse from the workhouse, Susan Bartlett, said she had seen Margaret after her birth at the workhouse, and she had been a fine, healthy baby girl and when she saw her again, after her death, she had not recognised her shrivelled, emaciated body. She also stated that there had been two other children in Binmore's house, both were thin and emaciated. The boy, who was 5 months old, had also been born in the workhouse and he had left as a fine, healthy child, but when she found him, he weighed only 7 lb and a few ounces and she had feared for his life. However, after spending time in the workhouse being fed every hour, he now weighed 11 lbs.

Betsy's neighbour, Mrs Mudge, said she had visited the prisoner's house and Betsy had seemed very fond of the children in her charge. They had always been clean but when she saw baby Margaret lying on Betsy's lap on 5 January, the child had looked very ill and wasted. Betsy said she had tried to send for the doctor, but he would not come.

That Betsy had tried to send for a doctor to attend the baby in December was confirmed by her daughter, 16-year-old Sarah Jane. She said she had asked Dr Haydon to visit but he had asked for a parish paper that would ensure payment from the parish. He was told this was not a parish case and that the mother would pay; however, he refused to visit until he had been paid as he had attended three other babies at Binmore's house and had not been paid for any of them. Betsy had also tried to get a Dr Jayne to visit. Sarah Jane spoke of the other babies that had died, saying that they had been attended by Dr Haydon and Dr Drake and that they had been fed bread and sugar as well as milk and cornflour, and they had been fed three or four times a day and a bottle at night.

Evidence was given by the dairyman, John Webber, and his wife, Sarah, as to the quantity of milk purchased by the prisoner.

When giving evidence, Dr Haydon, said the amount of milk that Binmore was buying was not sufficient for the number of babies in the house. He stated that children brought up by the poor and fed by hand were quite likely to die in infancy. Dr Drake agreed with Dr Haydon's opinion about the quantity of food needed for a baby. He had also attended babies at Betsy's house, both of whom had died, but he believed the cause of these deaths had been atrophy caused by disease. Again, he had not been paid for his services in these cases. He had also been called to attend baby Margaret but had also refused.

Betsy appeared to try to find help for the sick baby as she said she went to the relieving officer three times, but he had not been at home. When Margaret eventually gave up the struggle for life, Betsy called PC Nicholls, who did not know there was a baby farm at the house. She told him she did not know what to do as she had called three doctors and none of them would attend. The registrar refused to give a death certificate and PC Nicholls had informed the coroner. When the remaining two children were taken into the workhouse the following morning, both had been so weak, they had been unable to cry. The boy had weighed 7 lb 11 oz and the girl only 4 oz more.

Dr Gay of Newton Abbot carried out the post-mortem and had found only a small quantity of fluid in the child's stomach and that there was no food in either the child's stomach or her intestines. He found no evidence of disease to account for this and the baby's brain was healthy. He attributed the girl's death entirely to lack of nourishment. He noted that the two other living children in the house were also starving, and he recommended to Mrs Binmore that she feed them. He stated that the quantity of milk purchased by the prisoner was sufficient for one child but totally inadequate for three.

The defence solicitor, Mr Bompas, called a witness, Mary Waycott, who stated Betsy had always been very kind-hearted to the children. He then stated there was no evidence that the prisoner had intended to harm the children in her care, and he did not think there enough evidence to put to a jury. The judge, Mr Justice Lush, thought this was a matter for the jury to decide. In his closing speech, Mr Bompas said Mrs Binmore had been guilty of omission and had no intention to cause harm to the child.

In his summing up, His Lordship said that in order to find the prisoner guilty of murder there must be evidence of intent to kill and that, in this case, it was in the prisoner's interest to keep the child alive as she was receiving 2 shillings and sixpence a week that would stop should the child die, although it was in her interest to spend as little of this money as possible on the child in order to make a larger profit for herself. He said that should they find her responsible for the child's death but without intent to destroy it then they could find her guilty of a lesser charge.

After a short deliberation, the jury found Betsy Binmore guilty of manslaughter.

In passing sentence, His Lordship said he thought the verdict a just one on the evidence given but that he should make an example of her by sentencing her to a heavy sentence as a warning to others. He sentenced her to twelve years' hard labour.

Betsy was removed from the dock crying bitterly.[6]

This case highlighted the lack of enforcement of the Infant Life Protection Act 1872 and the Home Secretary, Viscount Cross, was asked in parliament if he would circulate to all local authorities named in the Act calling on them to enforce the enactment. He stated that there was no way to enforce the Act and that the authorities should be asked to provide the returns of all baby farmers who were registered.[7]

After her release from prison, Betsy lived with her daughter, Sarah Jane, now Mrs Honeywill, for many years.[8]

John and Catherine Barnes

John Barnes was born in Tarporley, Cheshire in 1838. He had worked at the post office in Holywell and, it was said, he had worked as a clerk in solicitor's office and letter carrier in Birkenhead.[9] By the 1871 census, he was married to Catherine with an 11-month-old son and was working as a barman in a public house in Birkenhead.[10] Over the next few years, Mr and Mrs Barnes, calling themselves Mr and Mrs Howell, appeared to be moving in improving Liverpool society circles, John often appearing in fashionable dress and smoking a shilling cigar whilst frequently displaying a pocket full of banknotes. However, John Barnes also borrowed large sums of money, usually paying them back accompanied by a bottle of champagne, but there were times when he lied about monies he expected to receive in order to buy himself time before absconding without repaying his debt.[11]

The Barneses had been known to the police for many years through various fraudulent schemes, but they had always managed to slip away from prosecution.

By 1879, it was believed that John and Catherine Barnes had been baby farming for ten years.

The police believed they had had between nine and twelve children a year in their care and the authorities had been directed to investigate them by complaints from their neighbours, who were much disturbed by the distressing cries emanating from several children, and from the police, although nothing had been discovered to justify interference. It was found that the Barneses were not registered under Infant Life Protection Act – but this was 'all but a dead letter' in Cheshire.[12]

In 1877, they had sub-farmed out a child to a Mrs Walker of Newton by Tattenhall, Cheshire. When the baby arrived, it was noticed that it was in a weakened state. The child died soon after its arrival and a certificate was given stating death had been caused from starvation. Later, during the trial, a letter was sent to the prosecuting solicitor informing him of this case.

In 1877, a Birkenhead police officer on holiday in Southampton saw an advertisement with the address 'E. Hall, Post Office, Birkenhead' asking for babies to adopt for a small premium. He realised that the advertiser was Mr and Mrs Barnes, so he answered the advert. Several letters were exchanged, and the deal was all but done, but nothing ever came of it, and no further light was shed on the baby farming operations of John and Catherine through this subterfuge. However, an operation was set up after a gentleman from Sheffield notified Birkenhead police of an advertisement he had seen in a Sheffield newspaper. The police asked that the gentleman reply to the advert, and, after an exchange of correspondence, a meeting was arranged at the Exchange Station, Liverpool. The gentleman was to meet a man wearing a white hat bound with crepe. Instead of the Sheffield gentleman attending, a plain-clothed police detective waited in the first-class waiting room, only to identify John Barnes wearing the said hat with his wife Catherine. Following this, a letter was received in Sheffield saying they had waited for three trains to pass and had been disappointed that no one had shown up.[13]

The police now felt they had enough evidence to apply to the magistrate for a warrant to search the house at 124 Church Road, Tranmere, Cheshire. Although the application had been supported by evidence given by neighbours that they had heard babies crying, the magistrate decided there was insufficient reason to issue a warrant. Not to be thwarted by this, the police decided to carry out the search without the permission of the magistrate. Being aware that Mr and Mrs Barnes might become violent at the intrusion, the police ensured they arrived with plenty of officers and the visit took place on 3 August 1879.

Asked by the police if a search of the house of the house could be carried out, John Barnes agreed. Catherine Barnes, meanwhile, ran upstairs and reappeared clutching the dirty, emaciated baby Florence in her arms. She said she had cared for this child for six or seven months. When Florence was examined, it was noted that she had a bruised lump on her forehead. When entering the filthy room just vacated by Catherine, no furniture was found but a bit of rug on the floor that was soaking wet. It was presumed that the child had been lying on this. In another foul-smelling room, an iron bedstead and mattress without other coverings was found. Lying on this were two naked infant girls about 3 or 4 months old, Alice and Mabel, just wrapped in little pieces of rug. All the girls were in an emaciated condition and were sent to Birkenhead workhouse, where Mabel and Alice quickly died, on 17 and 20 September, respectively. Although Florence had appeared to be the most emaciated of the three babies, she seemed to rally but, sadly, she too succumbed to diarrhoea and soon followed the others on 11 October.

In addition to these three girls, the police also found three older children who were said to be the Barneses' own. No bedclothes, feeding bottles or provisions of food for the children were found in the house. On 4 August 1879, John and Catherine Barnes were charged with providing insufficient food for three infants in their care. Catherine stated that the child, Florence, who was a little older than the other two, had been placed on the rug while she cleaned the room and that all the girls had been fed properly as she had bought two or three quarts of milk each day.

Alice Maria Rodenhurst of Hereford, who was single, gave birth to a daughter, Alice Mabel Emily Hamilton, on 15 April 1879. After advertising in a Liverpool newspaper for a person to adopt the healthy infant, she entered into some correspondence with Mrs Barnes, who was using the name 'Hamilton', and Miss Rodenhurst was assured that Mrs 'Hamilton' was childless and wanted to bring a child up as her own and was more keen to have the child rather than the money, she handed her child over to Catherine Barnes at Hereford Railway Station on 20 May, paying £30 and £1 expenses and providing clothes for the baby. Miss Rodenhurst next saw her baby daughter at the workhouse after being contacted by the police but had not been able to recognise the child as hers due to its changed appearance.

Baby Alice had been at the workhouse for three weeks being fed on milk, corn and flour, and milk and bread before she succumbed to diarrhoea and died. The post-mortem found she had died from long continued malnutrition. Dr Laidlaw stated that the treatment she received at the workhouse could not have caused her death.

Evidence given at the inquest into the infant's death said she had entered the workhouse in a dirty, emaciated condition and covered in flea bites. The child's mother had visited her offspring several times in the workhouse and appeared at the inquest wearing mourning clothes. She showed an agreement signed by Mrs Barnes using the name Hamilton:

> I agree to take your little girl forever and bring her up as my own for £30; never to trouble anyone belonging to her again from this date 17 May 1879.
>
> (signed) C. Hamilton

Miss Rodenhurst also identified baby clothes shown in evidence as those she had made herself and had handed over to Barnes. These had been acquired by the police from two pawnshops, having produced pawn tickets found at the Barneses' house.

Unmarried Emma Green of Wigan gave birth to a daughter who was registered as Emily Green at 17 Portland Crescent, Leeds, home of Ellen Long. When the baby was a month old, Emma left Leeds to take up a position in Manchester and left baby Emily with Mrs Long, where it stayed for two months, with the child's father paying 7 shillings a week for its keep. The father agreed that Mrs Long should hand the baby over to Catherine Barnes on 18 July. This little girl was the baby known as 'Mabel'.

Samuel Blythe gave evidence at the inquest. While not admitting he was the father of the little girl, he did say he had arranged for the Mrs Barnes, calling herself Mrs Hall, to adopt the infant after visiting her at her house in Church Road, Tranmere. She had assured him she was keen to adopt a little girl as she had a son and had little interest in payment and her husband was a merchant in Liverpool. In letters sent between the Barneses and Mr Blythe, they asked for £50 but he said he was unable to pay that much, and they agreed £15 (although in the event he only paid £10).

The inquest juries for all three deaths found John and Catherine guilty of wilful murder and the couple were committed to trial.[14]

When the police visited the Barneses' home, there were six children in residence. Two boys, John and Henry, were said to be the Barneses' own sons, and a girl, 13-year-old Louisa, was said to be the Barneses' own daughter; however, it transpired that her name was really Maria Louisa Waller, whose parents lived in Leeds. She had been given to the Barneses with a premium of £60 through an agreement that had been drawn up by a firm of solicitors and was said to be an heiress to the sum of £1,200. The Barneses had tried to claim the interest on this inheritance. This claim continued to be investigated but it was later found that no such inheritance was due, and Louisa continued to be confined to the workhouse.

On 29 November 1879, it was reported in the *Cheshire Observer* that the guardians of the Birkenhead workhouse had received a letter regarding Maria. The letter was signed Jane P. Westcott of Torquay and contained all the indications that it was from another baby farmer.

Gentlemen – A paragraph in the *Western Weekly News* of the 15th *inst.* having come under my notice in reference to a little waif in the union, and it being my intention to advertise for a child to adopt, I respectfully beg to state before doing so, I would inquire if you are disposed to part with the little thing? – and if so, would you let me have it? My husband is a respectable, steady working man, employed constantly by the local board of Torquay, for whom he has worked for several years, and is well known to the principle manager. We have no family and are both very fond of children – myself in particular, and should be happy to adopt as our own the little one which is now in your care. Of course we could not adopt any child without a premium, as we have my husband's father, who is very aged, to entirely maintain. The child would be kindly treated and respectably brought up.

The reading of this letter was greeted with laughter, and it was suggested that Mrs Westcott could have any of the children from the workhouse who were not due an inheritance of £1,200, but not this one. This, again, was greeted with laughter by the gentlemen present.[15]

Louisa believed that John and Catherine Barnes were her parents. In her clothes, letters were found regarding babies taken in by the Barneses and she gave evidence at their trial saying she had often visited the pawnshop to pawn articles of baby clothing. She also said she had nursed the babies and had always been given plenty to eat, as had everyone else. She said she had bought milk for the babies every day.

The police continued their search of the Barneses' home and found seventy letters relating to children from Hull, Leeds, Wigan, Bristol, Bath and Hereford and about twenty other towns and two insurance policies. Between thirty and forty children had been entrusted to the Barneses, four or five children had been buried, three others were found in workhouse schools, but the others had not been traced. Evidence was also found that the Barneses used other names; Howell, Hall, Banks, Hamilton and Beard, and lived in various houses in Bootle, Birkenhead and Tranmere.

At Birkenhead Police Court, John and Catherine Barnes were first charged with wilful murder of two children and failing to provide sufficient nourishment to another. This was later changed to the wilful murder of three children.

Evidence was given at the trial of John and Catherine Barnes, held at Chester Crown Court, of the interment of several children at local cemeteries and the finding of the bodies of two children in the district, both believed to have come from the Tranmere Baby Farm.

Catherine also answered an advertisement for babies from a Hannah Devine from Liverpool. Two infants were given into Miss Devine's care by Catherine. One of these was a child from Bradford from a woman, Elizabeth Ann Thompson, who had agreed to pay 10 shillings to Catherine but only gave her 5, agreeing to pay the rest in instalments. This child was in a healthy state while in the care of Miss Devine but was taken from her by Catherine for a month and, when returned, the child was so emaciated it was unrecognisable. Eventually this child was reclaimed by its mother, who sold the blankets from her bed in order to keep the baby.

During the trial, John appeared to be cool and composed while his wife seemed acutely affected by the proceedings.

The prosecution argued that the three children were taken by the prisoners under the pretence of adoption but once in their possession, being desirous to use the money paid to them for their own use, they systematically neglected and starved them, knowing, and even desiring, that the infants would meet their death. However, a nurse from the workhouse said that the younger two of the three girls taken there were not in such a poor condition, and she thought they would be well. She had fed them on bread and milk for three or four days until they were afflicted by diarrhoea, when they were fed milk and cornflour and medicine was prescribed by Dr Laidlaw.

Evidence was given that the copy of the advertisements given to various newspapers was written in John Barnes's handwriting.

The jury were instructed that they should not find the prisoners guilty of wilful murder unless the Barneses had the intention of causing death.

After considering for just twenty-one minutes, the jury found John and Catherine Barnes guilty of manslaughter and the judge sentenced them to penal servitude for life, stating that the prisoners had 'for years and years carried on the vilest trade that human malignity could have invented, and though the jury had by his direction found them not guilty of murder, they had committed a series of premeditated and reiterated crimes which were within a hair's breadth of murder.'[16]

In 1887, Catherine claimed she had carried out the crimes because she owed money to a money lender.[17]

On 16 October 1899, John Barnes was freed under licence from Dartmoor Prison and Catherine, on the same day, was released under licence from Aylesbury Prison.

Initially both John and Catherine lived with their son, assisting in his shop at 88 Duke St, moving to 113 Old Chester Road, Birkenhead, with him until John claimed he would get a fortune of £47,000. The son found that John had been claiming credit from various places and had lied about the fortune. This led to a fight breaking out, after which the son threw John out.

John then moved in with a Mrs Smith, after claiming he was a widower and promising marriage. He had told Mrs Smith he had been in Australia for a number of years.

In 1906, Catherine was still living with her son at his shop. The son obtained a large amount of goods on credit and tried to evade his creditors. Catherine was said to have assisted her son in this. Nevertheless, Catherine asked to be taken off licence, but this was refused.

She continued to report to the police until 1911, when she was keeping a small grocer's shop. She was said to be a drunkard but had never been charged with drunkenness. Police didn't think she would revert to baby farming, so she was taken off licence.

In 1911, John Barnes died in the workhouse.[18]

Louisa Noble

In February 1887, unmarried Charlotte Padfield of Westmorland Buildings, Bath saw an advertisement in the newspaper inserted by needlewoman Louisa Noble offering to care for a child. Wishing to continue working as a domestic servant and requiring care for her son, Reginald, who had been born the previous May, Charlotte contacted 38-year-old Mrs Noble of Malvern Buildings, Bath, and agreed to pay 5 shillings a week and provide clothes for young Reginald. The bright and healthy child joined the two other children Mrs Noble cared for in March of that year.

Miss Padfield visited the child about a month later and noticed that the boy was getting thinner but thought no more of it and didn't then visit for some time until she was communicated with, when she took him from

Birth certificate for Reginald Padfield.

Mrs Nobel and gave him to Mrs Abbott of Westmorland Buildings. At this point the boy was described as being of just skin and bone and he ate ravenously. A bruise was on his leg, along with a scar from a burn, and a cut was seen on his forehead. Given the boy's condition, a surgeon, Mr W. S. Walker, was called in but, nine or ten days later, on 15 March 1888, he died.

Mr Walker carried out a post-mortem on the child and noticed several signs of neglect and injury on the body but no sign of diseased organs. However, there was great emaciation, and he weighed only half of what should be expected of a child of his age. The immediate cause of death was diarrhoea, which Walker attributed to neglect.

Alice Gertrude Davis, Mrs Noble's servant, gave evidence at the trial at Wells, Somerset, saying that there had been five children at the house and Reginald was the youngest. The children were not given breakfast but would crawl about the floor eating crumbs and cinders found there. For dinner they had a broth made from bones, salt and bread that had been sold for fowl food. She also said she had witnessed Mrs Noble half drowning and beating the young boy and heard her say, 'If the child is so dirty it shall not have so much to eat; I will starve it.'

The Inspector of Nuisances in Bath, Henry Montague, had visited the house in August 1887 and found two children suffering from diphtheria and two emaciated children crawling about the floor and he thought these were starved.

Mrs Noble's defence counsel suggested that the boy's condition was due to diarrhoea. However, the judge pointed out in his summing up that if that were the case, a doctor should have been called.

The jury found Louisa Noble guilty of the manslaughter of Reginald Padfield. The judge stated that no blame could be put of Reginald's mother as she had paid handsomely and regularly for his maintenance. This was a case of child cruelty that came to court too frequently. He sentenced Louisa Noble to five years' hard labour. On hearing the sentence, the prisoner became hysterical and was assisted from the dock.[19]

As a result of her incarceration, Mrs Noble's 6-year-old daughter, Lilian May, was admitted into the Girls' Industrial School at Walcot.[20]

By November 1890, Louisa Noble had become delusional; she imagined herself to be the Empress Eugenie and the visiting surgeon to be her stepson. She refused to eat as she thought her food was poisoned and imagined she heard people talking about her outside her cell door. In light of this behaviour, she was removed from Woking prison to Broadmoor Hospital for the Criminally Insane, where she remained until September 1892, when she was deemed to be sane and transferred back to Woking prison.[21]

William and Elizabeth Pearson

On 18 November 1889, Jessie Beamer of Chatham Road, Birkdale, Southport visited her neighbours, William and Elizabeth Pearson, in order to view the body of 4-year-old May Oldfield. May had been in the care of the Pearsons for several months prior to her death. As she was leaving, another neighbour, Mrs Knight, took her to one side and drew her attention to 17-month-old Rosina Elizabeth Norris Oldfield, another of the Pearsons' nurse children, who was wrapped in an old coat and crying 'like a pigeon'. Mrs Knight lifted one of Rosina's arms, which looked like a shapeless piece of bone. Mrs Beamer was so exasperated with Mr Pearson, she berated him for not feeding the child and a drunken Pearson told her to 'mind her own business'. The following day, arguing was heard from the Pearsons' house and Mrs Beamer sent for the police. Rosina was found by Police Inspector Cross in an emaciated condition and, on searching the house, he could find no food fit for the little girl to eat. Mrs Knight took the tiny Rosina into her own home, but the baby died soon after. Mrs Oldfield, the girls' mother, had been to the house on the day May had died and had cried and said that no expense should be spared in sending for a doctor for Rosina.

Elizabeth Pearson was remanded in custody under the newly passed Prevention of Cruelty to, and Protection of, Children Act 1889. It was stated that in the previous June, Mrs Pearson had taken charge of three children for 18 shillings a week. Two were the daughters of widow, Mrs Sarah Oldfield, and the other, Alfred Joseph Rimmer Talbot, 4 months, was the son of Oldfield's servant, Annie Talbot. Alfred had died soon after arrival.

Mrs Pearson accused Mrs Oldfield of asking her to let the children die. The magistrates who heard the case put by the police decided in Mrs Pearson's favour and discharged her from custody. However, an order for the disinterment of the two deceased children, May and Alfred, was received and they were exhumed from Southport Cemetery and the stomach contents were sent for analysis.[22]

All the children had been insured with the Prudential Assurance Company. Charles Andrews, 60, agent for the company for thirty years, stated that he was unaware of the children's illegitimacy as the proposal forms said that the father had been killed by falling into a ship's hold. After the deaths of the two children, he had paid £4 insurance money in respect of May Oldfield to Mrs Pearson, even though he knew that Mrs Oldfield had not signed the receipt as, after he realised the receipt he had been given by Mrs Pearson had been signed in the wrong name, he had got his niece to sign as Sarah Oldfield. There had been 19 shillings arrears owing on the policies and he had stopped this from the £4.[23] The coroner said that Mrs Pearson had been wrong to insure the children but that she could not be blamed when such temptation had been placed in her way by the insurance agent.

In January 1890, Charles Andrews was reported to have left his home with his wife and children. The house and furniture were in the possession of a money lender who had no knowledge of Mr Andrews's whereabouts, but it is thought he had left the country.[24]

After the exhumation, William Pearson, 51, and Elizabeth Pearson, 38, were arrested and charged with manslaughter. Mrs Pearson said she had only neglected the children in the last week as she had been abused by her husband. She also said she had been to Mrs Oldfield and suggested calling a doctor as the children had measles but had been told that Mrs Oldfield would not pay for a doctor and that Mrs Pearson was to let the children die.

Evidence was given at the coroner's court as to the amount of milk purchased by the Mrs Pearson and that she had bought a pennyworth of laudanum from the chemist.[25]

Dr Maule had visited Alfred in October, but the child had died of malnutrition six days later. He also visited May on 12 November, but she had died the following day. He had certified her death as being from catarrhal pneumonia, although he said that neglect would have accounted for the symptoms. Dr Moore had seen Rosina on 20 November and came to the conclusion she was being neglected.

Dr Newsham and Dr Moore carried out the post-mortems on all the children and they concluded that death had been accelerated by neglect in the cases of May and Rosina, but they were unable to state the cause in Alfred's case and an open verdict was found in his case. Traces of morphia had been found in the bodies of May and Alfred. May's stomach and intestines were found to contain no food and it was said she could not have eaten for several days prior to her death.

After two retirements, the inquest jury found Mr and Mrs Pearson guilty of manslaughter and Mrs Oldfield, now Mrs Brade, having re-married, guilty of being an accessory before the fact. Although the coroner had disagreed with the verdict as far as Mrs Brade was concerned, he committed all three to trial at the Assizes. Neither of the Pearsons was represented by legal counsel at the trial but Mrs Brade was represented by counsel.

At the Assizes in March 1890, it was stated that Mr Pearson was a mason's labourer, and the household income was supplemented by caring for children.

Mrs Brade was a woman of independent means who had been widowed four or five years earlier; however, since then she had led an irregular life and had given birth to two illegitimate children. After the birth of May Oldfield, the baby had been sent to a Mrs Harvey for 7 shillings and sixpence a week. Mrs Harvey had had the girl for more than two years but in all that time Mrs Oldfield had only visited twice and she had never handled or nursed the child. In fact, Mrs Oldfield had expressed the wish that the child should not live but in Mrs Harvey's opinion Mrs Brade had a 'slate off' due to her rambling conversation. After Rosina's birth, it was reported that Mrs Brade said she would give the midwife a 'handsome present' should the child be left to die, an offer that was rejected. The midwife also declined Mrs Brade's offer of £5 to register the girl as her own.

In October 1888, May was taken from Mrs Harvey to Mrs Brade's house, where she was unable to eat. The doctor was called by Mrs Brade and she was told that the child should be given generous nourishment in order to recover its health. Later May was sent to live with the Pearsons for 6 shillings a week, where baby Rosina was already staying. Both girls were said to be in good condition when they went to the Pearsons and there was no neglect until the end of July 1889. The prosecution claimed that from that time until their deaths they were neglected in such a way as to amount to culpable neglect by the Pearsons with the connivance of the mother. It was said that the neighbours saw the filthy conditions of the children's clothing and that Mr Pearson beat young May with a belt and, while she was suffering from measles, put her into a cold bath. Rosina was said to spend most of the day tied to a rocking chair that frequently got knocked over during the Pearsons' rows. Witnesses claimed they had implored the Pearsons to bring a doctor to the sick children some time before their deaths but had been ignored. The Pearsons were said to mostly drink, quarrel and fight.

Mrs Brade was said to have visited a week before May's death and had been drinking with the Pearsons and paying not the slightest attention to the children. The day May's body was exhumed was the same day Mrs Oldfield had re-married. However, it was stated that Mrs Brade had sent clothes and money for her daughters and had visited on a weekly basis but that the clothes had been used by the Pearson's own child except on the days Mrs Brade visited. Mrs Brade's solicitor said that although his client had shown little affection for her two illegitimate daughters, she had provided for them amply and had been deceived by the Pearsons as to the girls' health. When she had been told of May's death, and discovered how ill Rosina was, she had provided port wine for the child (which Mr Pearson had given to his own daughter) and had paid for a doctor to be called. Mrs Pearson disagreed with this evidence and stated that she had visited Mrs Brade's home in order to tell her of the children's ill health but had been greeted by the house being full of men and stinking of rum. She had been told by Mrs Brade (then Oldfield) that she would not pay for a doctor but to take the girls to the infirmary. On a second visit, Mrs Brade told her that if the girls did not die, she should let them die.

It was alleged that Mr Pearson had lived in the same house and had witnessed the state of the children but had not taken steps to relieve their suffering and had taken out insurance on the children while not informing their mother.

Two local doctors said they had not seen signs of emaciation and one stated that the condition he saw could be accounted for by measles and pneumonia.[26]

On 27 March 1890, William and Elizabeth Pearson were convicted of the manslaughter of May Oldfield and Rosina Oldfield. Mrs Brade had been acquitted at the magistrate's court. The judge said that they had tried to implicate Mrs Brade by suggesting she had instigated their neglect of the girls but that what they had said was not evidence against Mrs Brade. He sentenced William to seven years' and Elizabeth to five years' penal servitude.[27]

Ellen Barnard

The life of women associated with lying-in homes and baby farming is full of pseudonyms and this case is no exception; here, in a case that went to court in 1893, almost all of the protagonists used a pseudonym at some point, and it is often confusing trying to keep up with who is who!

Cast of characters:
- Forty-two-year-old Ellen Barnard aka Mrs Carter aka Mrs Cox aka Mrs Painter: charged with manslaughter; found guilty of neglect.
- Sixty-year-old Sarah Baker aka Mrs Beta aka Mrs Weston ran a lying-in house and seems to have traded babies.
- Mother unknown aka Mrs Weston.
- Mrs Lydia Robinson: nurse.

Ellen Barnard was charged with the manslaughter of Albert Victor Weston. Ellen, accompanied by Mrs Lydia Robinson, a nurse, received baby Albert in the waiting room at Victoria Station, London from Sarah Baker after replying to an advertisement from a 'Mrs Weston'.

We first meet Sarah Baker, wife of a railway porter from Willow Walk, Bermondsey, advertising in the name of Beta or Walker running a lying-in house where ladies go in order to give birth. Ladies who stayed at Willow

Way were all given the name 'Mrs Weston' – because it was the name known at the stationer's shop at Newington Butts, Walworth, that was run by a Mrs Matthews, where letters for them were sent. Mrs Matthews received letters addressed to Mrs Weston, Mrs White or X, Y, Z that were collected by Mrs Baker, who she believed to be the wife of a police officer. Clearly neither the expectant mothers nor Mrs Baker could be easily identified in these letters. As the case against Ellen Barnard developed, it became clear that Sarah Baker also carried out an extensive trade in babies; as she had given three babies out to nurse to a Mrs Whitehorn from Morden. Of these three only one was still alive, the others having died; one at Spalding and the other at Aldershot. Mrs Baker had refused to give any information and Detective Inspector Morgan had had to search her house, where he found letters and papers that proved she carried out an extensive baby farming operation. During the trial, Mr Babey, inspector under the Infant Life Protection Act, proved that Sarah Baker had been convicted at Lambeth on 22 December 1890 of contravening the Act; although, while giving evidence in this trial, Mrs Baker made the point of saying that she did not 'keep babies in the house'. Mr Babey also asked Mrs Baker questions referring to ladies that had been confined at the house and what had happened to their babies, all of which Mrs Baker refused to answer.

On 29 October 1892, a baby boy, Albert Victor Weston, was born at Mrs Baker's house to a woman known as 'Mrs Weston'. Mrs Baker claimed she had no knowledge of where the woman came from as she had had no correspondence with her. When 'Mrs Weston' decided she would have to find a home for the baby, she advertised for one and received several replies and from these she chose 'Mrs Carter'. Throughout her evidence, Mrs Baker frequently stated that she had nothing to do with the rehoming of babies and this was all down to the mothers; one wonders if she does protest too much!

'Mrs Carter' was actually 42-year-old laundress Ellen Barnard, a woman who was living in Kilburn not with her clerk husband but with another man, painter and pavement artist Robert Carter! Mrs Barnard, using the name Mrs Cox, had previously cohabited with the man at the Kilburn home of certified nurse, Mrs Lydia Robinson. When there she had had a 13-month-old boy with her, but the boy was not now with her at her address in Beethoven Street.

During the first week of November, on a cold evening, Mrs Baker, using the name Mrs Weston, met Mrs Barnard, using the name Mrs Carter, who was accompanied by Mrs Robinson, at Victoria Station to hand over the young, healthy, well-dressed baby plus £2 and some silver. Mrs Baker said the baby had not been baptised or registered from her house as 'Mrs Carter' had wanted to register the child in her own name. Mrs Barnard and Mrs Robinson claimed that they had been told the boy had been the child of Mrs Baker's daughter, which Mrs Baker denied.

Mrs Baker had said the mother was in straightened circumstances but when asked in court how much she had charged 'Mrs Weston' for staying at Willow Way, she admitted that she had charged her £3, which was 10 shillings more than the normal rate!

Robert Carter said he had had no knowledge of the baby until he had arrived at the house he shared with Barnard. This seems to be a plea by many of the men living with baby farmers as a way of denying any responsibility for what went on in the house. He said that although the baby had been brought to his house without his agreement, he could not turn it out. He also said that he did not know Barnard had received £2 with the baby and that he only earned between 5 and 7 shillings a week. He had spoken to a boot maker, Thomas Cleaver, about being very poor, and having no food for the child and asked for advice as the nurse child was ill. He was told to go to the relieving officer. When discussing that there was another child in the house, Carter was informed that he was infringing the Infant Life Protection Act.

The inquest jury found Mrs Barnard guilty of manslaughter and asked that Mrs Carter be severely censured as they believed her to be morally more guilty. After the inquest, Ellen Barnard was arrested and charged with manslaughter.[28]

At the trial at West London Police Court, Mrs Robinson said she had accompanied Barnard to the meeting in order to ensure the money was paid along with the child, which suggests that she knew Barnard was involved in the baby farming business. She said the baby had been taken to her house where she changed it and noticed it was clean and healthy, and about a week old. It was wrapped warmly and had a bottle of milk with it. It then left with Barnard, its adopted mother. When she saw the child later, it was small but healthy. Some weeks later, a change had taken place and the baby was thin and looked ill. Mrs Robinson advised Barnard to take the child to a doctor as it looked so wasted it looked like a different baby. That was the last she saw of the baby but heard of its death. She was not aware of its birth being registered by Barnard and there appears to be no evidence of his birth being registered. The coroner revealed that Mrs Robinson used to keep four children at a house in Willesden.

It seems from questions put during the inquest that it was thought that the babies in Barnard's care were not getting sufficient food and evidence was given as to how much milk was bought each day; it appears to have averaged one pint a day. No condensed milk was purchased and at the later trial, in answer to the jury, it was stated that condensed milk was not an appropriate food at this age, although it was known that it was often given in poorer neighbourhoods; nevertheless, there was no evidence of this in the stomach of baby Albert.

By 15 December, just six weeks after receiving the child, baby Albert was so ill that Barnard took him to the parish doctor, Dr Alfred Leete Griffiths. The boy was emaciated, and she was told she wasn't feeding him properly; he should have a pint of milk and half water per day and to keep him warm and well covered up. The doctor saw him again two days later but didn't see him again until after his death on 29 January. Barnard had taken Albert to another doctor, Dr Rainsford, on 25 January. She said the baby had been vomiting and purging for some time and the doctor gave her some powders to give to him and advised her to take him to the hospital as he thought the child was dying. Five days later Barnard returned to Dr Rainsford, saying she had not taken the baby to the hospital and asked for a death certificate. He gave a partial certificate stating the cause of death to be wasting but did not certify the cause of the wasting. It was at this time that the second child was seen by the coroner's officer in the house, but it was explained that this was a neighbour's child. The following day this child was absent; no doubt to avoid being in trouble for being unregistered by the Infant Life Protection Act. Dr Griffiths carried out a post-mortem. He discovered the remains of milk and starch in the stomach, which was not appropriate food for a child this age and decided the cause of the wasting was lack of food; the boy had only weighed 4½ lb when the normal weight for a child that age should be 11 lb. When asked by the jury if the baby could have become ill due to leaving its mother so soon and during cold weather, he replied that symptoms would have started much earlier.

In amongst the letters found at Mrs Baker's house, Inspector Morgan found one in Barnard's handwriting asking for more clothes and money for the baby as he was not as healthy as had been stated. There was no evidence given as to the answer to this.

The jury found Barnard not guilty of manslaughter but the following day she was tried again on the charge of unlawfully neglecting the child. The evidence was given again and this time she was found to be guilty and sentenced to two years' imprisonment.[29]

Henry and Beatrice Hatchard

When NSPCC Inspector Sygrove visited a house at 2 Carlton Road, Leytonstone, London in July 1919, he found the body of a child lying in a pram in the back room. The occupiers of the house were Henry Melville Hatchard, aged 52, and his drunkard wife Annie Beatrice, 47, known as Beatrice.[30] The Hatchards had been married for twenty-eight years.[31] Henry had been employed for the previous thirty-nine years by a law stationer in the City to write wills, earning a salary of £270 per annum. Henry worked from early morning to late at night Monday to Friday; on Saturday he went to his allotment and Sunday was spent attending Salvation Army meetings. He said he slept downstairs and had not been upstairs for two years. The couple had six living children of their own, three of whom paid their mother for their board and lodgings. It was stated that there was ample money to allow for a comfortable life.[32] The deceased baby was later named as 7-month-old Iris Mayes, daughter of Daisy Mayes from Gravesend, and had been taken to Mrs Hatchard by Mrs Mayes's husband, Frederick, who had doubted the child was his. He had met Mrs Hatchard in her sitting room, which he said appeared to be clean and nicely furnished, and paid a £10 premium. Nine more babies were found in the house, which was in a filthy condition; four of these children appeared to be dying and all were emaciated, filthy and verminous. Both were charged with manslaughter, despite Mrs Hatchard claiming her husband knew nothing about the children. While they were in custody, one more of the babies, 10-month-old Joyce Sutton, also died. Joyce's mother, Emily Sutton, had paid a £15 premium when she handed her daughter over to Mrs Hatchard. They were now charged with the manslaughter of both children and with the neglect of four others. Both pleaded not guilty to the manslaughter charges, but Mrs Hatchard pleaded guilty to the charges of neglect, stating that she wouldn't have neglected them had she not been drinking. It was suggested that she should plead not guilty to this charge as well.

It seems that Mrs Hatchard kept the babies upstairs and refused to allow anyone access to the upstairs rooms. Hatchard's daughter, 13-year-old Annie, said she washed the babies every other day and fed them barley milk. Baby Iris had arrived fatter than the others but had soon wasted away. Two women who had been employed to clean the house gave evidence that they had been told not to go upstairs and had seen vermin.

In giving evidence, both Henry Hatchard and their daughter, Violet, claimed they had implored Beatrice to stop taking in nurse babies, to no avail. Violet said her father was a teetotaller, but her mother drank and had pawned almost everything in the house. Henry said that Beatrice had only recently started pawning furniture; before that she had been 'everything a man could desire his wife to be'. She had promised him the babies would go by the end of the week that they had been arrested in.

The jury found Henry not guilty of all charges and Beatrice guilty of the manslaughter of the two babies and the neglect of four others. She was sentenced to five years' penal servitude on the manslaughter change.[33]

It seems that Henry Hatchard closed his eyes to the chaos taking place in his home as his wife's drunkenness became more and more pronounced. One cannot help but feel sorry, not just for the children and their birth families, but also for the Hatchard family, as its cohesion unravelled around the family members.

Chapter 11

Murder

Ten baby farmers were found guilty of the murder of innocent babies. All were sentenced to death, as the law of the time gave no other option. However, not all were executed, some were reprieved and there are two cases where the murder charges were dropped, and the case against Charlotte Winsor was one of them.

Charlotte Winsor

One of the most complex cases taken to court was that of Charlotte Winsor. This case was notorious at the time, raising questions about the legality of retrials.

During the years of the nineteenth century, the south Devon town of Torquay was fast becoming a tourist destination, firstly as a health resort for visitors to recuperate during the winter months and, later, as a summer resort. The railway had come to Torre in 1848 and was extended to the sea in the 1850s and this made Torquay an easier destination to visit. In 1863, the first large hotel, the Imperial Hotel, was built to supplement the rooms that were being let in smaller establishments.[1]

However, Torquay had acquired a reputation for infanticide as many tiny bodies had been found one after the other, but no one had been held responsible for these deaths and the local police were ever vigilant in their endeavours to find the culprit.

Charlotte Winsor was born in Halberton, just outside Totnes, and was the second child of William and Elizabeth Shepperd (Will and Betsy). Will was a hard-drinking labourer and Betsy travelled the neighbourhood asking servants for money to tell their fortunes. Charlotte's brother had been transported. At an early age, she obtained employment on a farm and, as she grew older, was said to have enjoyed the company of men. She married three times. Her first husband was John Caseley, a farm labourer, who was killed whilst digging a tunnel. Her second, William Reynolds, a labouring quarry man, died from the effects of the cold while working in a well. Her third husband was James Winsor, a farm labourer. It was said she had always lived a dissolute life.²

On 15 February 1865, beside a snow-covered road outside of Torquay, Devon, Thomas Millman and Edward Selby saw a cloth-covered bundle. When they unpicked the blue worsted stitches holding the parcel together, they found, wrapped in papers from the *Western Times* dated 6 May 1864, the body of a boy of 3 or 4 months old. The parcel was taken to the police station and given to PC W. Ford and Sergeant John Edwards.

The police discovered by searching the register of births that a woman named Mary Jane Harris had given birth in October the previous year to a boy named Thomas Edwin Gibson Harris whilst she was lodging with a Mrs Gibson in Upper Union Lane, Torquay. The police located Harris at 1 Tamar Villa, Warren Road, where she was working for Mrs Wansey as a cook and she freely admitted to giving birth to the boy, Thomas, and stated that: 'There has been a child picked up: I hope you will not think it is mine.' On the way to the police station, she said: 'If I cannot give an account of my child do you think I shall be hung?'

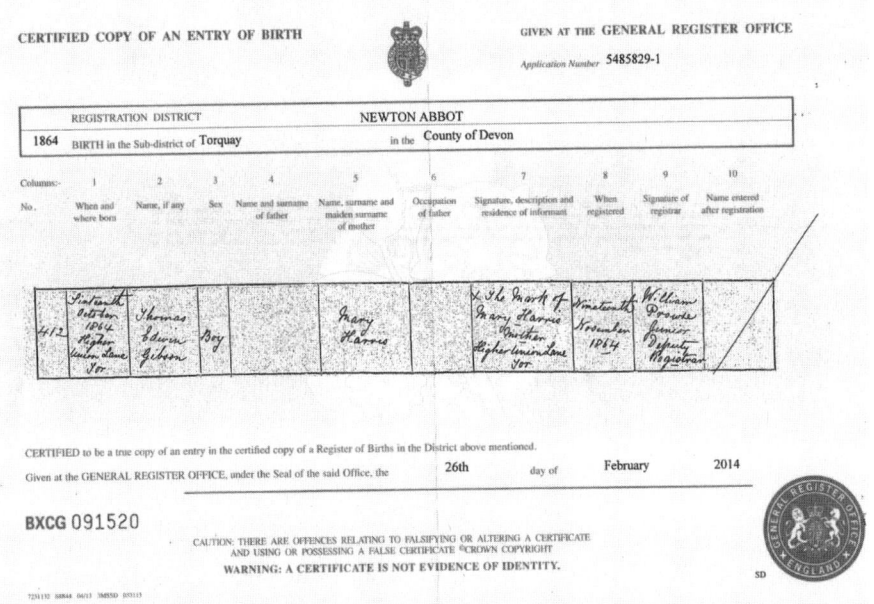

Birth Certificate of Thomas Edwin Gibson.

Mary Jane Harris was 23 years old. She had stayed with Mrs Lucy Gibson until the middle of December when she had procured her present post. Whilst staying there, Mrs Gibson said she had been a kind and attentive mother who had looked after the baby well and, on 19 November 1864, had registered the child's birth. Mrs Gibson described the baby as a 'fine child, very fair, round featured, auburn hair. There was more behind than in front.' Harris stated that after visiting with Mrs Gibson, she had given the child into the care of Charlotte Winsor on 12 December 1864 for the fee of 3 shillings a week but had later given the boy to an aunt, Mrs Stevens, who lived on the moor.

Mrs Winsor, 45, lived in a lonely spot just outside of Torquay with her husband, James, and her 8-year-old granddaughter, Charlotte Selina Pratt, known as Selina. When police questioned Mrs Winsor, she said she had heard Harris had been charged with murder, but she didn't believe she had done it because she had looked after the child for a few weeks, but Harris had then given the boy to an aunt, Mrs Stevens, who lived on the moor. Winsor denied having any blue worsted wool. Charlotte Winsor was taken to the police station where, on seeing Harris, she put her hand to her neck and jerked on her neckerchief, to which Harris nearly fainted. Winsor was taken to identify the child. She stated that 'Little Tommy' had a wart on his toe and a lot of hair on top of his head but little at the back. On seeing the child's body, she said this was not the boy she had looked after as this boy had no wart and a lot of hair at the back of his head. When Winsor's house was searched, there were balls of blue worsted thread found along with old copies of the *Western Mail*, but none dated 6 May 1864.

Selina was taken by PC Ford to see the boy's body and she recognised it as 'Tommy'. She was subsequently taken by PC Ford to some crossroads she had been to with her grandmother.

When the child's body was examined by a surgeon, Mr Stebb of Torquay, no signs of external violence could be found, except a mark on his face where rats had been gnawing, and there was food in the boy's stomach. He decided that the boy had died as the result of exposure to the cold. He couldn't rule out the possibility of drowning, but he would not say the child's death had not been of natural causes. However, at the inquest the jury's verdict was that the boy had been wilfully murdered by Mary Harris and Charlotte Winsor.

Mary Jane Harris and Charlotte Winsor were tried together for the murder of Thomas Edwin Gibson Harris in March 1865.

At the trial, Selina Pratt, Winsor's granddaughter, told of one evening, early in February, when Harris had visited 'Little Tommy' at Mrs Winsor's abode. Selina was present. The little girl was sent out on an errand by her grandmother. When she returned, she saw Mary Jane Harris and Charlotte Winsor but there was no sign of the baby. She was then sent on another errand and when she returned for the second time, the baby was still absent. She was told that Harris had been to the station and had given the boy to her aunt who had taken him to the other side of Exeter. When questioned, she stated that two days later her grandmother had washed and ironed Tommy's clothes and put them in a carpet bag. She had then walked with her grandmother, who carried a bundle and the carpet bag, to some crossroads, which were later to be shown to be the exact place where the child's body had been found, and then on to see Mary Jane Harris, to whom she gave the clothes. She also mentioned that there was a cellar in the house where rats often came. As February 1865 had been very cold and it was stated that had the boy been taken elsewhere, he would have gone with his clothes.

Harris's aunt, Betsy Stephens, stated at the trial that she had not known that Harris had had a child until the police came to see her and she had not gone to Winsor's house to collect the said child. She did say that Harris had two other aunts.

In his closing speech, Harris's defending solicitor, Mr Prideaux, pointed out that the surgeon had not thought the death had been caused by exposure to the cold and that, if this were the case, Harris could not have been responsible for that. He then called a witness, Mary Barber from Teignmouth, who had employed Harris for more than three years, who stated that Harris was kind, attentive, truthful and honest.

On 13 March 1865, after five hours' deliberation, the jury were discharged as they could not agree – eight in favour of an acquittal and four a guilty verdict.[3]

In July, a second trial commenced but this time Mary Jane Harris gave evidence for the Crown against Winsor and, due to this, the trial continued against Winsor alone. The judge was asked if he would therefore acquit Harris before she gave evidence; he said he saw no reason why that should be done. Mr Folkard, Winsor's solicitor, then brought up a point that he was to return to in the months after the trial: that as Winsor had already been tried for this crime and the jury discharged without reaching a verdict, she could not be retried. Mr Justice Keating considered this point and even consulted with a fellow judge, Mr Justice Willes, who was sitting in the neighbouring court and came to the conclusion that Mrs Winsor could now be tried again. He also praised the learned and cautious nature of the judge from the previous trial.

At this trial, Selina's evidence was very different to that which she had given at the first trial. Now she stated that she had visited the crossroads (where she had taken PC Ford) with a friend but had not been there at any other time. She also said she had visited Harris with her grandmother to give her clothes from the carpet bag but didn't mention carrying a bundle and she confirmed that the baby had had a wart on his toe. There was a suspicion that Selina had been coached to give contrary evidence. Selina was cross-examined but stuck to her story and it was noted that since the previous trial she had lived with her mother in Plymouth and had not seen her grandfather.

Harris went into some detail that Winsor had given her about how she had been paid to murder two other babies, one she had flung into the bay and the other she had left on the moor and said she 'would do the same for anyone who wouldn't split on her'. Later Winsor had asked Harris for £5 to kill the child but Harris had not got £5. Winsor suggested she contact the father and ask him for the money, but Harris said she couldn't do that. Sometime later, Harris was visiting the boy at Winsor's house and, when Selina was sent out on an errand, the offer was again made, and this time Harris had agreed. Winsor then said she would put the child 'between the bed-ticks' and that it would soon die. She then took Tommy into Selina's bedroom and returned ten minutes later without the boy. When the child was later brought out from the bedroom, he was dead. They then undressed him and put him into a box that was then locked. Harris declared she had not wanted to have her child killed but that Winsor had 'filled my mind up, and I was led away by her'. She related a conversation she had with Winsor while they were both awaiting trial where Winsor had confirmed she had taken Harris's child's body to the crossroads. On cross-examination, Harris said the father of the child was a Farmer Nicholls and that she had been having intercourse with him for six and a half years and had had a child by him previously. She said she had never tried to procure an abortion and that

Nicholls had allowed her 3 shillings and sixpence for the previous child and had given her an allowance for this one until it had gone to Mrs Winsor. She continued to deny wanting her child dead. Harris gave her evidence calmly, but Winsor sobbed bitterly for several hours when she heard Harris was to give evidence against her.

Winsor had previously said that Harris had visited her and the child one night and had given the child 'some sweetstuff' but when she tried to taste what it was, Harris had told her not to as it would poison her and admitted it was used to clean brass. Winsor had told Harris that if it would poison her, it would also poison the child. She then said she left the room for a short time and when she returned, Harris was holding the child's head in a pan of water. Harris stated that she had not given the child stuff that poisons rats and mice but had been present when Winsor murdered the baby. She said she had not given Winsor the boy in order for him to be murdered.

In Mr Folkard's closing speech, he pointed out:

> the woman Harris came from beneath the very shadow of the gallows, and, therefore, let them receive with great caution any statements she would make against the prisoner in order to save her own life ... The atrocious history described ... looked like an invention on the part of Harris against the prisoner merely concocted to save her own life.

He pointed out that the prisoner received only 1 shilling and sixpence for committing this crime and said this was no motive for murder; indeed, she had more motive for keeping the child alive and receiving a weekly payment for its care.

Mr Justice Keating, in his two-hour summing up, stated that, if Harris's evidence were believed, she was complicit in the murder and the jury should consider whether she was telling the truth. After considering its verdict for an hour and twenty minutes the jury returned a verdict of guilty on Charlotte Winsor for the murder of Thomas Edwin Gibson Harris and she was sentenced to death. The judge cautioned her to expect no mercy. Winsor wept bitterly at this, but she was the only person in the courtroom to show any emotion.[4] Her execution was to take place at 8.00 am on 11 August 1865.

Winsor continued to protest her innocence, claiming Harris to be guilty.

This, however, was not the end of the story. The *Pall Mall Gazette* of 2 August 1865 questioned the thoroughness of the trial. It pointed out that Winsor was not examined in court and therefore Harris's story was not contested. It wondered at the speed in which the trial took place after the event and how much evidence was collected.[5]

Two days before the execution date, Winsor had an emotional meeting with her husband, mother and two sisters. Her daughter had been unable to attend due to being close to her confinement date. The afternoon prior to the execution, hangman Calcraft travelled to Exeter by train. However, the journey was not needed as a respite was allowed until November due to a wrangling of legal points about whether a jury once sworn in could be discharged without the prisoner's consent, as was the case in the first trial. This would mean that Winsor had been improperly tried at the second trial.[6] In November, the sentence was respited again until February. Mr Folkard, Winsor's solicitor, continued to argue his client's case and the date for a decision was extended and extended. In May 1866, Mrs Winsor appeared at the proceedings in London. Her physical appearance had much deteriorated: the previously stout and robust woman was now thin and of a careworn appearance. She kept her eyes downcast during the appeals by her solicitor and she refused to eat any luncheon. On Monday, 7 May, it was decided that the original trial had been lawful and, as the prisoner had not been acquitted or convicted, the charge had been not proven and so it was appropriate to be retried. The prisoner was then returned to Exeter prison to await execution.[7]

It now seemed all hope of a reprieve was over but still the story continued. Throughout the months of legal arguments, Mrs Winsor had suffered by the continual indecision and she simply wished to know her fate. The news media, while decrying her actions, showed some compassion to the suffering woman and, due to the length of time that had passed since the original death sentence, the Secretary of State for the Home Department, Sir George Grey, requested that the Queen exercise the royal prerogative of mercy and, on Friday, 11 May 1866, Charlotte Winsor's sentence was commuted to life imprisonment.[8] She is seen on the censuses for 1871, 1881 and 1891 as an inmate at Woking Women's Prison.[9] Despite continuing to claim Mary Jane Harris had been responsible for the child's death and many pleas for her release, stating she would live with various friends or family, including her nephew who wanted her to sit with his children, and suffering from chronic bronchitis, she died in prison in 1894 aged 74.[10]

While fate of Mrs Winsor was being debated, Mary Jane Harris was still waiting to find out what would happen to her. It was decided that she could not be pardoned for her part in this crime but that she should stand trial; however, the prosecution should offer no evidence against her. The jury were then directed to find her not guilty, and she was, therefore, discharged.[11]

Exactly what did happen on the day that little Tommy lost his life we will never know. It appears that Mary Jane Harris's decision to turn Queen's evidence allowed her to avoid conviction for her part in this horrendous deed. Also, consideration must be given to what Mrs Gibson's role was in this: why did Tommy have 'Gibson' as a middle name? Did she know of Mrs Winsor's ability to dispose of unwanted babies? Again, we shall never know.

Margaret Waters and Sarah Ellis

Born in Nottingham, Margaret and Sarah Forth[12] in 1833 and 1841 respectively were the daughters of hatter Jacob Forth and his wife Mildred.[13] The family moved to London at some time between 1841 and 1851. Jacob then had a series of different professions and is shown in 1851 to be living in Ludgate, London as a boarding housekeeper[14] but by 1861 he is a commissioning agent.[15] In March 1861, Margaret married draper Charles Edward Waters; however, just weeks later, she is still living with her parents but there is no sign of Charles.[16]

In August 1868, Sarah married carpenter John Ellis at St Saviour's, Southwark.[17]

During the trial of their wives, neither Charles Waters nor John Ellis was present. Mrs Waters was said to be a widow, Charles having died in Glasgow, and Mrs Ellis had separated from John.[18]

It was said Margaret Waters had been well brought up and well educated.[19]

By 1869, the two sisters were living together at a variety of addresses throughout south London. The women had left their Peckham address owing rent and without paying the local tradesmen before moving to Camberwell, Clapham Junction and Battersea before fetching up at Frederick Terrace, Brixton, where the rental agreement was in the name of Mrs Margaret

Blackburn. It was noted that two babies had been abandoned in Battersea at the time they lived there, one of which was found dead.[20]

Both women were identified as having placed advertisements in *Lloyd's Weekly Newspaper* almost every week between January 1869 and June 1870.[21]

When musician Robert Tassie Cowan discovered his youngest daughter, 16-year-old Jannette, was expecting an illegitimate baby as the result of being violated, he was anxious to ensure she was well looked after. He had her stay with him in his lodgings at 1 Langholme Villas, Loughborough Road, Brixton until her confinement when she moved into Mrs Castle's establishment. Midwife Mrs Castle ran an accouchement house at 164 Camberwell Road, Brixton for pregnant women. Jannette's healthy baby boy, John Walter Cowan, was born on 14 May 1870. Robert intended to hire a wet nurse to bring the child up but when this advertisement in *Lloyd's Newspaper* was pointed out to him –

> Adoption – A respectable couple desire the entire charge of a child to bring up as their own. They are in a position to offer every comfort. Premium required, 4l. Letter only. Mrs Willis, P.O., Southampton Street, Camberwell.

– he saw it as the answer to Jannette's problem. He had no idea that this action was to involve him in one of the most notorious cases of baby farming that was to hit Victorian Britain. He wrote to 'Mrs Willis' and eventually met with her at Brixton Station. She told him she had been married for many years but had not had any children and her husband was a representative of a large shipping firm in the City and was passionately fond of children. She said she didn't want any money to take the child. Robert was impressed by the woman and gave her his name and address and ensured she knew the baby was illegitimate as he didn't want her to take the child without knowing this. 'Mrs Willis' refused to give her address to Robert as she did not want the child to be reclaimed after she had become fond of it. The same evening, Robert's landlady, Caroline Guerra, called at Mrs Castle's house and took the baby away and gave it to 'Mrs Willis' at Walworth Road railway station, along with a small parcel of clothes. A few days later, 'Mrs Willis' called at Robert's home, and he offered her £4 for taking the child but 'Mrs Willis' refused the money, eventually taking £2 after much persuasion and agreeing to return for the other £2 at a later date. Robert was also willing to provide clothing for the infant. 'Mrs Willis' never did return.[22]

In early March 1870, Police Sergeant Relf had been instructed by his Superintendent to investigate instances of baby farming around Brixton due to a large number of infant bodies being found deposited in the area. Around about the same time as Jeanette Cowan's confinement to Mrs Castle's establishment, Relf had been watching the house and had found out that Miss Cowan had been confined.[23] He had also seen an advertisement in *Lloyd's Weekly Newspaper*, this time it read:

> Adoption. A good home, with a mother's love and care, is offered to any respectable person wishing his child to be entirely adopted; premium 5l., which sum includes everything. Apply by letter only, to Mrs Oliver, P.O., Gore Place, Brixton.

Calling himself Mr Martin, Sergeant Relf arranged to meet 'Mrs Oliver' at Camberwell New Road Station, where she told him she had been married for some years, her husband had a good business, and they had no children of their own, but she refused to give him her address. Relf agreed to give her his son and £5 the following evening. When they parted, Relf started to follow but she turned, and being next to a public house, Relf invited her to take a drink with him. After some conversation, no doubt Relf trying to elicit more information, she left and headed back to her house at 4 Frederick Terrace, Gordon Grove, Brixton, successfully followed by Relf. It was said that when she arrived home in a tipsy condition, Waters saw the man watching the house and told Ellis, 'You ungrateful cat, you have ruined me,' and certainly the cat was out of the bag!

When the time of the handover came, at Sergeant Relf's request, Mr Cowan was in the neighbourhood, and he saw Sarah Ellis aka Mrs Oliver wearing the same dress that 'Mrs Willis' had worn when he had met with her.

The next morning, Friday, 11 June 1870, Sergeant Relf, Robert Cowan and Caroline Guerra went to Frederick Terrace. Robert waited outside while the others went in. The outside of the house looked very nice but that belied what was to meet them when the door was opened by Sarah Ellis. Inside they found the house had hardly any furniture and smelt offensive. When asked if 'Mrs Willis' lived there, Ellis replied that she didn't and she also denied that children were taken there to adopt. After initially denying that Robert's grandson was there, she then asked Margaret Waters aka Mrs Willis to bring the boy up. The child was very emaciated and filthy dirty, wrapped in old clothes, merely skin and bone and very quiet. Mrs Guerra cried, 'You have been starving this child to death.' Mrs Waters stated the boy had been ill and had been attended by Dr Harris.

Relf then asked if any other babies were in the house and Waters said there were 'a few' and Relf asked to see them. He was taken downstairs into the front kitchen where he saw nothing at first but then saw a shape that looked like a head under some black clothes on the sofa. As he removed the clothes, he saw five infants huddled together. All were quiet and appeared to be asleep. All wore clothes that were saturated and smelt very offensively. There was no sign of any food. Relf thought two of the babies were dying. Waters said when questioned about their parentage that she didn't know who they were but that all had been adopted.

Relf asked if there were any more children in the house and Ellis replied that there were some older ones in the yard. These were in a better condition, and it appeared that these were paid for with a weekly sum.[24] One of these children was 'Little Emily', who appears to have arrived into the care of Waters via a Mrs Harding. This was one of the pseudonyms of Amelia Dyer, who was hanged for murder in 1896. Little Emily's mother, Elizabeth Gilbert, had been attended at the birth by Dr Harding, who, it is thought, also carried out illegal abortions. Dr Harding passed the baby on to Mrs Harding for a weekly payment of 5 shillings. It hardly seems likely that this woman would be Dr Harding's wife. The following June, Mrs Gilbert removed the child from Mrs Harding and placed her with 'Mrs Arthur'. There was no doubt that the 'Little Emily' found at Frederick Terrace was Mrs Gilbert's daughter.[25]

Relf left the house, returning later with Mr Cowan and Dr Puckle. In the meantime, baby Cowan had been dressed in clean clothes, although he was still unwashed, and his head had the appearance of a little shrivelled up monkey. Robert Cowan shed a tear at his grandson's state and cried, 'Mrs Willis, you have been murdering this child.' Waters said that as the boy had been ill, she was about to send for a wet nurse, Mrs Rowland, to feed him naturally.

On going downstairs, Relf found the other five babies in clean clothes with feeding bottles by their sides and teats in their mouths, but all appeared to be in a state of torpor. There was a bottle on the table and the contents smelled of laudanum.

Robert Cowan paid for Mrs Rowland to wet nurse baby Cowan that day. Ellis claimed one of the babies was hers and took it. The following Monday, Mrs Castle and Mrs Rowland attended Frederick Terrace with the police and were given charge of the four other babies who were initially taken to the Police Court. Mrs Castle gave evidence that the child she had been given during this time had been very dirty and had been in a sleep and was impossible to wake for the whole time it was in her care – approximately six or seven hours. All the children found in the house were taken to Lambeth Police Court and were later removed to Lambeth workhouse. As none of the children had names, they were numbered 1, 2, 3, 4, 5, 6, 7, 8 and 9! Numbers 1, 2 and 3, the older children, were in fair health and were later claimed. Numbers 4 and 5, aged approximately 18 months and a little older, were in poor health when taken to the workhouse but recovered, much to the surprise of the medical inspector of the workhouse, but the other children, the youngest, all were in a very emaciated state and appeared to be in a stupor and all died during the following weeks. During the coroner's inquest on three of the babies taken from Waters's house, two of the babies were named, John Walter Cowan and Frederick Hundane, but the identity of the girl was still unknown. It was concluded that they were poisoned with lime and narcotics and died from extreme wasting of the body and congestion of the brain caused by either disease or starvation.

Sergeant Relf also took possession of a large number of pawn tickets and other articles from the house, in addition to a number of letters detailing the adoption of babies. He took Margaret Waters into custody for not providing proper food and nourishment to the child of Jannette Tassie Cowan, thereby endangering its life. Sarah Ellis was charged with being concerned, with her sister, in the lack of providing food and care to the four other babies. Waters claimed her sister only did as she had been directed. Both sisters were tried for the wilful murder of John Walter Cowan.

Dr George Puckle, surgeons Henry Harris and Edward Pope and Dr Henry St John Bullen all gave evidence at the women's trial in relation to the condition of the children found at Frederick Terrace. All agreed that they were very poorly indeed and suffering from diarrhoea and there was great discussion about the difficulties of feeding babies by hand. All asserted that the death rate in such infants was higher than those fed naturally. Medical opinion at the time believed that babies fed by bottle should be fed cow's milk with the addition of sugar and cornflour.

When giving evidence, Dr Puckle claimed that the stupor that was exhibited by baby Cowan appeared to have been caused by the baby having been given laudanum. He also stated that the baby seemed to have been improperly fed or given food that had not nourished it. He judged that the baby's death had been caused by receiving insufficient food early on and being improperly administered a narcotic.

Ann Rowland gave evidence about the condition of baby Cowan when she took over his care. She said he had diarrhoea and thrush and looked as if he had never been washed; he was dirty around his bottom, thighs, underarms and behind his ears and she had been unable to get him clean throughout her time with him. His body was very thin, his bones were showing, and he was wet and sore. The clothes he was wearing were clean and looked brand new. She had been unable to rouse him for four or five hours after he had been put in her care. Although she had four children of her own, she had never seen a baby in such a condition. Dr Puckle had attended the baby every day and Mrs Rowlands had followed his instructions. Once the baby had aroused enough to be able to feed, she had given him the breast every ten to fifteen minutes and he improved for two or three days but after the third or fourth day he had gradually gone back into his state of stupor until he died on 24 June.

Mrs Castle said she had come across Mrs Waters once before, about six years earlier, when she had called upon her in answer to an advertisement to take a nurse child from one of her patients, although the child had not been placed with Waters. This seems to suggest that Waters had been in the baby farming business for at least six years. Waters and Ellis admitted to having been in the baby farming business for about four years and had about forty infants in their home during that time. Neither woman could say where any of these babies were now.

Ellen O'Connor worked for the two women, and in her evidence, she claimed that the children were fed whenever they required food and, although they were kept in their beds longer than she thought appropriate, all were properly attended to. She said baby Cowan had not been washed due to his illness. She did comment that all the babies in the house were very quiet.

Ellen was sent to collect lime from a local builder and then put some into water which was then added to the babies' bottles. This was said to stop the milk becoming sour. From Ellen's evidence, it was clear that both Waters and Ellis were in the habit of taking infants from the house at night and returning without them, telling her that they had 'taken them home'. Another of Ellen's tasks was to collect letters from various post offices in the names of Mrs Oliver, Mrs Furley and Mrs White.

Prior to the arrest of Waters and Ellis, several babies' bodies had been found in the area and this had been the reason for Sergeant Relf's investigation. During the trial, clothes found with these children had been identified as coming from the accused's house, also a piece of slate-coloured cloth that had wrapped one of the bodies had matched a piece torn from a cloth found at the pawnbroker using one of the tickets found in the house.[26]

It was found that Waters had been advertising under the names of Watson, Hurley, Fort, J. W., M. T. and Stewart in addition to those already stated. A search was made in the local area. A decomposed baby's body was found under a wood pile,[27] and another body was found in a pond adjacent to the Frederick Terrace house.[28]

Towards the end of the trial, Dr George Newport Pickstock said he had attended Mrs Waters's establishment when she lived in Bournemouth Road. He had never seen more than four children there and had attended two women who had difficult births and the children were left with Waters when the women left – this suggests that Waters was acting as a midwife at times. He also said that Mrs Waters had always seemed to conduct herself with kindness and motherly solicitude.[29]

After the inquest had ended, but before Waters was taken away, several women demanded of her to tell what had become of their babies. Two of those were thought to be the babies taken to the workhouse. Some of the women asked for return of monies paid by them for the care of their children and one woman claimed she had been given a child to take care of by Waters. Waters denied all knowledge of any of these women. The judge was asked if payment could be made to the women asking for the return of money. He ordered only £3, saying that persons who gave up children in that way did not deserve much consideration.[30]

Regardless of this defence, Margaret Waters was found guilty of murder and sentenced to death. Sarah Ellis was found not guilty.[31] However, on 19

September 1870, Sarah Ellis was tried for unlawfully conspiring with Margaret Waters to obtain money, from various persons, by false pretences, to which she pleaded guilty and was sentenced to eighteen months' imprisonment.[32]

Sergeant Relf was awarded £20 by order of the judge, and it was suggested that he be solely occupied with solving this type of case.[33]

An appeal was made on her behalf, with Ellis saying that unknown to Waters she had administered the laudanum to the infants as she had hated children while her sister had passionately loved them and her brothers asking for leniency. Her solicitor also pointed out that the coroner's inquest jury had found the deaths to have been caused by manslaughter, not murder. It was also claimed that sickly children were taken by Waters and passed to another woman whose name and address were not known, and it was this woman who dumped decomposed bodies of infants wearing clothing that could be traced to Waters in order to save burial fees, thereby evidencing all children taken from the convicted woman's house were alive when they left.[34]

Despite this, on 11 October 1870 at Horsemonger Lane Gaol, after a sleepless night and much prayer, Margaret Waters became the first baby farmer to be hanged.[35]

After her execution, a letter that she had written was published. In it she claimed that she started taking in children after she had got into debt to a Mr Hollingsworth and was having difficulties repaying the high rate of interest he was charging. She also claimed that she had no intention of killing any of the children and had washed them daily. She denied administering any narcotic and said if she had given improper feeding it had been an error of judgement on her part. She also criticised the parents of illegitimate babies, saying, 'What do they care what becomes of the poor little things? They have only one care, to hide their shame – all love, if any, is stifled.'[36] Although this last statement seems to be shown to be mistaken in the cases of the women who demanded after the trial to know what had become of their infants.

This case became so notorious that thirteen years later, Margaret Waters's baby farm featured in a play, *Rachel*, written by Sidney Grundy and shown at the Olympic Theatre.[37]

We would expect this to be the last we heard of Sarah Ellis, Waters's sister; however, less than three years later, Sarah made the news again. It appears that in May 1873, using the name Ellen Harwood, she was working as a housemaid to a Charles Marston Stretton of Surbiton, Surrey when she was dismissed for stealing a bottle of whisky and becoming drunk. The following day, she returned to the house and begged forgiveness, which was denied; instead, her wages were paid, and 2 shillings were given to pay for her fare. Some hours later it was realised that ten silver spoons, a gold jewelled brooch, a pair of boots and other items of value were missing. The information was given to the police and the missing articles were found in Ellen's possession, when she was charged with larceny.

During the trial, Inspector Relf was called to give evidence of her association with Margaret Waters and her subsequent conviction and sentence for fraud.

Ellen pleaded guilty to the charge and was sentenced to seven years' hard labour and seven years' police supervision.[38]

In the 1881 census we find her, still using the name Ellen Harwood, working as a general domestic servant for Elizabeth MacKey, the Lady Scripture Reader at Woking Prison.[39] We can presume that this is part of her police supervision.

After this she disappears, as so many of our baby farmers do, into the mists of time.

As an amusing aside, in the *Hull Packet and East Riding Times* on 8 July 1870, underneath an article about the inquest on the deaths of three infants who were under the care of Waters and Ellis, is an advertisement for Mrs Winslow's Soothing Syrup for calming sick children.[40]

Mrs Winslow's concoction was made up of morphine sulphate, sodium carbonate and aqua ammonia. It is thought it easy to give an overdose that would lead to death.[41]

Frances Rogers

I find the most heart-wrenching cases are those where children were found being kept in appalling conditions. In this case my heart went out to the 8-year-old girl who had been living with this heartless woman for two years.

In March 1871, Frances Rogers, 34, of 156 Knightley Street, Queens Road, Manchester and Edward James appeared before the magistrates charged with wilful murder of a child and attempted murder of three others by not giving proper sustenance.[42]

It was decided that there was no case to answer for Edward James and he was discharged but Frances Rogers was committed to trial at Manchester

Assizes[43] charged with neglecting and ill-treating several infant children with intent to murder them and do them grievous bodily harm.

Rogers had, until two years previously, lived in Keswick but had left her husband and had taken her son to live in Manchester, where she started to nurse two babies. Both had been small and died in her care. Using a variety of names, she had had three other addresses before moving to Knightley Street.[44]

Agnes Murray of Chorley had answered an advertisement in the *Manchester Examiner and Times* and had been contacted by Rogers, who was using the name of Irving. She had given birth to a baby and, the following day, was visited by Rogers, who was given £8 to entirely adopt the child. Rogers had told her she would be able to visit the baby whenever she chose. She had dropped by thirteen days later without informing the prisoner first and had surprised Mrs Rogers, who informed her that she should have written in advance. After waiting four hours, Agnes was allowed to see her child, who was in a very poor condition. She remonstrated with Rogers and ultimately took the baby away by force while Rogers attempted to prevent her from doing so. She then took the baby to Mrs Holmes, a monthly nurse, who sought medical advice from Dr Royle, who thought the baby in a comatose state and that it wouldn't live another couple of hours. Fortunately, with proper care, the baby recovered.

As a result of this encounter, PC Haslam and PC Slater visited the house on a Sunday afternoon and in the kitchen found a boy of 8 or 9 months old was being nursed by a boy of approximately 9 years of age, who, it later transpired, was Rogers's son. The baby boy was sucking an India rubber tube that had no milk bottle attached to it. Rogers said she thought the baby was the illegitimate child of a Miss Kate Gallagher, a domestic servant, and that she had been nursing him for three months at a rate of 4 shillings a week.

In an upstairs room, an 8-week-old baby girl was lying on some dirty straw that was covered with a damp rug along with a girl of approximately 8 years of age, both covered with an old, damp blanket. Rogers said she received 5 shillings a week to look after the baby but didn't know who the mother was. She said the little girl was a distant relation who she had had living with her for two years. In an adjoining room there was some straw in the corner but no furniture.

Edward James was in his shirt sleeves in a downstairs front room with a jug of beer. He said he had lodged at the house for two weeks.

Rogers took the policemen into the cellar where they found a pile of dirty napkins. Rogers went into a corner with her back towards them and stooped down. At that point, a very bad smell emanated from that part of the room. She turned around holding some napkins and a coal bag. When asked about the smell, Rogers said she had had a little dog there and presumed this to be the cause of the noxious odour; however, she seemed anxious to leave the room. Having searched the cellar without finding anything else, the policemen returned to the kitchen and noticed for the first time a very bad smell there. PC Slater asked if she was concealing something under her dress. She said it was nothing, but when a parcel was wrested from her, it was found to contain the body of a dead baby. Rogers stated that she knew nothing about this, and, at this moment, Edward James appeared and he, too, said he knew nothing of the dead child.

No bed had been found in the house and the only food found was a small loaf, a little piece of mutton, a few ounces of flour and there had been a wine glass that contained water and milk.

Both Rogers and James were taken to the police station. On the way there, James said he hardly knew the woman, and she had confirmed this. Rogers said she had no other nurse children and that one had been taken away by its mother the previous week after she had only had it a week, although she had been paid £8 to adopt the child. No doubt this was Agnes Murray's baby. Both were remanded in custody. When searched, a small bottle was found secreted in Rogers's clothing.

Surgeon Mr R. D. Fox of Lever Street carried out a post-mortem of the dead baby, which he thought had been about 6 months old when it had died approximately ten days earlier. He said the body was in a state of much decomposition, particularly the head and upper extremities. He could find no evidence of violence and the body was not much emaciated. The stomach contained a teaspoonful of dark, decayed fluid, which he identified as opium. Mr Fox described the effects of opium poisoning in an infant and stated that not all of these had been present in this case, but that opium could accelerate convulsions that were caused by some other means. He said the brain was congested but he could see no sign of disease and he thought the cause of death had been convulsions caused by lack of food. He supposed that the child did not appear emaciated because it had previously been well fed.

The local chemist, Mr Robert Maunder, gave evidence that Rogers had visited his establishment daily and had purchased laudanum, which she said was for a toothache, although he later thought she had been addicted to it. When analysed, the bottle found on Rogers was shown to contain traces of laudanum.

Two of the children found in the house were taken to the Crumpsall Workhouse, where surgeon Mr W. A. Patchett examined them. He noted the girl was but a little emaciated, but the 10-month-old boy's eyes were red and sunken, his face was pale and wore a pained expression, his limbs were wasted, the skin shrivelled, and he weighed little more than a newborn baby. He took food ravenously and appeared to be suffering from starvation. He said the boy showed no signs of disease and that the boy suffered from insufficient food. In the short time the boy had been at the workhouse, he had gained over a pound in weight.

Mrs Rogers's defence counsel said the boy had been in the charge of the police for several hours before being taken to the workhouse and this would account for him being so hungry. Mr Patchett replied that three weeks of insufficient nourishment would be needed for the skin to appear shrivelled.

In court, the mother of the baby boy, Miss Kate Gallagher, gave evidence against Mrs Rogers. She said she had paid the prisoner 4 shillings a week to look after her son, who had already suffered at the hands of another nurse. She had offered 5 shillings; however, Rogers had said looking after the boy would be a comfort to her as she had no other baby in the house, and she only wanted 4 shillings. Miss Gallagher had already removed her son from another nurse as she had been dissatisfied with the care he was receiving. She said he had been very ill and had visited regularly after informing Rogers she was coming. She had taken the boy to doctors and the hospital several times. When Kate saw her son in the workhouse, she had hardly recognised him as he appeared so ill. When questioned, she stated she would not have given her baby to Rogers had she known there was another in the house, and it was proposed that the magistrate should commit Rogers for taking money under false pretences, although this charge was not used in the Assizes Court.

A young lady of 24 years of age, Rachel Bennett, gave evidence privately to the magistrate but did not appear at the Assizes. She said she had advertised for a nurse and Rogers had called upon her. It was agreed that Rogers would nurse her baby for 5 shillings a week and had taken the child with her. A few days later, she had seen newspaper stories about the baby farming case and had proceeded to the workhouse, where she had found her child looking much worse that when she had last seen it.

In summing up for the prosecution, Mr West QC said that it was noticeable that the care given to Miss Gallagher's child was much different to that given to Agnes Murray's. This could be accounted for because Miss Gallagher paid a weekly sum, and it was in the prisoner's interest to keep this child alive, whereas Agnes Murray had paid a lump sum, so Rogers was anxious to be rid of that child as soon as possible.[45]

The judge, in his summing up, told the jury to only look at the case of Agnes Murray's child. He asked them to consider these points when reaching their verdict: (a) Did the prisoner administer laudanum to the child with the intention to kill it? (b) Did she supply insufficient food to the child with the intention to killing it? (c) Did she administer food to the child in an improper manner with a similar intent of killing?

The jury answered all these questions in the affirmative and the judge took it that they had found her guilty.[46]

Frances Rogers was found guilty of feloniously causing grievous bodily harm with intent to murder. She was sentenced to twenty years' hard labour.[47]

In passing sentence, His Lordship said:

You have been engaged in the most abominable trade ... This is a trade that cannot be permitted to be carried on in this country with impunity, and it is my duty to see the punishment you receive for that offence is proper and adequate. One of these offences is to administer laudanum to this child with the intention to get rid of the trouble of keeping it. The opinion of the jury is that you administered this laudanum for the purpose of taking away its life. The sentence of the Court, therefore, is that you be sent to penal servitude for 20 years.

Rogers appeared to be astounded by the severity of her sentence.[48]

Mr Foard, for the defence, applied to the court for an appeal on the grounds that the answers to the three questions did not meet any offence in the indictment. This was allowed.

At the appeal, Mr Foard argued that the questions asked by the judge didn't match up with the offences on the indictment. Therefore, she had not been convicted of a criminal offence.[49]

It would appear that her appeal, although allowed, did not benefit her at all, and ten years later she can be found residing in Fulham Women's Prison.[50] One wonders if she was grateful she hadn't been hanged for murder.

Sophia Martha Todd

Using the name Mrs Jackson, Sophia Martha Todd took lodgings at Gilbert and Mary Ann Oldham's house at 24 Springfield, Liverpool in November 1875. Todd was a respectable-looking woman who spoke several languages and had worked as a governess and teacher. It was said she had been born on the Isle of Wight and had married a farmer called Jackson with whom she had moved to Liverpool, but the marriage had not lasted long.[51] She placed a box in the corner of her room and two weeks later walked out of the house, never returning to pay her rent or to collect the box. However, she did write three times. In the last letter she said she had been completing business in London and would return to pay her dues and collect the box. Six months later she had still not returned, so Mrs Oldham forced the lock of the box and looked inside. All she saw were dirty, unpleasant-smelling napkins.

When in November 1876 Mrs Oldham moved to Devon Street, she took the closed but unlocked box with her. In March 1877, she and her servant, Lucy Wells, decided to remove the contents of the box and, to their dismay, they found wrapped in the bundle of rags the mummified body of an infant. Quickly they replaced the bundle and waited until Mr Oldham returned home, when the police were called.

Detective Strettell took the box and its contents away and, after taking the body to the mortuary, he found two letters in amongst the papers left in the box. One, dated 29 March 1875, was address to Mrs Jackson from Henry Thompson and the other, dated 9 July 1875, to Mrs Jackson from John Robinson.

A search was instigated throughout north-west England and Mrs Jackson was apprehended on 24 March 1877 at Old Trafford, near Manchester. She was found travelling in a gig with a Mr Todd, an agent-in-advance for the circus, who was said to be her husband.[52]

Twenty-eight-year-old Sophia Martha Todd was charged with the murder of an unknown female child.

Sophia Martha Todd was, in fact, the daughter of Mr Wilson, a civil engineer. He settled in Barbados and married the West Indian daughter of a wealthy planter, and they had baby Sophia in 1849. Sophia's mother died while the baby was very young, and Mr Wilson returned to England with Sophia. Sophia was sent to school in Brussels but, on leaving school, she discovered that her father's means had become reduced and that she needed to earn a living. She had obtained the post of governess to a Polish noble family and through this had lived in Poland and Russia and had learned both languages in addition to French, Italian, Spanish and German. On returning to England, she had lived with a relative who was headmaster of a school in Yorkshire and had travelled with them when they moved to Bowness in Cumbria, where she found employment as a governess to the family of Lady Decies. When she left this post, she moved to Lancaster, where she became a teacher. It was reported that whilst here she met and married a small farmer, Thomas Jackson, and adapted well to a life that she had not been brought up to. However, Thomas had to give up the farm and move to Ulverston where he started working for the railway. It was said Sophia moved to Liverpool where she worked as a barmaid under her maiden name[53] but in 1871 a Martha Sophia O. Wilson is shown on the census as a teacher of languages boarding at 20 Cable St, Lancaster.[54] It was during this time that her husband died, and she took up baby farming.

Letters found in Sophia Todd's box (Lancaster Gazette, *18 April 1877*)

At Todd's trial, Mary Jane Jolliffe was called as a witness. Mary Jane had lived with her father at 20 Prospect Street, Liverpool and, in 1875, Todd and a little boy had lodged in the same house. Todd had said she was married but that her husband had left her. In June of that year, Todd had received a visitor who had left a baby wrapped in a red and black shawl with her. Todd had said that the child was given to her by a Dr and Mrs George, who had been staying at the Washington Hotel, and had asked her to take care of the healthy baby boy until they returned later that evening and that the Georges had planned to sail the following day on *The Achilles*. She had been given the sum of 5 sovereigns in payment for Mrs George's keep while she had stayed with Todd at New Ferry. Mary Jane had stayed with Todd until 2.30 in the morning in the expectation of Dr George's return but, when he hadn't arrived, she went to bed. She said the baby was awake when she left Mrs Todd, but she had not heard the child cry. Mary Jane had held the baby and remarked how fine and healthy he looked. The child had not been fed or changed while Mary Jane was with Todd. This evidence was repeated by the next witness, Mrs Fletcher, who also boarded with the Joliffes.

In the morning, the baby was not to be seen and Todd told Mary Jane that Dr George had collected it after Mary Jane had gone to bed. Todd was later seen wearing the baby's shawl and had explained this by saying Dr George had given it to her.

Mary Jane said Todd had had a box with her when she arrived at her lodgings and had sent for it after she had left. There had been nothing unusual about the box.

Dr Cormack and Dr Bligh carried out a post-mortem on the mummified remains and decided the child was a full-grown, well-developed female that had been about 2 days old when she died. It was in a mummified condition and the umbilical cord had been skilfully tied with silk thread. The bones of the head were mostly perfect, but the lower jaw was missing and dried-up maggots had been found both inside and outside of the corpse. There had been staining on the cloths covering the upper part of the baby and these stains contained blood and were more than would have been caused by natural means. However, they do not seem to have been able to form an opinion as to the cause of death.

In a statement made by Todd after her arrest, she stated that she had been advertising in the newspaper for babies to care for. The baby in question had been delivered to her at Prospect Street for the premium of £10. She said she had been undressing the child and found her to be cold and as she held the baby close to her body it died.

After her arrest, enquiries were made to ascertain whether a Dr George had been staying in Liverpool and particularly at the Washington Hotel 1875, but no trace could be found.

A letter had been found on Todd that offered to pay a premium of £30 for the adoption of a boy and the police had found that a child had been sent from Whitehaven but had not been seen since, although in 1875 a boy had been found by Detective Nelson wandering in Birkenhead and since then had been taken care of by Detective Nelson. It was also ascertained that five other children had been sent to Todd at different times and, when questioned, Todd said they had all died natural deaths, but it was claimed in court that one of these children had been smothered.

In her defence, Todd claimed that the child had died of convulsions a few hours after it had been given to her and that she had concealed the body for fear of being accused of causing its death.[55]

Sophia Martha Todd was found guilty of the murder of a child entrusted to her care and sentenced to death.[56] Her execution was scheduled for Monday, 13 August 1877.

However, this was not the end of the story. Mrs Todd's defence team raised a petition that was sent to the Home Office requesting clemency as they claimed there was no evidence to show that Todd had caused the child's death, only that she concealed the body. The petition was signed by many barristers and members of the press who had been present at the trial.[57]

On 9 July 1877, while awaiting execution, Mrs Todd made a statement to the chaplain of the prison that said that a man named Lord, who had been with her husband when the baby had been delivered, had given her an address of a George Henry Thompson, General Post Office, Liverpool. (In 1880 an Elizabeth Thompson of Liverpool was prosecuted for being in contravention of the Infant Life Protection Act. She was said to be separated from her husband. Could there be a relationship?) On the back of this address was the name 'Mrs Castle', a midwife, without an address.

The Home Secretary, Mr Cross, was very interested in the names Mrs Todd had mentioned and asked that an urgent police enquiry be made about Mrs Castle, Lord or George Henry Thompson or John Robinson or Dr

George or Thomas Jackson or Henry Thompson. This turns out to be the same Mrs Maria Castle that was the midwife whose Brixton lying-in home had been under surveillance by Sergeant Relf in the Margaret Waters case and on 11 August information was sent to the Home Secretary about Mrs Castle. She had been traced to 9 South Place, Kennington. She admitted that she confined ladies who wished to have their identities kept secret in her house and that she didn't keep any record of the women's names. She also admitted to placing such children out to nurses or sending them to places for adoption. She had advertised in the *Christian World* and *The Times* but these papers now refused to take her advertisements. She said she had no recollection of any of the men's names that were put to her or any knowledge of Mrs Todd. Police Inspector Clarke said that suspicion had fallen upon Mrs Castle after the Waters case and her house had been under surveillance from time to time over the course of two or three years, but nothing could be found that could be used by the police against her. Inspector Clarke thought that these observations had been known to her and that she had ensured her conduct had been within the law. He opined that he did not believe anything improper had taken place.[58]

The Home Secretary, Richard Assheton Cross, after receiving the Queen's mercy, commuted Sophia Todd's sentence to life imprisonment.[59]

However, this still wasn't the end of this story.

In December 1877, Todd asked for her case to be taken into consideration as she admitted to concealing the death of the child but only because she was forced to by the violence of her husband. This appeal was not granted.

In July 1878, she asked to be excused going to the laundry but was told she should go where she was sent, but it appears she was never asked to work in the laundry but at sewing tasks.

In 1882 and 1883, she was petitioning for release on the grounds of ill health and that she had friends who were willing to receive her and send her abroad. This was not granted.

In May 1883, the medical officer of Fulham Women's Prison wrote that Mrs Todd was in the prison infirmary in a weak condition with a vascular disease of the heart and that she was seriously ill. By the end of June, it was said that she was unlikely to live more than a few days if left in prison. On 9 July 1883, Sophia Todd was released on licence into the care of the Rev.

James Davidson of Bristol. Rev. Davidson had been writing to and visiting Mrs Todd ever since her incarceration.[60]

While there was no direct evidence that Todd was responsible for the death of the baby, it seems remarkable that Todd's death sentence should be commuted to life imprisonment and then that she should be released after five years. It is interesting that the Home Secretary should be so involved in tracing the names Todd gave after her trial and gives rise to the suspicion that the child may have had noble parentage.

After her release, Mrs Todd disappears from records.

Annie Tooke

When the dismembered body of a child was found at Powhay Mills, Bonhay Road, Exeter on weekend of 17/18 May 1879, a murder investigation was mounted. The post-mortem examination was carried out by Mr Bell, the police surgeon, who said the child had been stunned by a blow to the head, possibly swung by the legs to hit a hard object, causing a fracture of the jaw and collar bone and then allowed to bleed to death after his throat was cut. The body was then decapitated and dismembered. Mr Bell stated that the body had been put into the water four or five days after death. It appeared that the child had also been cut in an attempt to cover an identifying disfigurement in his 'private parts'. This peculiarity led police to carry out enquiries in North Devon and eventually arrested Mary Hosking, the 25-year-old daughter of a mining engineer from Camborne, Cornwall. Miss Hosking was described as being 'considerably under middle height, with a thin, dark-featured, but rather interesting face'. Going under the name of Mrs Hede, Mary had taken, with the help of her brother, lodgings in Ide, a village about 2 miles from Exeter, for several months until she gave birth to her son, Reginald, in October 1878.

During the investigation, it transpired that Miss Hosking's brother and her sister, Mrs Elizabeth Tonkins, had, in November 1878, arranged for middle-aged widow and former cook Annie Tooke, who was living in Bartholomew St, Exeter, to nurse their sister's child for the sum of £12 with the promise of continuing to visit the child but that there was to be no correspondence. On 10 November, after Miss Hosking had been persuaded to part with her son by her siblings, the baby boy was given to Annie Tooke.

In January 1879, Annie Tooke moved to South St, Exeter with her four children, aged between 12/13 and 4 years, and young Reginald.

During her time at South St, she had had a discussion with a neighbour about the sum of money she was receiving for nursing the boy and had said she was planning to put the child into the workhouse as she could earn more by going out to work.

On 16 May, Mrs Tooke had a conversation on the stairs with her neighbour's husband when she said she had passed the baby to a friend to look after for 4 shillings a week rather than putting the child into the workhouse as money had been due to her for the boy's keep.

In a letter to her daughter (who was living in a brothel in Plymouth!), Annie Tooke said she had trouble with 'the poor miserable child' and complained about the amount he ate.

When questioned on 22 May, after the baby's body had been found, Mrs Tooke admitted she had taken a child to nurse after advertising for a nurse child. She stated that a stranger had taken the baby shopping and was to return with it. She also denied that the nurse child she had looked after had any sort of deformity and was unable to identify the child from photos shown to her of the deceased infant. On 27 May, Mrs Tooke returned to see the police of her own volition. This time she identified the photos she was shown by the police as being the baby Reginald Hede and told them to visit her daughter in Plymouth. As a result of this, Annie Tooke was taken to Camborne to identify Mary Hosking as the mother of the baby. Miss Hosking was charged with being an accessory to murder and Mrs Tooke gave evidence against her at the magistrates' court stating that on 12 May, Miss Hosking had sent a woman to collect the child on her behalf, but she was unable to give the name or address of this woman. This was denied by Miss Hosking.

At the trial, much was made of Miss Hosking's lack of concern for her offspring after she had given him to Mrs Tooke to nurse but her sister, Mrs Tonkin, said family members had dissuaded her from visiting as they had not wanted their parents to learn of Miss Hosking's illegitimate baby. Her sister also swore that she had not been away from Camborne from 10–17 May. Hosking's defence counsel said that he had other evidence that confirmed Mrs Tonkin's claims. Regardless of Tooke's evidence, the case against Mary Hosking was dismissed and Miss Hosking was discharged to the applause of the court. Miss Hosking had shown hysteria in court at any mention of the fate of her son. There must have been some gossip amongst the general public speculating on the paternity of Miss Hosking's son, as her solicitor took the opportunity in court to deny that the father was Miss Hosking's brother.

The police continued to search Annie Tooke's home and there they found a razor, an axe, a feeding bottle, pieces of blood-stained clothing and a well-scrubbed trunk (that had previously been seen with marks on the lid). These were analysed by Frank Perkins, the Public Analyst, who found traces of a floury substance on the bill hook and the razor that was the same as deposits found on the inside of the baby's bottle. Threads of cotton and traces of blood were under the handle of the razor. Blood was also on the clothing and inside the trunk along with filaments of what seemed to be human hair. As a consequence, Annie Tooke was charged with murder.

The public who were present at the trial of Annie Tooke were shocked when her confession was read to the court. In it she described in great detail how on Monday, 12 May, she had smothered the boy then put him into the trunk in her bedroom until the Friday when she took the lifeless body into the coal cupboard and used a knife (the one her son used to eat his dinner with) to disfigure and then dismember the boy's body. She then put the pieces into a box in her bedroom. That evening, she took the parcel containing the tiny body parts and threw them into the river near what she thought was Trew's Weir Mill.

Despite the detail of the evidence given against Annie Tooke in court, she denied the charge and refused to acknowledge the confession she had made while being remanded in prison. Nevertheless, after considering the case for an hour, the jury found her guilty of murder and she was sentenced to death.

While waiting for the sentence to be carried out, Tooke admitted that the evidence of her confession had been the truth.[61]

On the wet morning of 11 August 1879, a little before eight o'clock, a crowd of several hundred people waited outside Devon County Gaol as Annie Tooke was executed by William Marwood after the executioner insisted that new temporary alterations be made in the prison hospital to allow a drop of eight foot rather than the four-foot structure that had been erected in the prison yard by the prison authorities.[62]

Jessie King

When unmarried servant Catherine Gunn (later, after her marriage, she was known as Mrs Whyte) of Huntly St, Cannonmills, gave birth to twin boys, Alexander and Robert, in May 1887, she knew that, as she was in service, she would be unable to take care of them herself, so she paid Mrs Margaret Henderson of Rose Street 4 shillings a week each to care for them. There the children thrived for ten or eleven months; however, Catherine was unable to continue to pay for their keep and she sought the help of Mrs Euphemia McKay, who was the nurse that had attended the birth, to find the boys adoptive parents. Mrs McKay advertised, and she arranged for two different people to take a boy each. Catherine then handed the children over to Mrs McKay, who carried out the adoption procedures. On 4 April, Alexander was adopted by a Mrs MacPherson for a premium of £3 and taken to her room in St Ann's Court, Cannonmills, while Robert was taken by a Mrs Henderson (this appears to be a different Mrs Henderson to the one who cared for the children from birth) for £5, although these sums of money were given in two instalments. The following year, Robert is seen with Mrs Henderson, although Alexander's fate is not so good.[63]

Mrs MacPherson and her 'husband' were really Jessie King and Thomas Pearson.

Jessie Keane or Kane (she was later referred to as King, seemingly due to an error on the part of the authorities when she was arrested, although she does sign her statements as 'King') was born in Glasgow on 27 March 1861. Her father was a cloth yarn warper and she had two brothers, Peter and John. Her mother had died when she was 18 months old and her father when she was 18 years old. It was then that Jessie went to work in the mills at Renton, but this does not seem to have been a settled life for her as she is later found working in the Magdalene Asylum in Edinburgh, where she was an inmate for 18 months, learning laundry work. It was rumoured that she had been imprisoned in Glasgow for concealment of pregnancy. After she left the asylum, she obtained work in various laundries and, eventually, she is found in lodgings with Jessie Taylor and her supposed husband, Thomas Pearson; however, she left after Pearson made advances to her. Jessie Taylor later died in such suspicious circumstances that an inquiry was made into her death. At this time, Jessie King was expecting a child by a man named

Calder, who had offered to marry her, but she appears to have been under Pearson's influence and moved in to live with him. She gave birth to a daughter, Grace, who was registered and vaccinated in September 1887; however, there is no trace of the little girl after that date. In October 1888, Jessie was delivered of a baby boy, Thomas, who was later taken into the care of the parish.

Thomas Pearson formerly had had a good position in business and had a grown-up family in the Western Metropolis before he fell into dissolute habits and took up with Glaswegian Jessie King.

Jessie King, 27, had lived with Thomas Pearson, 59, for seven years, often using the name Mr and Mrs MacPherson, during which time they had sunk further and further into degradation, spending all their money on alcoholic beverages. As a way of acquiring easy money, Jessie started a baby farm and this is how unmarried servant Catherine Gunn's baby Alexander came to be put into Jessie's care.

On taking the boy home to St Ann's Court, King told her landlady that this was her sister's child, and she was looking after him while his mother was poorly. Pearson was said to be fond of the child but complained about the burden King had taken on; however, after hearing that Jessie had received £3 for taking the child, he agreed to keep it for three or four weeks. Alexander was treated kindly by King, although she was admonished for feeding him whisky. Jessie claimed that by the end of May, she tried to find a children's home that would take the child but was unable to do so as the boy was illegitimate. Eventually, in a drunken state, Jessie told Pearson she had found a new carer for the child in Miss Stirling's 'Destitute Home'. Pearson went for an evening in the public house, and on his return the baby was gone, not, however, to Miss Stirling's establishment but lying strangled in a cupboard adjoining their single room. Sometime later, Jessie stated that once, when passing Miss Stirling's home, Pearson had wanted to visit the boy and she had had to tell him that men were not allowed to visit in order to stop him taking Alexander a toy.

When, three days later, they moved to Cheyne Street, Stockbridge, Edinburgh, King took the child's body with her and placed it in a closet in the lobby with the door locked, keeping the key on her person. After some weeks, the smell emitting from the closet became so bad that King decided she needed to remove the body. She wrapped it in Pearson's waterproof coat, which she told Pearson she had thrown out due to it being mouldy, and took it to the end of the street, where she left it on a piece of vacant ground. Here it stayed until some young boys playing in the street found the parcel. The children opened it up and when they saw what was wrapped inside, they called the police, who took the small body to the mortuary.

In the meantime, King realised that she had remained undiscovered and answered an advert that had been placed by the mother of another baby, unmarried servant Alice Maria Jane Stewart Tomlinson of 3 Coates Place, Edinburgh, who had recently given birth to baby Violet. Giving the name of Mrs Banks, King met with Mrs Tomlinson, the baby's grandmother. King said the baby was for her sister, who was married to the Duke of Montrose's piper (John McDonald, piper to the Duke of Montrose, later wrote to the *Glasgow Herald* stating he was unmarried and did not know Jessie King[64]) and was paid £2 and given a 3-week-old child. She dispatched this second child so quickly that Pearson was said to know nothing of its arrival. Initially, she gave it whisky to keep it quiet before she smothered the baby by putting her hand over its mouth, then she tightly tied a cloth around its mouth. She then put the body into the closet as she had before.

James Banks, King's landlord at Cheyne Street, remembered that Jessie King had told him she had got a child and £25 to keep it but that she had given the child to another for £18, thereby keeping £7 for herself. Finding this suspicious in light of the discovery of Alexander's body so close to Jessie's home, he reported the conversation to the police.

Detective James Clark went to the house and was shown Violet's birth certificate and vaccination papers. King told him this baby was with her sister. Clark realised that these papers referred to a girl and the body found by the boys was a baby boy, so he insisted on searching the closet when King said, 'Get a cab; it is there,' and on opening the closet door he found the body of Violet Tomlinson on the lowest shelf wrapped in canvas, a canister of chloride of lime and a piece of oilskin identical to that which was wrapped around the body of baby Alexander. King confessed to murdering the baby girl, Violet, and the boy, Alexander, saying Pearson had no knowledge of it. She said she had fed Violet with whisky before strangling her with a cloth.

The post-mortem of Alexander Gunn showed he had heathy internal organs, but his skin showed a mummified appearance. Death had been caused by strangulation.

Again, the post-mortem of Violet Tomlinson showed that all her organs were healthy; however, in this case, decomposition was advancing with maggots and small flies. Her skin was intact and uninjured. The cause of her death was strangulation.

Baby Walter, the son of Elizabeth Campbell and David Ferguson Finlay of Leith, had been born in May 1887. Elizabeth had died a week later, and her sister, Janet Anderson, had offered to adopt the child if the baby's father paid for its keep. Finlay refused and three months later he advertised his son for adoption. The advertisement was answered by a father and daughter named Stewart of Dalkeith Road, who were identified later as Jessie King and Thomas Pearson. Pearson had said his 'daughter' had recently lost a child and it was thought adopting another would give her some comfort. They took baby Walter and a premium of £5. A neighbour recollected the boy arriving at Pearson's home and disappearing three months later.

Jessie King was charged with the murder of three infants: Walter Anderson Campbell, 5 months, son of Elizabeth Campbell, deceased wireworker, of Prestonpans, at 24 Dalkeith Road, Edinburgh, in October or November 1887; Alexander Gunn, 12 months, son of Catherine Whyte, servant, from Huntly St, Cottonmills at in Ann's Court, Cannonmills, Edinburgh in April or May 1888; and Violet Tomlinson, 6 months, daughter of Alice Maria Jane Stewart Tomlinson, servant, of 3 Coates Place, Edinburgh at Cheyne Street, Stockbridge, Edinburgh in September 1888. Against the advice of the lawyer Jessie admitted the killings of Alexander and Violet but denied the murder of Walter. While making her confession, she was determined to clear Pearson of implication in these killings and was overjoyed when she was later told that he had been released, but then asked if she could take back her confession. She was told that she could in front of the sheriff; however, she did not do so.

Thomas Pearson was also charged with Violet's murder.

While awaiting trial in Edinburgh Prison, Jessie attempted suicide by taking the tape from her child's clothing and wrapping it tightly around her neck several times. It was then decided, after speaking to those imprisoned with her, that her child was in danger and should be removed from her and a watch should be kept on Jessie.

In her evidence, servant Catherine Whyte said she gave birth to illegitimate twins, Alexander and Robert Gunn, on 1 May 1887, attended by nurse

Mrs Euphemia MacKay. When the babies were 4 days old, they were taken into the care of a Mrs Henderson for a weekly sum. There they resided for eleven months until Mrs Whyte asked Mrs MacKay to advertise for someone else to take charge of the children. Mrs MacKay saw a different Mrs Henderson, who took baby Robert for a £1 premium, and a Mrs MacPherson, who took baby Alexander for a £2 premium. Mrs Whyte had not been present during these transactions but had given clothing and shoes over to Mrs MacKay along with the boys. While giving her evidence, Mrs Whyte appeared very composed, until she was shown shoes that she identified as being those she had handed to Mrs MacKay, when she began to weep.

Mrs MacKay then identified Jessie King as the Mrs MacPherson she had handed Alexander over to. She said she had seen the baby since, and he had seemed in good health and that both Mr and Mrs MacPherson had appeared to be fond of the infant, but she had been particularly taken by the fondness Mr MacPherson had shown when nursing the child. She did note that the house had been very untidy.

Mrs MacKenzie, landlady of the accused at St Ann's Court, said she had admonished King for giving the child whisky to quieten it.

Mr Finlay told the court that he had advertised for someone to adopt the baby and 'Stewart' had replied from 24 Dalkeith Road.

He visited them at their home and met the 'father and daughter'. He gave them £5 to adopt the child and a note to give to Mrs Anderson. Mrs Anderson identified Thomas Pearson and Jessie King as this couple. Finlay, too, identified them as Thomas Pearson and Jessie Pearson. Mrs Elizabeth Penman from Dalkeith Road identified Pearson and King as previously being her neighbours. She said in the summer of 1887, a child of about 3 months old arrived at the house but disappeared a few months later, after looking unwell. The Pearsons said the child had returned to its home and soon afterwards they left Dalkeith Road.

Both Pearson and King had been charged in connection with Miss Campbell's child but Pearson had been told if he gave evidence about Miss King with regard to the other charges, his charge in this case would be dropped, and so he stood in the dock and gave evidence against Jessie King. He said he knew of the child, Alexander Gunn, and had been told by Jessie that she had given him up into the care of Miss Stirling's home. He had asked if he could visit the boy, but Jessie had told him this would not be allowed. He denied having any knowledge of Violet Tomlinson, never having seen the child, and he never looked into the closet where the child had been found. He admitted collecting Walter Campbell and he had believed that Walter had also been taken to Miss Stirling's home and said had no recollection of passing himself off as King's father, although a letter from him had been found referring to Jessie as his daughter.

Although searches were made of the house in Dalkeith Road and at Miss Stirling's home, no trace had been found of Walter. It was suspected at the time that a body that had been left in a bonnet box at Abbeyhill Station had been deposited by King, but she denied having anything to do with this child, even though she had freely admitted to killing the other two children.

In her defence, Mr Fitzroy Bell said the jury must consider whether King had been under the influence of Pearson and acting in his control and for his benefit. In his summing up Lord Justice-Clerk said that, even if this were the case, it would not exonerate King or reduce the charge to culpable homicide.

The jury took just four minutes to return a unanimous verdict of guilty against Jessie King for the murder of Alexander Gunn and Violet Tomlinson and the death sentence was passed.

Jessie was seen to be leaning heavily on the policeman at her side after the verdict was given as the judge pronounced the death sentence when she groaned loudly and needed to be carried from the court.[65]

She was under the impression that she should have only been found guilty of manslaughter and sentenced to 18 months' imprisonment, despite having been told by her counsel that she would hang for murder if she admitted killing the two babies.[66]

It was reported that while Jessie King resided in Calton Jail awaiting her execution, she had become resigned to her fate, saying she would prefer death to life imprisonment, and she was carefully watched in case of suicide attempts, which the warders believed she wished to do. A petition of over 2,000 signatures was received by the Secretary of State for Scotland, asking for a reprieve. It stated she was of low intelligence and had lived in poverty, and also pointed out that it had been 58 years since a woman had been executed in Edinburgh.

Several jurymen wrote asking that her case be reinvestigated as there were strong feelings regarding Pearson's role in the crimes; indeed, there did seem to be many who believed it to be unlikely that Pearson had no knowledge of the fate of the children.[67]

A letter was received from Jessie Leslie, who had met Jessie King (who she knew of as Jessie Kean) in various homes and laundries, in one of which she was treated for melancholia. She thought Miss King was 'not all there' as she acted in peculiar ways, twitched her mouth and had an odd movement of her eyes. The matron of the Magdalene Asylum in Edinburgh said Jessie had been at the asylum from July 1883 to March 1885 and it was noticed that she had a silly, peculiar laugh and a strange expression in the eyes that were so unusual that it wasn't clear if she understood instructions or would carry them out. If she were scolded, she would go into the open air and sit without food for the best part of the day, regardless of the weather.[68]

There was even a letter from an A. Gordon requesting that they be hanged in place of Jessie![69]

In light of all the evidence given from her past and that given by the warders in the prison of her demeanour, her mental state was investigated, and it was deemed that she was not insane, either whilst in prison or when carrying out the murders of which she was convicted.[70]

In the event, a reprieve was denied,[71] and Jessie King was hanged by James Berry at 8.00 am on 11 March 1889.[72] Prior to the sentence being carried out, Jessie wrote her last will and testament, in which she appointed the priest in charge of the Roman Catholic Cathedral in Broughton St, Edinburgh as guardian to her son, Thomas.[73]

She also left a confession which implicated another person in the crime, presumed to be Pearson. However, as Pearson had turned Queen's evidence, the authorities were unable to rearrest him.[74]

A few months later, Jessie King's case is cited in an article in the *Pall Mall Gazette* about the dangers caused by using irrevocable penalties, where it states that Jessie had tried to screen Pearson from prosecution and had the full facts been known at the time, Jessie would not have been convicted.[75]

Amelia Elizabeth Dyer

Amelia Elizabeth Dyer is probably the most infamous of all the baby farmers.

Early life
She was born in 1837 in Bristol to Samuel and Sarah Hobley and was christened on the last day of the year.[76] She had three older brothers and

an older sister, and she later claimed that she was one of eleven children, many of whom had died young. Her father was a shoemaker, which was a good trade, living at Pyle Marsh, Bristol. In November 1861, she married master carver and gilder George Thomas. In the 1861 census, taken in April of that year, 57-year-old George is seen living with his wife, Elizabeth, and grown son, George, and was employing one man (probably his son).[77] By November of that year, Elizabeth had died and George had married Amelia, taking nine years off his age! Amelia also lied about her age, but she added years, making her 30 years old! Maybe an eighteen-year age difference was more acceptable than a thirty-three-year gap.

In 1863, she became a nurse, and in 1864 she gave birth to a daughter, Ellen. Around this time Amelia met midwife Eleanor Dane, who came from Southport. Dane was a baby farmer who took unwanted babies and passed them on to others. It was later said that in the late 1860s Dane's reputation reached the ears of the police and she left the country.[78]

Amelia starts baby farming
In 1869, George died. Amelia sent Ellen away to be cared for in a foster family (although she had returned to live with Amelia by 1879)[79] and Amelia started to take in babies after advertising in the names of Mrs Harding and Mrs Smith. Amelia would act as an intermediary, passing these infants on to other baby farmers.

In 1870, Margaret Waters was executed in London for the murder of babies in her care and letters were found in Waters's house relating to transactions between Dyer, using the name Mary Smith from Totterdown, and Waters.[80]

In the same year, letters from Mary Smith of Totterdown were also found in the home of Mary Ann Hall, who was convicted of fraud but was lucky to avoid more serious charges.[81]

In the 1871 census, we see Amelia has become nurse attendant at Bristol Lunatic Asylum.[82] Was this an attempt to distance herself from Margaret Waters and Mary Ann Hall?

In December 1872, she married illiterate labourer William Dyer at St Philip and Jacob Church, Bristol. A year later, she had her second daughter, Mary Ann (later known as Polly),[83] although she did later say that Polly was not in fact her daughter but had been adopted from a gentleman farmer named Francis William Dyer, who was a relative of Amelia's husband, followed in 1876 by a son, William Samuel.[84] It appears that soon after this, Amelia again took up baby farming.

Babies that were not breastfed were often fed boiled bread, water, cornflour and condensed milk and it was accepted that they had less chance of survival than breastfed babies. Baby farmers also often used opiates such as Godfrey's Cordial (a concoction obtained from the chemist that contained opium) so there was no crying, and it was easy to overdose or fail to feed the sleeping babies. Later Dyer's daughter Ellen stated that her mother had regularly given babies in her care five drops of Godfrey's Cordial before putting them to bed. Ellen was sent to the chemist for two-pennyworth of the cordial twice a week.[85]

First brush with the law
The deaths of babies were easy to register due to the high number of babies that died through not thriving; however, by 1879, it was noticed that too many babies' deaths were being registered by Dyer, so she got other women, Mrs Williams and Mrs Hacker, to care for the dying babies. These women lived in a different area of Bristol so when the babies died, local medical practitioners had no knowledge of the surrounding circumstances and issued death certificates. Dyer had even encouraged Mrs Williams to register the baby as her own.

By now the police were interested in Amelia Dyer as Mr Hacker had persuaded his wife to report her. The police tipped off the County Coroner and a post-mortem was ordered on one of the babies.

Dyer did what she was later to do so often when faced with difficulties: she tried to commit suicide, this time taking an overdose of laudanum. Needless to say, she survived and was arrested for the attempt.[86]

The jury at the inquest into the infants' deaths brought in a verdict that the children had died of natural causes but there was concern about the treatment Mrs Dyer handed out to those in her care.[87]

Amelia was arrested 26 August 1879 under the 1872 Infant Life Protection Act as she wasn't registered to look after children. She told the court she had not realised she needed registration but was found guilty and was sentenced to six months' hard labour.[88]

After her release
After her release, she went to work as a forewoman in a firm making ladies' corsets. In 1881, she was recorded on the census as working as a laundress and she was also said to have opened a small general shop; however, the shop failed to make money, so the family moved away to Fishponds, Bristol and Amelia restarted baby farming.[89]

In 1880, during the trial of Elizabeth Thompson in Liverpool, one of Dyer's aliases, Mary Smith, seems to have been one of the intermediaries that Thompson dealt with. Dyer appears to have had a network that stretched across the country.[90]

Not all of the children Amelia took in were babies: she took in a 12-year-old girl named Annie for a premium of £70. Amelia said this girl was a relative and she certainly kept in contact with Annie as she referred to her in a letter that she wrote the night before her execution.[91] She also took in a boy, Alfred, for an £80 premium, who was brought to her by a young woman in a carriage.[92]

Amelia moved from house to house in quick succession. According to the *Bristol Mercury* she had lived with William Dyer at Totterdown, Fishponds, Horsfield (advertising under the name of Wathen) and Eastville (advertising under name of Smith). She still took in women to have their babies in addition to advertising for nurse babies. Babies came and went quickly – she no longer seems to have kept them to sicken.[93]

At various times Amelia attempts suicide, although each time it was when she was in a difficult situation and may have been a ploy to avoid trouble as each time she was committed to the lunatic asylum.

In the 1891 census, Amelia Dyer is listed as a nurse in a middle-class boarding house in Portishead while her husband, William Dyer, is in Stapleton, Bristol with daughter Mary A., son William S., daughter Annie and son Alfred W. – the latter two are probably adopted children.[94] Was Amelia trying to avoid detection, as it was during this time that she took in a baby from a woman who later attempted to trace her child? On 13 November 1891, Amelia tried to avoid complications by cutting her own throat (a small scratch with a hat pin) and was committed to Gloucestershire asylum. She was released on 16 December and moved to Horsfield.[95]

The governess, her baby and Mrs Dyer's madness

While there, she took in an unmarried woman, a governess, to await the birth of her illegitimate child. When the child was born, the mother left the baby with Mrs Dyer, presuming the child would be adopted by the Dyers. Some months later, she requested to visit the baby and to pay the part of the premium still owing but, when she arrived, Dyer gave her a child that she did not recognise as her baby. When pressed, Dyer admitted she had handed her the wrong child but agreed to make another appointment when the correct baby would be there. In the interval between the two appointments, the governess married the child's father and returned with her new husband, wanting to reclaim the child. Dyer told them she had met a woman under the clock at Bristol railway station and the woman had taken a fancy to the child and adopted it. She gave them addresses in Bath, Cheltenham, Gloucester and London.[96]

Eventually the young couple threatened to inform the police and in 1893 Dyer again made a suicide attempt and was taken to Wells asylum on Boxing Day, only to be released on 20 January 1894. In April 1894, the *Bristol Mercury* reported she had been found lying unconscious in a stream that ran through Bedminster Park.[97] She was taken to hospital where she gave a rambling statement. The police believed she had attempted suicide, although she had apparently just managed to wet her skirt![98]

In December 1894, the couple decided they were not going to deviate from their quest and this time Dyer took laudanum in a suicide attempt.[99]

Again, she was committed to Gloucester asylum, where she stayed, on and off, having been released 'on trial' and returning after she was again met by parents seeking their child until 13 February 1895. She was discharged as recovered on 11 March, when she went into Barton Regis workhouse. In his letter to the police after her arrest, Frederick Hurst Craddock, medical superintendent of Gloucester asylum, stated that during her times at the asylum, Dyer had appeared to be suffering from mild depression and recovered within a few days of admittance and appeared to view the asylum as a haven away from the cares that troubled her at home.[100] There had been four children in her house at this point and these were taken to Barton Regis workhouse. The parents of two were found: one had paid Dyer £80; the other £40. One of the remaining children died soon after being admitted and the other, a girl, was sent to Canada.[101]

Murder   171

While all this was going on, life for the Dyers was changing. In April 1894, Polly married Arthur Ernest Palmer,[102] who was to feature in the baby farmer story later, and at some point in 1894, William Dyer and Amelia parted company and William placed an advertisement in the *Western Daily Press*, saying he would not be answerable for any debts contracted by Amelia. Amelia was later to say that William had not approved of her taking in children.

On being released from the asylum
While Amelia Dyer was an inmate at Barton Regis workhouse, she became friendly with a 74-year-old widow, Jane Smith, who was nursing smallpox patients in the workhouse. Dyer told Mrs Smith that she was planning to leave the workhouse and start to take babies in to nurse and she asked Mrs Smith if she would like to go to live with her.[103] According to the *Bristol Mercury*, when she left the workhouse she moved first to Fishponds, then Eastville where she took the name of Smith and had a small child with her but soon moved to Cardiff, where Polly and Arthur Palmer joined them. Before moving to Cardiff, she deserted a child, Bertie Palmer, on Durdham Down.[104] A warrant was issued for her arrest for desertion. She took another child living with her to Cardiff, but the police were unable to locate this child. Their stay in Cardiff only lasted a few weeks before Amelia was in debt and she is thought to have visited London as, while she was in the workhouse, she had received a letter from her daughter from Notting Hill and, soon after, the whole family moved to Caversham.[105]

It was reported in the *Hampshire Telegraph* of 18 April 1896 that Mrs Dyer had previously lived in Stafford and Newcastle-upon-Tyne.[106]

Police in Bristol had evidence that two children had been handed to Arthur Palmer, who had promised to find them a good home. Neither child had been heard of since, but a warrant had been issued for a man who had abandoned a child in Plymouth.[107]

Move to Reading
In August 1895, Dyer moved to Caversham, followed by the Palmers and Mrs Smith. Throughout this time, they moved house frequently; in Reading they had started at Pigott's Road, then Elm Villas, where they were joined by a 9-year-old boy, Willie Thornton, who brought with him a carpet bag, and finally, Kensington Road, Reading, where 10-year-old Ellen Maud

Oliver (Nellie) joined the household.[108] Elm Villas is close to a footbridge over Clappers Pool, which is lonely and unlit at night and close to both the river and the mill stream.

While at Kensington Road, an officer from the NSPCC visited and reminded Dyer that she should be registered under the Infant Life Protection Act if she was caring for more than one child.[109]

Willie Thornton
Young Willie Thornton said he had a mother and father living in Henley but had been taken from there by his godmother to a Mrs Dalton in London, who, in turn, passed him onto Mrs Dyer, who he referred to as 'Mrs Thomas'. Willie and his carpet bag joined the Dyer household at Elm Villas, Caversham and moved with them to Piggott's Road, Caversham and Kensington Road, Reading. He told of a baby girl who later died that had been looked after by Polly Palmer at Caversham and then the arrival of a boy, Harold, into Polly's care. He explained about children coming and going through the house at Kensington Road, some staying, as did 10-year-old Nellie Oliver, while others were reclaimed by their mothers and others being sent away.[110]

Willie had noticed a foul smell that had also been remarked upon by Mrs Chandler, the lodger, emanating from a kitchen cupboard at Kensington Road. On investigation, he found a brown paper parcel tied with string that was a little over a foot long. This smell continued until 30 March, when it disappeared.[111]

After the trial, Willie was reclaimed by his mother[112] and Nellie Oliver's mother was traced but was not in a position to care for her.[113]

Bodies in the river
Over the course of many months in 1895/6, the Thames police had had thirty or forty reports of the bodies of babies being found in the Thames between Battersea and Wapping. Many of these bodies were wrapped in brown paper and it was believed they had been murdered but there was no evidence to identify the babies or the culprit. A police surgeon in the East End of London believed that the bundles had been thrown into the river further upstream from London.[114]

On 1 April, a bargeman found a parcel containing the body of a baby. The brown paper in which the infant had been wrapped had a name and address written on it – Mrs Thomas, 26 Wigott's Road, Lower Caversham, Reading, Oxon.

After some investigation on the part of the police, they discovered that 'Mrs Thomas' was really Mrs Dyer, as there was no Wigott's Road it should have read 'Piggott's' Road, and that she had moved from Piggott's Road to 45 Kensington Road, Reading. A woman was taken into the confidence of the police and sent to the house in Kensington Road with the story she had a child to put out to nurse and that 'Mrs Harding' had been recommended. She discovered that Dyer had left to visit London but made an appointment to visit again when Dyer was back. The woman returned on 3 April and agreed that Dyer should adopt the 'baby' for £100 and exchange would be made the following evening after dark.[115] This ascertained that Dyer took in babies to nurse, and Detective Constable James Anderson and Sergeant Harry James then arrived to question her. Finding her answers to be unsatisfactory, they arrested her and remanded her in custody while they searched the house where they found a large quantity of pawn tickets, baby clothes, vaccination certificates, receipts for advertising and letters from parents wishing to have their babies adopted. By sifting through the latter, they concluded that the baby girl discovered in the river was Helena Fry, illegitimate daughter of Mary Fry. Dyer had collected a baby girl from the Bristol woman after advertising in the name of Thorley and it was thought this was the same child.

Amelia Dyer was charged on suspicion of murder of Helena Fry, although this charge was later dropped as the body was so badly decomposed it was impossible to make a positive identification.

Engineer John Toller, while returning home from work at the prison in the late evening of 2 April, greeted a woman he later identified as Mrs Dyer as they passed. She was not walking from the direction of the station but from the river.

On 10 April, a party of men were employed by the police to drag the river and a total of six bodies were eventually found. A carpet bag contained two bodies: these were identified as Doris Marmon and Harry Simmonds. Both had been given to Dyer for adoption just days earlier, both had been strangled with tape and bricks had been used to weigh the bag down.

Amelia Dyer was charged with the murders of Doris Marmon and Harry Simmonds.

A body had also been found in the canal in Manchester wrapped in brown paper and strangled with a knot under the right ear and police looked for similarities, but it appears that this was not connected to Mrs Dyer, even though the distinctive knot was Dyer's trademark, which was noted by the Manchester coroner.[116]

After the publicity surrounding her arrest, several women came forward enquiring about children they had placed in Dyer's care, and it was thought she had received twenty children aged between 2 months and 8 years between Christmas 1895 and her arrest in April. In each case she had charged a premium for taking them, one for as much as £100. Of these, nine had been traced, five having been taken from the river. No trace was found of the others, but clothing found at the house was identified as having been given to her with the children.

One of these women was domestic servant Miss Elizabeth Goulding, from Frampton-on-Severn, near Gloucester. The wife of the baby's father had written in answer to an advertisement in early 1895 and had received a reply from Mary A. Palmer, offering to adopt the illegitimate child for a premium of £10. Miss Goulding and her aunt then attended a solicitor's office at the request of the father and Mrs Palmer collected the baby girl, after signing an agreement, and had since written letters describing the child's progress. Although the mother had asked several times if she could visit her child, she had always been told that Mrs Palmer would not be in Reading at that time and, eventually, the letters to Mrs Palmer were returned marked 'gone away'.[117]

Polly and Arthur Palmer

The letters found in Kensington Road also led the police to Polly and Arthur's house at Mayo Road, Willesden where, on 6 April, Police Sergeant James and Detective Constable Anderson found many items of clothing including a pelisse (a type of cape) later identified by as being that which Doris Marmon had been wearing. PS James stated that there seemed too much clothing for the Palmers' one child. On returning to Reading, Chief Constable Tewsley issued a warrant for the arrest of Arthur Palmer as it was believed he had had knowledge of the murder of Helena Fry. Arthur Palmer was arrested and charged with being an accessory after the fact in the murder of Helena Fry.[118]

Clearly Arthur Palmer had some knowledge of his mother-in-law's trade as in January 1896, calling herself Mrs Stansfield, wife of a Reading farmer, Dyer had collected a child from a house in Cunningham Road, Shepherd's Bush and had been accompanied by Arthur Palmer.[119] This child was later found to be alive by an inspector from the NSPCC as the mother had removed the infant from Dyer and placed it elsewhere.[120]

Miss Goulding's baby
It had been thought that the seventh baby to be found in the river was Miss Goulding's baby girl and during the inquest of this baby, both Miss Goulding and her aunt were called as witnesses, as was Polly Palmer. Mrs Palmer stated that she had never intended to keep the child herself, despite the evidence given by the previous witnesses, and that she had been sourcing a child for a Miss Robb, who was an actress in Birmingham. Miss Robb had been promised an annuity from the father of her illegitimate child if the child lived, but it had died, and she wanted a child to replace it. Mrs Palmer said she had taken the child to Birmingham the day after she had received it and the letters of its progress she had written had been composed from information she had been given by Miss Robb.

At the end of the inquest into the seventh baby's death, the jury returned a verdict of wilful murder against Mrs Dyer and Mrs Palmer as an accessory before the fact. Mrs Palmer was then arrested.[121]

Amelia later claimed that she had taken this baby to London and had left it outside a church and that Polly's story of taking the child to Birmingham had been Polly's attempt to exonerate her mother without realising she would be implicating herself.

Doris Marmon and Harry Simmonds
Evalina Edith Marmon had given birth in January 1896 to a baby girl, Doris. In March, Evalina answered an advertisement in the *Bristol Times and Mirror*: 'Couple with no child, want care of or would adopt one: terms £10. Care of Ship Exchange, Bristol.' An exchange of letters (where Miss Marmon called herself Mrs Scott) took place where Dyer, calling herself Mary Harding, spoke of how she and her husband were plain, homely, religious people in fairly good circumstances with their own house in the country. She emphasised how she would give the child a good home with a mother's love

and care. Several times she stated she would be pleased for Evalina to visit and seemed very keen to arrange to collect the child. On 31 March, Dyer arrived at Evalina's home. Evalina was impressed by the kindly, well-dressed 'Mrs Harding' and, after signing an agreement and receiving £10, Dyer left carrying little Doris, who was dressed in a fawn-coloured pelisse and a white bonnet, on the 5.20 train from Cheltenham. At Cheltenham station, Dyer had collected a carpet bag from the cloak room. Evalina accompanied Dyer as far as Gloucester, where she handed over a box containing baby clothes and received assurance that 'Mrs Harding' would write to her that evening.

In the event, the letter that arrived on 2 April informed Evalina that 'Mrs Harding' had had to visit a sick sister and had taken Doris with her to Kensal Rise but that the baby had been very good during the journey and that she would write a longer letter next time. However, Evalina heard no more so wrote to Dyer on 4 April. The next she heard of Doris was when the police arrived at her home on 7 April. On 11 April, she attended Reading mortuary at the request of the police, where she identified the body of 10-week-old Doris. She also identified the box and some of the clothes she had given to 'Mrs Harding'.[122]

Undertaker's wife Amelia Hannah Sargeant was caring for Harry, the son of Mrs Lizzie Simmonds. Mrs Sargeant was later at pains to point out that she was not paid to do this but did it out of kindness. She had been asked to find a home for the 13-month-old boy as the mother had obtained the situation of lady's maid. On 15 March 1896, she saw an advertisement in the *Weekly Dispatch*, and, after some exchange of correspondence, she went to visit Amelia Dyer, who was using the alias 'Mrs Harding', at 45 Kensington Road, Oxford Road, Reading. When she arrived, she asked 'Mrs Harding' if she was 'in the habit of taking nurse children'. 'Mrs Harding' said she wasn't but that she had brought up two children, her niece and a young man, who was now a sailor. She said she had lived in Reading for twenty-two years and her husband was a goods guard on the railway. However, she did confide that her name wasn't actually Harding but 'Mrs Thomas'. This alias was, she said, due to her being well respected in Reading and wishing to keep her advertisement private. After some conversation, where Mrs Sargeant was impressed by the kind, homely, motherly woman, she agreed to hand Harry over to 'Mrs Thomas' for the fee of £10 without seeking further references.

On 1 April, Mr and Mrs Sargeant went to Paddington Station, where the child was given into 'Mrs Thomas's' care; also at this meeting were 'Mrs Thomas's' 'niece', Mrs Palmer, and a boy named Harold who was dressed in a fawn-coloured pelisse – later identified as the one produced in court as belonging to Doris Marmon. Mrs Sargeant paid £5 and an IOU for the other £5 and a parcel of clothing for which she received a receipt signed 'Annie Thomas'. Although Mrs Sargeant was encouraged by 'Mrs Thomas' to call upon her to see how the boy was doing, when she wrote to suggest a meeting to pay the outstanding debt, she was told 'Mrs Thomas' had a cold and to put the money into a registered letter.

The next time Mrs Sargeant was to see Harry was when she identified his body at Reading mortuary.

Both Evalina Marmon and Amelia Sargeant identified Amelia Dyer as the woman they handed the infants over to and both broke down in court when various articles were shown in evidence.

Doris and Harry's fate
On 11 April 1896, Amelia Elizabeth Dyer and Arthur Ernest Palmer first appeared at Reading Police Court. The case was adjourned as further bodies had been recently recovered and the police wished to investigate further. When the case resumed, charges relating to Helena Fry were dropped but the fate of Doris Marmon and Harry Simmonds was unfolded.

After taking charge of Doris Marmon, she was to visit her daughter, Mary Ann (Polly) Palmer, and her husband, Arthur, who were living in two rooms at 76 Mayo Road, Willesden, North London. She had been seen on an omnibus by Mary Ann Beattie carrying a bag, a parcel and a child. Mrs Beattie had been kind enough to help her carry the heavy bag to Mrs Palmer's front door after they had both alighted from the bus. Mrs Beattie saw Mrs Dyer enter number 76 as she continued on her way. At Dyer's trial, Mrs Palmer said she had seen Dyer with what she presumed to be a child in her arms when she knocked at the front door of her Mayo Road address, but Dyer refused to come into the house as she was waiting for a Mrs Harris, for whom she was holding the baby. Polly then went to the rear yard of the house, leaving Dyer on the doorstep. When she returned to the sitting room, her mother was already there putting the carpetbag under the couch and she saw no sign of the baby. Dyer did give Polly some child's clothes, including a fawn-coloured pelisse, from a cardboard box that had been in the parcel and a gammon of bacon.

The day after Dyer arrived at Polly Palmer's house, she went to meet the Sargeants at Paddington Station. According to Polly's testimony, she went with Dyer and her adopted son, Harold, but her husband, Arthur, did not. When they arrived back at Polly's house, young Harry got fractious and Dyer eventually gave him an India rubber teat to suck on, but this had not quietened him for long and she had no food for him, so Polly gave him some bread and butter. Dyer told Polly she would not keep the child.

At about 6 o'clock, Polly put Harold to bed and Dyer said she would do the same with Harry, who was crying again. After Polly had left the room, the child went quiet and by the time she had returned to the room, he was lying on the couch covered with a shawl. Polly said Dyer had stopped her from looking at the 'sleeping' child. When Polly's husband, Arthur, came in, he went towards the bundle on the couch and Dyer told him not to touch it because the baby was asleep. All three adults then went out of the house for between an hour and an hour and a half. When they arrived back, it was noticed that the child on the couch had not moved and Dyer went to look at him and said, 'He is still asleep; don't touch him.'

The following morning, 2 April, there was no sign of the baby. Polly noticed as she tidied the sitting room that there was a child-shaped parcel on the floor under the couch. She asked her mother if the baby was all right and was told not to worry about him. Later that day, Dyer asked Polly if she had a brick. Polly said she did not but when Dyer went into the backyard, she found a brick, which she put under the couch. That evening, before leaving the house for Paddington Station with her mother, Polly noticed the carpetbag had been packed and was so full it would not close properly, but the top was covered with brown paper and the whole was tied with string. There was nothing left under the couch. Strangely, Polly stated in her testimony that she had asked her mother what the neighbours would say at seeing her enter the house with a baby and leave without it. Dyer told her she could make an excuse! She also said that she had had a work basket in the sitting room of her house and, after Dyer had left, she discovered that a skein of tape was missing from it and neither of the babies that Dyer had brought to the house had been left there.[123]

While the investigation of Amelia Dyer's crimes was ongoing and widely publicised in national newspapers, police in Devonport, Plymouth, Devon were attempting to find a couple who had abandoned a 4-year-old girl, Queenie Baker, in the town. The couple had lodged with a Mrs Barber in May the previous year and, after deserting the girl, left town hurriedly. Mrs Barber was shown a photograph of Arthur Palmer who she identified as the man involved. It was ascertained that the woman could not have been Mrs Dyer. Police from Devonport waited outside the court in Reading for Arthur Palmer to be released in order to question him with regards to the abandonment of Queenie.[124]

Charges with relation to the deaths of Doris Marmon and Harry Simmonds against Arthur Palmer were dropped due to lack of evidence against him, only for him to be rearrested for the abandonment of Queenie Baker in Devonport, near Plymouth four years earlier as he left the court. He was taken to Devon. While being transported there by the police, he denied ever having been to Plymouth, but despite this he pleaded guilty to the charge, and he was sentenced to three months' hard labour.[125]

As the days passed, the police made more enquiries into these deaths and eventually arrested Dyer's daughter, Mary Ann (Polly) Palmer.

Amelia Dyer's trial
After a hearing in front of Reading magistrates, where evidence was heard and letters written by Amelia Dyer that confessed to her crimes but denying that Arthur and Polly Palmer were involved were read out, she was formally charged with murdering Doris Marmon and Harry Simmonds at Willesden, and she was committed for trial at the Central Criminal Court in London – the Old Bailey.

She was conveyed to London by train, and such was the interest in the case a huge crowd assembled to watch her departure from Reading and an equally large crowd was waiting to see her arrival at Paddington Station, London.[126]

When giving evidence at Dyer's trial, Jane Smith, 74, said Dyer had left Reading on 31 March carrying a carpet bag that had been owned by Willie Thornton, one of the children Dyer cared for, but when she returned, she no longer had the bag but said she had left it with Polly for her to pack her belongings in as she was moving to Bridgewater.

Mrs Smith also said that, although Dyer got into tempers sometimes, she never felt threatened by her, and she had never heard her talking to herself.

Young Nellie Oliver also gave evidence at the trial, saying that Dyer had treated the babies cruelly, hitting them and throwing them into the cradle, but she had been treated well, as had Willie, because they could talk!

During the trial, much discussion was made of Dyer's mental health. Her lawyer, Mr Kapaida, used insanity as her defence. She claimed to various specialists that she heard voices that told her to kill herself and pointed out that she had been committed to lunatic asylums after various suicide attempts and experts were called to give evidence of her insanity. She had also claimed her mother had been mentally unstable and had died in an asylum. A claim denied by her brother, James, who asked for his identity be kept secret. She was also examined by Dr Scott, the medical officer at Holloway Prison, who stated she was only feigning insanity.

When cross-examined, Polly related that Dyer had been confined to mental asylums in 1891, 1893 and 1894. She said Dyer had tried to commit suicide and that she was very violent on these occasions, hearing voices and thinking Polly was trying to murder her, but in between she was kind and affectionate. Polly suggested that when her mother had visited her on 31 March, she had seemed calm until she came into the house, when she was 'flurried'. When Polly had tried to look at the baby, Dyer had pushed her away and that had frightened her.

During this cross-examination, Polly said two babies had been brought into the house but earlier she had suggested that Dyer had only been holding Doris until she had been collected by 'Mrs Harris'. It seems strange that she had shown so little interest in the babies, and it appears evident that Polly knew a lot more of the demise of these children than she was willing to admit. Given that both Polly and her husband had been arrested in connection with these murders, it seems clear that Polly did not want to be associated with the deed.

The jury deliberated for just four and a half minutes before finding Amelia Elizabeth Dyer guilty of murder and she was sentenced to death.[127]

After the trial
While awaiting execution, Mrs Dyer made a statement where she again exonerated Polly from any knowledge of, or complicity in, any of the murders or abandonments committed by her mother.[128]

There was a slight problem in that Amelia Dyer was subpoenaed to give evidence in the trial of her daughter, who was charged with being an accessory before the fact in the case of Miss Goulding's baby, but the date of the trial was 16 June, ten days after the date of Mrs Dyer's execution on 10 June. It was decided that the subpoena was not to be presented and the execution should continue as planned.[129]

The day before Dyer's execution, three other prisoners were executed at Newgate. In order to spare Dyer hearing or seeing anything of these executions, she was transferred to Holloway Prison until the deed was done, when she was returned to Newgate to await her own demise.[130]

On the morning of 10 June 1896, she was executed at Newgate prison by James Billington.

Despite all the monies paid to Dyer during her spell as a baby farmer, when the possessions from Kensington Road were auctioned, they only raised £7/15s.[131]

More about Polly and Arthur Palmer

On 17 June 1896, at Berkshire Assizes, no evidence was offered by the prosecution on the charge against Mary Ann Palmer of assisting Amelia Dyer with the murder of Francis Jessie Goulding, as the body of the child who was the subject of the inquest was not identified as that of Francis Goulding. Baby Goulding had been collected from her mother from Frampton, Gloucestershire by Mrs Mary Palmer and, although there had been correspondence since outlining the child's progress, all attempts to visit the child had been 'inconvenient'. Polly was released and was said to leave the courtroom with a 'jaunty air'.[132]

However, this is not the end of the story for Polly and Arthur Palmer. On 19 October 1898, they were sentenced to two years' hard labour at Devon Quarter Sessions for abandoning a 3-week-old baby in a railway carriage. It appears that Arthur had advertised for a child to adopt, and it had been answered by a Mrs Hill, who handed the child to Polly with £12. Polly was seen leaving the train at Newton Abbot and, the following morning, the baby was found wrapped in brown paper under a seat. The child was cold but had recovered.[133] Clearly having seen her mother executed had not deterred Polly from carrying on the family's darkest business.

So infamous was Amelia Dyer that after her execution, a ballad was written about her:

The old baby farmer has been executed,
It's quite time that she was put out of the way,
She was a bad woman, it is not disputed,
Not a word in her favour can anyone say.

CHORUS
That old baby farmer the wretch Mrs Dyer,
At the Old Bailey her wages is paid,
In times long ago we'd have made a big fire,
And roasted so nicely that wicked old jade.

It seems rather hard to run down a woman,
But this one was hardly a woman at all,
To make a fine living in ways so inhuman,
Carousing in comfort on poor girls' downfall.

Poor girls who fell down from the straight path of virtue,
What could they do with a child in their arms?
The fault they committed they could not undo,
So the baby was sent to the cruel baby farm.

To all these sad crimes there must be an ending,
Secrets like these forever can't last,
Say as you like, there is no defending,
The horrible tales we have heard in the past.

What did she think as she stood on the gallows?
Poor little victims in front of her eyes,
Her heart, if she had one, must have been callous,
The rope round her neck – how quickly time flies.

Down through the trapdoor quick disappearing,
The old baby farmer has come to her harm,
The sound of her own death bell's toll she was hearing,
Maybe she went to the cruel baby farm![134]

Later discoveries

About four years after Dyer's execution, in the garden of a house she had occupied in Bristol the remains of four children were found.[135] No evidence was found to associate these with Dyer. However, in 2019, the owner of another house occupied by her in Totterdown was building an extension that required the removal of the garden subsoil. The soil was excavated and sent for disposal before he found out who had lived in the house. He remembered seeing a great number of small bones in the soil. There had been no skulls or pelvises, so he thought nothing of it.[136]

Babies' skulls and pelvises are much less durable and decompose quickly. Was this where Amelia Dyer was disposing of the remains of babies she had 'adopted'?

Ada Chard-Williams

When unmarried Florence Jones was delivered of a baby girl, Selina Ellen Jones, in December 1897, at a lying-in home, a Mrs Muller was recommended to her as a woman who would be able to nurse the baby. Baby Selina stayed with Mrs Muller until March 1898, when she was removed to a Mrs Wetherall for 5 shillings a week. During her weekly visits, Florence saw Selina flourish. In July, the baby's father ceased payments for his illegitimate daughter, so Mrs Wetherall accepted half of the original payment until August when Florence saw an advertisement in the *Woolwich Herald*: 'Adoption.—A young married couple would adopt healthy baby; every care and comfort; good references given; very small premium. Write first to Mrs. Hewetson, 4, Bradmore Lane, Hammersmith.'

Florence wrote asking what the premium would be. After an exchange of letters, a meeting was arranged at Woolwich Railway Station between Florence and Mrs Hewetson, who was then taken to Miss Jones's mother's house. Mrs Jones said that they only wanted Florence cared for for a while and would, in time, wish to have her returned. It was agreed that Florence and her mother could visit the little girl each fortnight and that Florence would provide clothes for the child. It was believed that Mrs Hewetson lived at the address shown in the advertisement.

Subsequently, Florence received a letter saying that the Hewetsons had moved house and a meeting was organised at Charing Cross Station on the day baby Selina was to be handed over. Mrs Hewetson was keen that it should be thought the baby was her own. All three went from the station to Hammersmith by bus and then an unoccupied house on The Grove was shown to Florence. This was to be where the Hewetsons would be living. They then proceeded to 2 Southerton Road, where a Mrs Woolner was introduced as Mrs Hewetson's sister-in-law. Tea was drunk and Florence handed over the little girl, a bundle of clothes and £3 with a promise to pay a further £2 the following week. Florence left, expecting to receive a letter telling her where to meet in order to pay the outstanding money.

No letter arrived but, the following week, Florence travelled to Hammersmith, first going to the house in The Grove where she found another unknown family living. She then went to Bradmore Lane and found it to be a newsagent's shop. Finally, she returned to Southerton Road, where she saw Mrs Woolner, and then back to Bradmore Lane before returning home without having located Mrs Hewetson.

The following day, Sunday, 4 September, Florence continued her search for the missing woman and child but, eventually, made a complaint to the police. On 27/28 September, Florence was asked by the police to go to the mortuary at Battersea, where she identified the body of young Selina. She also identified various items of clothing that she had given to Mrs Hewetson.[137]

As in the case of Amelia Dyer's victims, the body of toddler Selina Jones had been thrown into the river Thames and was found by a boatman.

William Stokes of Fulham was working his barge off Church Dock, Battersea on the morning of 27 September 1899 when he saw a brown paper parcel tied with string. He pushed it ashore and saw a child's foot sticking out of the parcel. While it was still in the water, he called to Police Constable David Voice.

Constable Voice took the parcel to the mortuary at Battersea, where he removed the outer paper wrappings. The child had pink flannelette sewn around its body and a white napkin between its legs and over its haunches. Over its head was a white cotton bag that was tied around its neck using a strip of the selvedge from the cotton. When the flannelette was removed, the child was found to have been tied up with cord. The knots tying the cords were distinctive sailor's knots, known as the fisherman's bend.[138]

It was found during the post-mortem that Selina had a bruise on the left side of her head that extended from her temple to the base of the skull. This would have rendered the girl unconscious when she was then bound up and strangled. There was no water in her lungs, so death had occurred prior to her being put in the river.

Two other bodies had been found in the Thames at Mortlake and Barnes in July. Both had been tied up in the same way as Selina.[139]

During the inquest, Mrs Woolner gave evidence that she had advertised a room to let at Southerton Road, Hammersmith when she was asked by Mr and Mrs Hewetson if they could hire the room for one night as they were moving house and Mrs Hewetson had not wanted to stay in a hotel overnight with her baby. Mr Hewetson would not be staying. It was agreed that the room could be rented for 3 shillings. The couple then left to collect the baby. Mrs Hewetson returned with the child and Miss Jones, who was introduced as her sister-in-law. A while after Mrs Hewetson and Miss Jones had left, Mrs Hewetson returned with the baby and said she no longer needed the room as her husband had managed to put the bedstead up in the new house and so she could stay there.[140]

It is unclear how the police managed to find the address in Grove Road, Barnes, but in doing so they discovered the Hewetsons' name was actually Chard-Williams.

Dagmar Loughborough gave evidence that Mr and Mrs Chard-Williams had lived next door to her at Grove Villas, Grove Road, Barnes. At first the Chard-Williamses had a little 10-month-old boy, Freddie, with them, then a 2-year-old girl, Lily. This latter child was identified by the witness as Selina Jones. Mrs Chard-Williams had said the girl was her sister's child. The girl was often heard to scream, and Mrs Loughborough said she heard her being beaten with a stick and, the following day, saw welts on the child's back. The girl disappeared on 25 September, two days before her body was found in the river. She had been told the girl had gone back to her mother, Mrs Chard-Williams adding that it was a 'good job she has gone'. She was then given some of the girl's clothing. A week later, Mrs Chard-Williams left but her husband had stayed on for another five weeks, leaving at night without paying his rent.

Detective Inspector Scott visited the house in Barnes and had found sash cord tied with the same sailor's knots as those found on the girl's cords. He had traced the couple back for the last six years and had found they had always had children with them and had never paid their rent.[141]

The inquest jury found Mr and Mrs Hewetson, alias Chard-Williams, guilty of wilful murder but neither of the accused had been located at this time and three detectives were tasked with finding the couple.[142] The chase had taken the police to Brighton, then to Lewes and on to Haywards Heath. Each time they arrived at an address, they would find the couple had fled just hours earlier.[143]

A fortnight later, Detective Gough, dressed as a navvy, visited a coffee shop in South Hackney where Mrs Hewetson had gained employment as a waitress while claiming to be a widow with a young son and lived above the shop. Having ordered coffee and bread and butter, he made conversation with the servant but there was no sign of his quarry.[144]

On 5 December, the police received a letter from Ada Chard-Williams.

To the Secretary, Criminal Investigation Department, New Scotland Yard, W. Sir,—I must apologise taking this liberty, but I see by the papers that I, in conjunction with my husband, are suspected of murdering the little female child found at Battersea on September 27th. The accusation is positively false. The facts of the case are these: I, much against my husband's wish, in August last advertised for a child, thinking to make a little money, the result of which was the adoption of this little child, with whom I received the sum £3. My next act was to advertise for a home for a little girl; I used some shop in Warwick Road, West Kensington, I forget the number, but I used the name of Denton, or Dalton, I am not sure which. I received about 40 replies, from which I chose one, from George Street or George Road, Croydon. The lady from Croydon, Mrs. Smith by name, agreed to take the child for £1 and clothes. I met her at Clapham Junction, the Falcon Hotel, on a Saturday about the middle of September; we were to meet at 7 o'clock. I arrived at time, but Mrs. Smith was 20 minutes late. I handed the child over to her, and she was then quite well. That is the last I saw of her. I have, it is true, been carrying on a sort of baby-farm; that is to say, I have adopted babies, and then advertised and got them re-adopted for about half the amount I had previously received. I have had five in this way; two died while in my care, but I can prove that every attention and kindness was shown them; no money was grudged over their illness. I can prove this by the people with whom we lodged, and also by the doctors who attended them. Two I have had re-adopted; one went to Essex, the other to Bristol, and the last one I parted with as above stated. From the accounts in the papers I am alleged to have carried on this system for six years; now, that, too, is utterly wrong. I am evidently mistaken for someone else, as the first one I ever adopted was in November, 1897. You will say, 'If innocent, why not come forward?' There have been innocent people hanged before now, and I must admit that at the present things look very much against me, but it is not fair to go entirely on circumstantial evidence. I am trying to find the woman to whom I gave up the child, but, unfortunately for me, I destroyed her letters, and if I came forward there would be no possibility of clearing myself unless I could find some clue about her. In conclusion, I must tell you that my husband is not to blame in any way whatever; he has always looked upon the whole matter with the greatest abhorrence, but only gave way to me because he was, through illness, out of employment; he never, however, once touched any of the money I made by these means.—Yours truly, (Signed) M. HEWETSON. P.S.—We left Barnes simply because we were unable to meet the rent, and some time before we heard of this lamentable affair. The shop in Warwick Road is a newspaper shop, the Hammersmith Road end, and only a few doors down on the right hand side.[145]

The police tried to find 'Mrs Smith' of George Street, Croydon but the only person matching that description was found to have had nothing to do with the child.[146]

On 8 December, when visiting the coffee shop for a second time, Detective Gough spoke to Mrs Hewetson and located her 'brother-in-law', William Chard-Williams, who was waiting in the kitchen, having come to collect her. Detective Inspector Scott and Detective Gough arrested Mr and Mrs Chard-Williams. Mrs Chard-Williams said she had delivered Selina to another woman as she had stated in her letter and that she was quite well. Ada said that her husband had not been present when she had taken Selina from the house. Neither of them had appeared to be worried by the accusation of murder. It was found that they had sold their household goods, packed their belongings and were ready to travel to Liverpool on route to New York.[147]

William Chard-Williams was born in 1853 and was described as a clerk and artist and said to have had a university education, and was a Cambridge coxswain in the University Boat Race.[148]

During the trial at the Central Criminal Court, London, Miss Jones repeated the evidence she had given at the inquest into baby Selina's death, adding that she had taken Selina from Mrs Weatherall as she had not liked Mrs Weatherall's conduct to the child.

Mrs Weatherall stated that while taking Selina to be vaccinated she had accidentally put her thumb into the little girl's face and had removed a piece of skin. The wound had bled and left a scar. She said the girl had golden curly hair and a large navel. She had identified the body at Battersea mortuary as Selina by the scar on her face.

The newsagent from Bradmore Lane, William Canning, identified William Chard-Williams as being the person who collected letters addressed to 'Hewetson'.

Dagmar Loughborough repeated the evidence she had given at the inquest but added that she had heard the child crying and Mr Chard-Williams telling his wife 'Don't do that!' and Mrs Chard-Williams replying, 'You mind your own damned business, or I will serve you the same.' Mrs Loughborough had then been told by Mrs Chard-Williams that she had beaten the girl with a stick for dirtying on the floor and that it 'Served it right'.

It was clear that the child had been 'done to death' but what was not so clear was who had carried out this dreadful deed. It was stated by Ada Chard-Williams that her husband had had nothing to do with her business with children; however, it was known that William had been involved with collecting the mail, he lived in the house where the children had been taken and he had a practical role in the deception of Miss Jones. Ada had tried to lay the blame at the door of 'Mrs Smith', who had not been found, and there was no corroboration to her story.

Despite the defence claiming there was no evidence against either Mr or Mrs Chard-Williams and asking for the jury not to be swayed by the abomination that was baby farming, the jury only took thirty minutes to find Ada guilty of murder and while William was found not guilty of that offence, he was found guilty of being an accessory after the fact, which the jury was told was not allowed as he hadn't been indicted for that offence.

Ada was sentenced to death, and, after some consultation, William was discharged.[149]

It seems there was an application to the Home Secretary for a reprieve for Ada, but this was denied for, although it was felt that William was probably fully implicated in this murder, the jury had found him not guilty and this could not be overturned; it was felt that a false impression of the severity of the crime would be given and, consequently, would lessen the deterrent effect of the sentence.[150]

Ada Chard-Williams gave every appearance of being in control of her emotions. The only time she was seen to cry was during her last meeting with her husband, and, although she spent a restless night, she ate a light breakfast and went to the gallows with composure on the morning of 6 March 1900 to be executed by James Billington. At no time did she confess to her guilt.[151]

Just a month after the execution, William Chard-Williams appeared in court again. This time he was charged with obtaining £8 from a pawnbroker under false pretences. Mr Chard-Williams had been in the habit of taking the tenancies of houses for three years and furnishing them under the hire purchase system using forged references. After paying just £4 to the hirer, he then took the furniture to the pawn broker and, using forged invoices, pawned the goods for £8. Each time he left the house he was renting without paying rent and set up in another establishment. He was found guilty and sentenced to twenty months' hard labour.[152]

Annie Walters and Amelia Sach

When on 17 November 1902 Annie Walters made her way to South Kensington carrying a bundle, she had little idea she was being followed by a police officer. When she was stopped and asked to open the bundle in her arms, it was discovered to contain the body of a baby boy.[153]

Annie Walters certainly seems to fit the pattern associated with baby farmers in that she was known at different addresses by different names: in

Church Road, Upton and at Glasgow Road she was known as Mrs Laming; in Crossley St, Islington she was known as Mrs Merith; and when in Danbury St she was Mrs Walters. She also was known to have communications with Amelia Sach while at all these addresses.[154]

Fifty-four-year-old Walters had taken a room in at a house in Danbury Street, Islington on 29 October,[155] where a police officer, PC Seal, lived with his wife.[156]

It was while living in this house that suspicion about her dealings arose. She explained that she had worked for a midwife, Amelia Sach, who got children from women who could not afford to keep them and rehomed them with wealthy women. Walters said she would collect the babies from the midwife and take them to their new homes and she was waiting for a telegram asking for her to collect a child from Mrs Sach to deliver to a lady in Piccadilly who was giving £100 for the baby, of which Mrs Sach was to receive £45 and she would get 30 shillings.[157]

On 12 November, Walters, aged 54, arrived back at Danbury Street carrying a baby, which she said was a boy. She asked Mrs Spencer, another lodger at the house, to buy a bottle of chlorodyne (Dr Collis Browne's Compound) and some carbolic acid for her. Two days later, during which time the baby had not been heard by anyone in the house, Walters left the house in the morning carrying a bundle. Mrs Seal then went into Walters's room, only to find the baby was missing. The child was never seen at the house again. However, during that afternoon, Walters was seen in Lockhart's Cocoa Rooms, Whitechapel, where the wrapping slipped off the bundle and a baby was seen by Miss Ethel Jones, one of the attendants. Miss Jones initially thought it was a doll as it was not moving or making any sound. Walters said the child had had an operation for a double rupture so was under the influence of chloroform and she was taking it to Finchley.[158] Miss Jones then thought the child was dead.[159]

On 15 November, Walters received a telegram asking her to a meeting that evening. PC Seal contacted another police officer, and it was decided that PC Seal's son should follow Walters. A tramcar was taken to Archway Terminus, Islington, where she met Mrs Amelia Sach. Walters and Sach then took a cab that was seen driving up Archway Road in the direction of East Finchley. Later Walters returned to Danbury Street with a baby that she described as a girl who was to be rehomed with a coastguard living in

Kensington. Leaving the baby in the care of Mrs Seal and Mrs Spencer, Walters left the house. While she was gone, the two women discovered that the child was a baby boy, not a girl.[160]

Clearly suspicions about Mrs Walters had arisen and Detective Wright was posted in the neighbouring house, where Police Sergeant White lived, to keep watch for Walters. At 9.00 am on 17 November, he saw Walters leaving 11 Danbury St carrying a bundle. He followed her on the omnibus to South Kensington Station, where they got off the bus. Walters walked up and down outside the station then went into the ladies' lavatory. When she came out, Detective Wright asked to see in the bundle and found the body of a baby boy. He then took her into custody on suspicion of murdering the boy, which she denied, saying she had only given the baby two drops of chlorodyne, as she would have given herself.[161]

Amelia Sach, nee Thorne, married Jeffrey Sach in 1896, and they had one daughter, Lillian, born in 1899.[162] Sach was said to be a certified midwife and ran a nursing home from Claymore House, Hertford Road, East Finchley, which she advertised, often using the name Nurse Thorne. She had previously had a house in Stanley Road, East Finchley. Sach's clients were women awaiting the birth of their babies, many of whom had discovered Mrs Sach from newspaper advertisements that claimed to be able to rehome unwanted babies.[163]

When police visited 29-year-old Mrs Sach at Claymore House, she initially denied knowing Mrs Walters. She explained she ran a nursing home and had a woman there who had recently given birth. At first, she said both mother and baby were in their room; however, when asked if the police could see the lady, Mrs Sach stated that the woman was too unwell. Dr Russell was called, and he said he would see the lady. After entering the room, the doctor returned to say that there was no baby in the room. Eventually, Sach admitted that two babies had recently been taken away. The police informed her they would be taking her into custody for accessory to murder. She stated, 'Murdering? Never! Do you really mean to say these babies are dead – that she has killed them?' When at the police station, Sach admitted knowing Walters but denied ever giving her any babies.[164]

On 2 December 1902, Annie Walters was charged with murder and Amelia Sach with conspiring with Mrs Walters to commit murder.[165]

When unmarried servant Rosina Pardoe found herself pregnant, she saw an advertisement for Mrs Sach's establishment in *The People* newspaper. After contacting Sach, she arranged to stay at Claymore House for a fee of £1 1 shilling a week until her confinement and £3 3 shillings for a fortnight during confinement. She was asked by Sach what she intended to do with the baby, and said she wanted to put it out to a nurse. Sach said she knew a well-to-do lady who would adopt the baby for £30 and a complete set of clothes but refused to name the lady. Rosina asked what the money would be used for if the lady was wealthy and was told it would be for presents for the baby. On 12 November 1902, Rosina was delivered of a baby girl that was taken by Sach as soon as it was born. It was later thought that this was the baby Annie Walters was seen with at Lockhart's Cocoa Rooms. The £30 was provided by the child's father, who had noted the numbers of the banknotes he had given. One of these notes was later given to the police by Mrs Sach's husband. On Sunday, 16 November, Rosina felt unwell and Dr Wylie saw her. When he asked where the baby was, Sach told him it was with Miss Pardoe's mother.[166]

Ada Charlotte Galley was also an unmarried servant who had found herself expecting a child. She saw an advertisement in *Dalton's Newspaper* and agreed with Sach for the same fee as Miss Pardoe. Again, she agreed to have her child adopted by 'a lady of good position', this time for £25, which she also obtained from the child's father, who also made a note of the numbers on the notes. These were given to the police by Mr Sach. On 15 November, Ada Charlotte Galley also gave birth to a baby boy. Miss Galley's confinement was difficult, and Dr Wylie had been called to attend. The baby was born with the use of forceps and a bruise on the dead baby's head was thought to be from the forceps birth, thus identifying the child found with Annie Walters at Kensington as Ada Galley's son. When Dr Wylie came again the following day, the baby had already been taken away and the doctor was told it was with Miss Galley's sister.[167]

From June 1901 until August 1902, Teresa Edwards had lived at the Stanley Road house both during her confinement and after, when she worked there as a servant. During this time, she witnessed five babies being taken, with agreement, from their mothers. At Mrs Sach's request, she had taken one of these babies to a Mrs Layman of Plaistow. The babies were taken for a fee to cover expenses and Mrs Sach had been keen to keep the transfer of babies to Mrs Layman secret. Could Mrs Layman be Annie Walters, as she is known to have been living in Plaistow from May 1901 to June 1902 using the name Laming? Miss Edwards also confirmed that Mrs Walters, known as Mrs Laming, had been a visitor to Stanley Road. Miss Edwards also stated that all the mothers had provided clothes for the children, but these stayed at Mrs Sach's house after the children were removed and some were later sold to other patients.[168]

Detective Constable Kyd found about 300 articles of clothing in the house and bank books that showed sums of money being deposited.[169]

Mr Augustus Pepper and Mr Lawrence Caunter carried out a post-mortem on the baby found with Walters and decided that death had been caused by asphyxiation, possibly caused by an overdose of a narcotic, but more probably, due to the lack of milk in the child's stomach, by the direct interference of air into the child's lungs.[170]

Although the charges only related to the death of Miss Galley's baby, the prosecution also described the birth and disappearance of Miss Pardoe's child. It was later questioned whether this should have been related at the trial; however, it was said that it was used as it showed a systematic criminality whereby babies were regularly passed by Mrs Sach to Mrs Walters for the express purpose 'of being put out of the way', and this was a joint design. Were this not the case, the defence could have convinced the jury that the death of Miss Galley's baby was accidental.[171]

After the prosecution had put forward its case, no evidence was put by the defence but, during the defence summing up, it was said that Claymore House was run as a legitimate business and there was no evidence to suggest children were illegally disposed of. Mrs Sach's defence argued there was no evidence connecting her to any crime, even assuming a murder had taken place.[172]

During his summing up, the judge remarked that, although both women referred to wealthy ladies, there was no attempt made by the defence to produce any wealthy women who adopted the children. After the judge's summing up, the jury took just forty minutes to return the verdict of guilty on both women, but they recommended mercy as both prisoners were women.[173] Despite this, the judge stated that the verdict was the only one possible and, as he passed the death sentence, told the women to make their peace with God as he did not believe a reprieve would be granted. Clearly the judge was convinced of the guilt of both women.[174]

After the verdict, some letters were received suggesting that Mrs Sach was under the influence of an older, evil woman, and should, therefore, be saved from execution. Her husband, Jeffrey Sach, petitioned the Home Secretary for clemency, stating that his wife was innocent of the charges brought against her and, although she had worked as a midwife and had sometimes arranged for babies to be adopted, she had no knowledge of the real fate of babies given to Annie Walters, and that there was no direct proof that she had anything to do with the death of Miss Galley's baby.[175]

Whilst awaiting execution, Mrs Sach wrote a letter to Mrs Walters asking her to confess the truth of the matter that she had no knowledge of the true plight of the babies as she had thought Mrs Walters had placed them in comfortable homes. The authorities decided that it would not be appropriate to deliver the letter to Mrs Walters.[176]

Nevertheless, no reprieve was forthcoming for either woman.

Prior to the execution, Mrs Sach thanked the chaplain who had promised he would look after her child.[177]

Amelia Sach and Annie Walters were hanged in Holloway Prison on Tuesday, 3 February 1903 by William Billington. They were the first women to be hanged in Holloway Prison.[178]

Interestingly, amongst the letter found in Claymore House was a letter from a Laura Bracey living in Woking, Surrey, dated 22 November 1902. She was a married woman who gave her husband's place of employment. She said they were unlikely to have children of their own and would like to have a nurse child or to adopt a child. She wondered if there was the possibility of getting a child from the maternity home.[179] Given the date, it is doubtful she received a reply, but she can be found on the 1911 census living with her husband and an adopted daughter.[180]

Rhoda Willis aka Mrs Leslie James

In January 1907, Rhoda Willis, aka Leslie James, went to live as a housekeeper to a shoe repairer, David Evans, in Pontypool, although this relationship appears to have become very friendly. Some weeks later, she told him that she had had a child that had been adopted by a Mrs Carruthers for £10, but that they now wished to give the child back with half the premium. Mr Evans had been willing to have the child in his house, but after a week he was told that Mrs Carruthers would keep the child and, instead of bringing this child in, James suggested she advertise for a child to adopt for a premium of £10. Having initially objected to this, Mr Evans eventually agreed and in March, Mrs James had placed an advertisement in the *Evening Express*, a newspaper with a wide circulation in the area surrounding Cardiff. It was to run for several issues.[181]

> Married couple, Christian people, good position wish to adopt Baby entirely as Own; every comfort and care; must be healthy; small premium. Apply C90 Evening Express, Cardiff.[182]

A reply was sent from Mrs Stroud of Abertillery and on 10 April, Willis received a 2-week-old baby boy with a premium of £6. The baby was wrapped in an expensive rug that was to be returned to Mrs Stroud; however, despite writing to ask for its return several times and receiving excuses each time, the rug wasn't returned, and the police later discovered it in James's possessions.[183]

She also received a reply to this advertisement in March from a Mr Stanley Rees of Salford and she arranged to take his illegitimate child as soon as it was born.[184]

On 7 May, James left Mr Evans, having led him to believe she was going to visit a relation who was to give her several hundred pounds from an inheritance. She took Mrs Stroud's son with her. This child she left at the Salvation Army Home in Cardiff with an anonymous note in which she had disguised her handwriting. It is interesting to note that the police brought in a handwriting expert to conclude that the writing had similarities to that of the prisoner. The child was taken to the workhouse where, despite it being said to be well nourished and healthy when it was in the care of the Salvation Army, it died a week later of diarrhoea.[185]

The following day, Mrs James took lodgings at the home of Mrs Hannah Wilson. The Wilsons took in lodgers but at that time had only one staying, Rose Smith.[186]

Having agreed to adopt Mr Rees's baby, but not yet taken possession of it, Mrs James went to her new lodgings in Portmanmoor Road, Cardiff and asked Mrs Wilson if she would adopt a baby from James. Mrs Wilson agreed providing she could meet the child's parent, whereupon Mrs James convinced her that the child was her own. James then met with Mr Rees and took possession of the baby that had been born just three days earlier, for which she received a premium of £5 and a promise of a further £5 at a later date. She had told Mr Rees that her family had wished her to have a child and she intended to pass this baby off as her own. This is the child she gave to Mrs Wilson, along with a sovereign. James continued to lodge with the Wilsons and assisted Mrs Wilson with the care of the baby.[187]

Eventually, this child was taken back by its mother in Manchester.[188]

While this was going on, Mrs James had received another answer to her advertisement from a Mrs English. Consequently, Mrs James met with Mrs Lydia English and her sister, Miss Maud Treasure, at Ivy Cottage, Fleur-de-Lis, Nr Hengoed, where an agreement was made for Mrs James to adopt Miss Treasure's child as soon as it was born for a premium of £8, with £6 being paid when the child was handed over and the remainder paid at a later date.

On 3 June, a telegram was received with the information that Miss Treasure's child had been born. Mrs James left for Hengoed, telling Mrs Wilson that she was going to see the father of her child (the one Mrs Wilson had taken). In fact, she travelled to Hengoed by train, where she was met by Mrs English and was taken to Mrs English's house. A healthy, well-developed child was handed over to her by Mrs English and her mother, Mrs Mary Treasure, a certified nurse, who had been present at the birth and had washed and fed the healthy baby girl. Leaving Hengoed at about 6.00 pm, she returned to Mrs Wilson's two hours later carrying a parcel, when she went to her room for around half an hour. She later showed Mrs Wilson some gold she said had been given to her by the father of Mrs Wilson's baby. That night, she slept in Miss Smith's room. Around this time, she wrote to Mrs English saying that she had just bathed the baby and that she was lovely. The truth was that the child was already dead.[189] The following day, she went out with Miss Smith and Mrs Wilson's baby, only returning mid-afternoon, carrying the baby upside down and in a very drunken state, whereupon she was put to bed in her own room. There she stayed until the following morning when she fell out of bed. The thud was heard from Mrs James's room and Mrs Wilson and Miss Smith went to investigate, only to find Mrs James on the floor. They were unable to lift Mrs James and Mrs Wilson started to straighten the bedclothes when she found a bundle wrapped only in a towel, fastened with a pin. Inside this bundle was the naked body of a baby girl. Despite Mrs James's pleas, police and a doctor were called, and it appeared that the child had been suffocated by being tightly wrapped in the shawl.[190]

While being transported to the police station, Mrs James was heard to say, 'I am not going to stand all the blame, someone else is in it as well as me.' James confessed to the murder whilst claiming that 'others' were implicated.[191]

The post-mortem concluded that death was caused by suffocation, the baby had been between twelve and twenty-four hours old and had been dead for between twenty-four and forty-eight hours. The opinion of the surgeon, James Buist, was that death may have been accidentally caused by wrapping the child tightly, although considerable pressure would have been needed.[192]

When giving evidence, Mrs James said she had received the baby already wrapped up and had not looked at it until she arrived back at her lodgings, when she discovered the child was dead. However, after this she had written to Mrs English saying that the baby was lovely, and she had given it a bath. This story was refuted by Mrs Wilson's son, David, who had seen James arrive back at her lodging on the evening of 3 June carrying only a parcel wrapped in paper, which she said contained baby clothes.[193]

It was argued that Mrs James had not intended to bring a living child to her lodgings as she had not told Mrs Wilson she would be, but instead had invented the tale of her seeing the father of Mrs Wilson's baby. It was thought she had not disposed of the child on her way home due to the need to remove the clothing that would have identified the baby.[194]

In July 1907, Leslie James, also known as Rhoda Willis, was brought before Glamorgan Assizes Court at Cardiff charged with the murder of an infant girl, daughter of Maud Treasure. The comely, black-clad prisoner pleaded not guilty to the offence.[195]

During her two-day trial, her defence barrister, Ivor Bowen (who was only appointed after the trial had begun), argued that the child had been accidentally smothered. He also asked the jury to ignore the suggestion of alleged baby farming as this would prejudice the jury.[196]

The jury retired for just twelve minutes to consider their verdict. On returning to the court, they pronounced the prisoner to be guilty of murder, without any recommendation for mercy. The judge pronounced the only verdict possible – death.[197]

There seems to have been a feeling amongst some members of the public against the death penalty and, in particular, the execution of women.

The Lord Mayor of Cardiff drew up a petition signed by members of Cardiff Council to be sent to the Home Secretary asking for the sentence to be commuted to life imprisonment. This led to some discussion about whether the death sentence should be carried out in this case as it appeared this murder of a newborn infant was the first that James had carried out.[198]

James's barrister truly believed the prisoner should not be hanged and campaigned hard for her sentence to be commuted, even writing to the Home Secretary. As did the coroner, E. B. Reece, who had doubts about whether the child was intentionally killed or accidentally suffocated, especially as a verdict of manslaughter had been brought against her at the inquest into the child's death.[199]

The Home Secretary, H. T. Gladstone, considered whether to recommend leniency to the king. Was Leslie James 'completely in the hands of unscrupulous people'? This was presumed to mean Mrs English and Miss Treasure, although the Home Secretary believed the women to be truthful. Who put the child in the parcel? Was Mrs English involved? Was the crime committed whilst drunk and not in cold blood? She had previously left a child on a doorstep and was there a deliberate predetermination to murder? The cases of other baby farmers who were found guilty of murder were looked at while applications for leniency were considered. However, no recommendation was made.[200]

Despite much campaigning on her behalf, Leslie James was executed on 14 August 1907 by Henry Pierrepoint, assisted by his brother Thomas. On the morning of her execution, she confessed to the crime and stated that the sentence was just and that she had killed the child in the train.[201]

It is difficult to trace the background of Rhoda Willis/Leslie James. There even seems to have been some confusion as to her correct name, with Inspector Willian Davey of the Cardiff Police saying he believed her proper name to be Rhoda Willis, but she was calling herself Leslie James.

According to the *South Wales Daily Post*, she was born Rhoda Leselles in Sunderland, and this seems to be confirmed by the 1901 census, where she is listed as Rhoda MacPherson, living with Gregor MacPherson, although there is no record of her birth in Sunderland. Her father was said to be a hotel proprietor, who moved the family to Birmingham, and she was privately educated in a boarding school close to London.[202]

In her late teens, she fell in love with marine engineer Thomas Willis from Sunderland and moved to Cardiff in the 1890s with their daughter, 6-year-old Emma Willis. They lived in Grangetown, Cardiff with a Mrs Carew and it was here that she gave birth to two children. In 1896, her husband died while at sea. At this time, her in-laws moved from Sunderland to Cardiff and took the younger two children into their care. She then took the position of housekeeper to, and later that year cohabited with, Stewart MacPherson, with whom she had three children, Stuart, who died, Dorothy and Bessie. They resided in Cardiff, Newport and Bootle until 1901 when James left Stewart to live with his brother, Gregor. They moved to Bryn-Glas Road, Newport, Monmouth. Around 1903, she returned to Cardiff and started living with the son of a previous landlady, Thomas Carew, a blacksmith.[203]

In 1905, a Mr and Mrs James had lodged with a Mrs Eliza Goodchild in Kennington. Mrs Goodchild said the prisoner was a drunken woman, who used drugs to prevent conception, but she did not believe her to be capable of murder. Mrs James had told Mrs Goodchild her name was Rhoda Mabel and that she had been a widow, her first husband being a Mr Willis. She said she had a 13-year-old daughter who lived with her mother in Cardiff.[204]

In 1906, Mrs James was knocked down by bike and taken to the workhouse hospital with a head injury.[205]

At the end of 1906, she moved to Railway Street, East Moors. She was arrested at this address under the name Rhoda Willis and charged with stealing money, war medals and clasps. She was sentenced to one month's hard labour. It was after her release that she took the position of housekeeper with David Evans.[206]

During her time in Cardiff, she was known as a woman with a low moral character and drunken habits. Reading letters sent by her prior to and after her arrest, Leslie James seems to be a habitual liar and it is difficult to tease the truth from the lies she tells.

He daughter, Emma Willis, was, by the time of Mrs James's conviction, a servant of good character and she had not been informed of Mrs James's conviction. No other relative had been found and the Head Constable of Cardiff Police states that, although James carried photographs of the three children claimed to be hers, he did not find any likeness to the prisoner.[207] Who can tell what the true life of Leslie James, or even her true name, is?

Chapter 12

The Fight to Protect Children

After Caroline Jagger's infamous appearance at the coroner's court in September 1867, *The Lancet* called for baby farms to be placed under inspection and control. While admitting illegitimacy was a social evil and recognising that women in such a position were using baby farms as a means of ridding themselves of the burden of a child, it was thought the state should stop the situation becoming a 'snare for the helplessness of infancy'. It pointed out that lodging-houses were registered and inspected and hospitals and 'homes of all kinds' were open to enquirers but that baby farms were not regulated in any way.[1] Dr Curgenven wrote a letter to *The Times* pointing out that although the issue of baby farming had been talked about in medical circles for some time, it took cases such as Charlotte Winsor and Caroline Jagger to bring the matter to the attention of the majority of the public. He mentions that between 60 and 90 per cent of children put out to nurse die within the first year and calls for nurses to be registered or licensed and supervised by the parochial medical officer. He suggests this be part of the Poor Law system and a small fee be charged.[2]

At the end of 1867, a coroner's jury in London requested that the coroner should write to the Home Secretary with regard to the case of Matilda Thorne and the death of Alfred Johnson in an attempt to have changes made in the system of baby farming.[3]

In 1868, the problem of baby farming was becoming so acute that the Earl of Shaftesbury raised a question in the House of Lords, asking if the government were planning to institute an enquiry into baby farming. The Duke of Marlborough answered that it was true that baby farming existed and that crimes were capable of being committed by baby farmers but that he didn't feel an enquiry was necessary as the police could deal with the matter, if the house was registered and inspected regularly, and that a bill was due to be put before parliament during the next session.[4]

In the same year, Lady Mary Petre had a different solution to the problem: she raised money to allow the foundation of a crèche in London for the children of the Roman Catholic poor in imitation of those institutions that were already set up on the Continent. It was to be run by the Sisters of Charity of St Vincent de Paul and would provide food and clothing free of charge.[5]

By 1869, newspapers had taken up the cry, demanding the licensing of baby farms, and reporter James Greenwood wrote his investigative piece *The Seven Curses of London*, where he traces a couple of baby farmers, Mr and Mrs Oxleek, and manages to trick his way into their house. After describing the scene, he found, he was rumbled and escorted from the building. As he is writing the article, he sees the report of the coroner's inquest into the death of Frederick Wood whilst in the home of Caroline Savill. He points out that Mrs Savill is quite at liberty to continue nursing babies for as little financial outlay as possible and regardless of the health and wellbeing of the infants as she left the inquest without a stain on her character. He suggests that a system of licensing, in the same way as cow-keepers were licensed, would put an end to the matter.[6]

In 1870, the Infant Life Protection Society was formed. One of the honorary secretaries was surgeon John Brendon Curgenven, who published many articles about the care of babies and was in the forefront of agitation to bring about legislation to protect young children.

In his publication *Waste of Infant Life* of 1867, he states that 75 per cent of illegitimate children that are in the care of nurses die. He quotes the case of baby Beatrice Lilian Harris, who died whilst in the care of nurse Mary Chard in Oxford the previous year. It was noticed that more than the usual number of children died when in Mrs Chard's care, so the coroner's officer visited the house and found children that were emaciated and dirty. The house was so filthy that the stench made it impossible to stay inside too long. The inquest jury decided that the little girl had died of debility in a house unfit for human habitation, although, in fact, she had died of slow starvation.

Curgenven claimed that should mothers be able to suckle their own children for one to four months, and still be able to retain employment; children would then be capable of living in the care of nurses.

He also believed that coroner's inquests should be held more often on the deaths of illegitimate children and all that had not had medical attention.

Curgenven agrees with the Harveian Society's recommendations with regard to the care of illegitimate children:

- All births to be registered;
- Still-born births to be registered;
- The registration of illegitimate children should be under their correct names;
- Single women should declare the name of the father before a magistrate if it is thought he would abscond;
- Pregnant women should be taken into the workhouse during the last month of their confinement and remain there for four months after the birth and show she has support for herself and the child;
- Workhouse guardians should have the power to recover any costs from the father of the child;
- Nurses of illegitimate children should be registered as fit and proper persons and supervised by the poor law medical officer;
- No nurse to have more than two children unless consent was received from the medical officer;
- No infant or young person be entered as member of a burial club or be the subject of life insurance.[7]

In 1867, a deputation from Harveian Medical Society went to the Home Secretary with this paper.

In 1868, the *British Medical Journal* published a series of articles about baby farming and recommended the licensing of nurses.[8]

In 1869, a paper by Curgenven was read to the National Association for the Promotion of Social Science: 'On Baby-farming and the Registration of Nurses'. In this he reiterates the points he made in 1867, while putting much more emphasis on the monitoring of each and every child throughout their childhood. He also points out that baby farming is far more prevalent than many would realise as he had found eleven advertisements for baby farmers in a single newspaper.[9]

The other Honorary Secretary was Revd. Oscar Thorpe, who was the vicar of Christ Church, Camberwell, close to the home of the notorious Margaret Waters, and it is probable that the Society was formed in the wake of the Waters trial.

During the 1870s, the Metropolitan Police received numerous communications from the Reverend and Mrs Thorpe with regard to suspected baby farms.

In November 1873, Revd Thorpe writes to the chief commissioner of police, with regard to the discovery of the bodies of several babies found wrapped in newspaper that had been packed with lime in the streets of Camberwell. At the inquest of one of these babies, the coroner expressed the opinion that a baby farmer was working in the area. Revd. Thorpe says he has written to the coroner asking him to consider that Mrs Barton, alias Mrs Castle, who was well known in connexion with the case of Margaret Waters, was involved, and he states that Sarah Ellis, Mrs Waters's sister, has also been released from prison. Now, Mrs Castle pops up again and again in relation to baby farmers. She was the midwife who was involved with the Margaret Waters case and her name was mentioned by Sophia Todd, although she was never charged with any offence.

While Revd Thorpe admits that the police are always very obliging when he approaches them with regard to a baby farming case, he suggests that they would be more effective if they appointed a detective to work incognito, as Sergeant Relf did three years earlier. He also mentions that they had some information about a suspected baby farming establishment in Frederick St, Caledonian Road, although he was rather sketchy on details.

In December the same year, the Thorpes again contacted the police and Chief Inspector George Clarke made enquiries about four places mentioned by them. The first was about a Mrs Shaw of Caledonian Road where no children were found to be residing and nothing was known of her.[10] However, in the 1871 census for her previous address of 70 Frederick St, Caledonian Road, we find Elizabeth Shaw living with an 8-year-old girl who is named as a 'boarder'. Perhaps this is the establishment referred to by the Revd Thorpe.[11]

The second woman to be mentioned by the Thorpes was Mrs Castle. When investigated by Ch. Insp. Clarke, he confirms she is a certified midwife, who advertises her lying-in house but that she doesn't generally take in nurse children, although she is about to take an infant for £50 per annum from a lady who is to join her husband in India. Clarke says the house appears to be reputable and sees no reason to suspect the woman.

The third mentioned is Mrs Ellis, sister of Margaret Waters, who the police seem here to have lost track of, although we know she had been working under a different name and had been found guilty of larceny and was in prison at this time.

The fourth woman mentioned is Sarah Huxley, who was discharged the previous year after being held in custody under suspicion of causing the death of her child. This woman has since left the neighbourhood and there is no more information about her.

Mrs Thorpe also forwarded advertisements, one apparently inserted by a Mrs Vaughan of Camberwell Road, but the address given in the advert is that of a grocer's shop, the owner of which states that Mrs Castle asked him to receive letters addressed to Mrs Vaughan, but none had been received for months. The inference was that the advertisement was an old one. Another advertisement was for Mrs Sinden of Thornhill Place, Wellington St. After investigation, it is found she is a certified midwife who works as a monthly nurse often away from home. She is of respectable character, no confinements take place at this address, nor are children taken in.

Mrs Thorpe also brought to the police attention a Mrs Waugh and her daughter, Sophy Williams, alias McGrath, who were 'people of the lowest class', and, while the mother occasionally helps women in their confinements, there was no indication that any baby farming was taking place. It was thought that P Division might keep some observation of Mrs Waugh and her daughter. These two were also mentioned in Thorpe's letter in November; however, the handwriting in that letter is virtually indecipherable.

At the end of this report, George Clarke states that the Revd and Mrs Thorpe

> take a very active part in these matters, but they are unable to give me particulars of any cases in which enquiry can be made and it appears to me that they are inclined to form very extreme opinions upon the subject [of baby farming].[12]

It seems from the modern viewpoint that the Revd and Mrs Thorpe were something of a thorn in the side of the police during this time.

In 1877, the Revd Thorpe contacted the police with reference to a Mrs Langman, who passed a 2-year-old girl called Emma Althrop to a Miss Rye. The police conducted enquiries and discovered that Mrs Langman was the wife of a former vestryman and Guardian for the Parish of Kensington and was now the Inspector of Nuisance for Kensington. Mr and Mrs Langman lived for part of the week in Notting Hill Gate, and partly in a farm in Woking. Mrs Langman had looked after a number of children at her own expense and treated them kindly. When they were old enough, she either put them into school or found situations for them. It was found that Mrs Langman had taken the girl from a home for deserted mothers in Notting Hill (Notting Hill appears to have had several such homes). Miss Rye then arranged for the girl to emigrate to Canada.[13]

The 1872 Infant Life Protection Act was passed.

Compulsory registration by the local authority was required by those houses keeping two or more infants for a period of longer than twenty-four hours for a period of one year. No charge was to be made to the baby farmer.

The local authority could refuse registration if it were considered the applicant, or the house, were unsuitable. The punishment for offences committed under the Act was limited to six months.[14]

The select committee acknowledged that other legislation would be needed. William Charley, MP for Salford, and a committee member of the Infant Life Protection Society, introduced a Bastardy Laws Amendment Bill on 9 April, which received Royal Assent on 10 August. It removed the 2 shilling and sixpence limit on financial support payable by the father, which may have gone some way to provide more effective support for infants.[15]

The Registration of Births, Marriages and Deaths became compulsory in 1874. This addressed some of the recommendations made by the Harveian Society that had not been deemed appropriate to be included in the earlier legislation.

Despite the registration of deaths being necessary for twenty-three years, in 1897, 40-year-old widow, Millicent Clifford, was taken in front of Edmonton Petty Sessions for failing to report the deaths of four children in her care. Mrs Clifford was registered under the Infant Life Protection Act as a baby farmer, but she pleaded ignorance of the need to register the deaths. During the previous thirteen months, six of the nine children she had received had died. She was fined 20 shillings and costs.[16]

The Prevention of Cruelty to, and Protection of, Children Act 1889 was heralded by Mr Benjamin Waugh of the National Society for the Prevention of Cruelty to Children as winning the war against cruelty to children. This Act covered all parents and guardians of children, and protected them against ill-treatment, neglect, exposure and the abandonment of children and, should cruelty be suspected, a warrant could be issued to search the house of the offender. This Act was amended in 1894 to tighten up technicalities and details.[17]

In 1890, Mr Waugh continued his campaign for children by stating that the Infant Life Protection Act was of little or no use in protecting children as it only covered two children under a year old who were living in the same house. He pointed out that baby farmers frequently advertised for children that were then passed on to others with no regard for the suitability of the recipient, as in the 1888 case of Jane Arnold, who avoided registration or arrest by 'sweating' babies.[18]

The Children and Young Persons Act of 1908 tightened many of the issues that had continued after previous Acts. All paid foster mothers now came under official supervision and authorities were obliged to appoint inspectors. The age of looked after children was raised to 7, and establishments with just one child were now included. Child minders were banned from insuring the lives of their charges, and contravention of this clause was applied to minders and to insurance officials.[19]

Baby farming was eventually stopped completely in 1939 when the Adoption of Children (Regulation) Act came into force. This Act ensured that adoption societies needed to be registered. Advertising was banned, except for registered societies and local authorities, and, finally, payments for children were outlawed.[20] These last two clauses made baby farming, as a means of making money, impossible and so, at last, the abominable practice became a thing of the past.

While all of these measures were needed to stop the cruelty of the baby farmers, we should remember that there were many women who cared for and nurtured children that were not their own to the best of their ability, and these children thrived in their care. These women would also have been classed as baby farmers.

Notes

Introduction
1. Charles Dickens, *Oliver Twist*, 1838
2. *Penny Illustrated*, 2 July 1870
3. Lionel Rose, *Massacre of the Innocents: Infanticide in Great Britain 1800–1939* (Routledge & Kegan Paul 1986)
4. Simon Fowler, *Workhouse: The People, the Places, the Life Behind Doors* (The National Archives 2007)
5. *The Pall Mall Gazette*, August 1865

Chapter 1: Reasons for the Rise of Baby Farms
1. Simon Fowler, *Workhouse: The People, The Places, the Life Behind Doors* (The National Archives, 2007)
2. Charles Dickens, *Oliver Twist*
3. Simon Fowler, *Workhouse: The People, the Places, the Life Behind Doors* (The National Archives, 2007)
4. *The Examiner*, 14 April 1849
5. Lionel Rose, *Massacre of the Innocents: Infanticide in Great Britain 1800–1939* (Routledge & Kegan Paul, 1986)
6. Dan Bogart, Leigh Shaw-Taylor and Xuesheng You, 'The Development of the Railway Network in Britain, 1825–1911'
7. www.oldbaileyonline.org, Margaret Waters, 19 September 1870
8. *Liverpool Mercury*, 19 May 1875
9. *Liverpool Mercury*, 29 October 1879
10. www.ancestry.co.uk, 1881 census
11. *Lloyd's Weekly Newspaper*, 19 February 1893
12. www.oldbaileyonline.org, Amelia Elizabeth Dyer, 18 May 1896
13. *Lloyd's Weekly Newspaper*, 18 September 1898
14. www.oldbaileyonline.org, William Chard Williams, Ada Chard Williams, 12 February 1900
15. *Lloyd's Weekly Newspaper*, 23 January 1898
16. www.oldbaileyonline.org, Annie Walters, 12 January 1903
17. *Liverpool Mercury*, 29 October 1879
18. Lionel Rose, *Massacre of the Innocents: Infanticide in Great Britain 1800–1939* (Routledge & Kegan Paul, 1986)
19. Lionel Rose, *Massacre of the Innocents: Infanticide in Great Britain 1800–1939* (Routledge & Kegan Paul, 1986)
20. *The Times*, 14 February 1889
21. Lionel Rose, *Massacre of the Innocents: Infanticide in Great Britain 1800–1939* (Routledge & Kegan Paul, 1986)

Chapter 2: Good Baby Farmers
1. *Sheffield Independent*, 12 December 1867
2. The National Archives, MEPO 3/96
3. *Illustrated Police News*, 4 November 1871
4. The National Archives, MEPO 3/96
5. *Nottinghamshire Guardian*, 20 August 1880
6. *Lloyd's Weekly Newspaper*, 20 November 1870
7. The National Archives, MEPO 3/96

Chapter 3: The Role of the Midwife
1. www.oldbaileyonline.org, Margaret Waters, 19 September 1870
2. The National Archives, MEPO 3/96
3. The National Archives, MEPO 3/96
4. The National Archives, HO 144/27 and PCOM 4/51
5. www.ancestry.co.uk, 1871 census
6. The National Archives, MEPO 3/92
7. *Daily News*, 30 July 1869
8. The National Archives, MEPO 3/92
9. The National Archives, MEPO 3/92
10. kingscollections.org
11. The National Archives, MEPO 3/93
12. The National Archives, MEPO 3/94
13. The National Archives, MEPO 3/93
14. The National Archives, MEPO 3/93
15. Alison Rattle and Alison Vale, *Amelia Dyer, Angel Maker: The Woman who Murdered Babies for Money* (Andre Deutsch, 2007)
16. The National Archives, PCOM 8/44 HO 144/267 CRIM 1/44
17. The National Archives, CRIM 1/44
18. *The Bristol Mercury*, 10 June 1880
19. *Lloyd's Weekly Newspaper*, 19 April 1896
20. The National Archives, MEPO 3/94
21. The National Archives, MEPO 3/94
22. The National Archives, MEPO 3/94
23. The National Archives, MEPO 3/94
24. The National Archives, MEPO 3/94
25. The National Archives, HO144/27
26. *Daily News*, 5 October 1888
27. *Daily News*, 5 October 1888
28. *Daily News*, 5 October 1888
29. *Reynold's Newspaper*, 2 September 1888
30. *Lloyd's Weekly Newspaper*, 7 October 1888
31. *Reynold's Newspaper*, 2 September 1888
32. *Reynold's Newspaper*, 2 September 1888

Chapter 4: The Role of the Coroner
1. Lionel Rose, *Massacre of the Innocents: Infanticide in Great Britain 1800–1939* (Routledge & Kegan Paul, 1986)

2. Lionel Rose, *Massacre of the Innocents: Infanticide in Great Britain 1800–1939* (Routledge & Kegan Paul, 1986)
3. Lionel Rose, *Massacre of the Innocents: Infanticide in Great Britain 1800–1939* (Routledge & Kegan Paul, 1986)
4. *The Standard*, 27 September 1867
5. *The Daily News*, 25 September 1867
6. *Sheffield and Rotherham Independent*, 12 December 1867
7. *Liverpool Mercury*, 24 December 1867
8. *Daily News*, 31 December 1867
9. *The Pall Mall Gazette*, 2 April 1869
10. James Greenwood, *Seven Curses of London* (1869)
11. *The Morning Post*, 27 May 1869
12. *The Standard*, 18 August 1869
13. *Lloyd's Illustrated Newspaper*, 7 November 1869
14. *The Standard*, 10 April 1871
15. *The Bristol Mercury*, 27 May 1871
16. www.ancestry.co.uk, 1871 census
17. *Liverpool Mercury*, 16 December 1871
18. *Western Mail*, 26 December 1871
19. *Nottinghamshire Guardian*, 14 November 1873
20. *Cheshire Observer*, 1 August 1874
21. *Liverpool Mercury*, 19 May 1875
22. *Belfast Newsletter*, 9 June 1876
23. *Dundee Courier and Argus*, 20 September 1877
24. *The Bristol Mercury*, 22 June 1880
25. *The Bristol Mercury*, 10 June 1880
26. *Lloyd's Weekly Newspaper*, 31 October 1880
27. *Hampshire Advertiser*, 9 March 1881
28. *Royal Cornwall Gazette, Falmouth Package, Cornish Weekly News and General Advertiser*, 5 December 1884
29. www.ancestry.co.uk, 1861 census
30. www.ancestry.co.uk, 1871 census
31. www.ancestry.co.uk, 1881 census
32. *Daily News*, 5 October 1888
33. *Reynold's Newspaper*, 19 May 1889
34. *Lloyd's Weekly Newspaper*, 2 June 1889
35. www.ancestry.co.uk, 1891, 1901, 1902 census
36. Hewines family
37. Hewines family
38. *Western Mail*, 7 March 1890
39. *North-Eastern Daily Gazette*, 1 May 1890
40. *Reynold's Newspaper*, 5 August 1894
41. *Reynold's Newspaper*, 7 October 1894; *Reynold's Newspaper*, 14 October 1894
42. *Reynold's Newspaper*, 3 February 1895
43. *Illustrated Police News*, 29 January 1898
44. *The People*, 3 April 1898
45. *The People*, 24 September 1899
46. *Illustrated Police News*, 4 August 1927; *Gloucester Citizen*, 10 December 1927

Chapter 5: Contravention of Life Protection Act
1. *Cheshire Observer*, 29 September 1879
2. *The Standard*, 1 April 1878
3. *Dundee Courier and Argus*, 30 August 1879
4. *Daily Gazette*, 22 April 1878
5. *Manchester Times*, 20 March 1880
6. *Berkshire Chronicle*
7. *North Wales Chronicle*, 14 July 1888
8. *Daily News*, 5 October 1888
9. *Lloyd's Weekly Newspaper*, 16 March 1890
10. *The Standard*, 24 February 1890
11. *Reynold's Newspaper*, 27 July 1890
12. *Illustrated Police News*, 26 April 1890
13. *North-Eastern Daily Gazette*, 14 September 1891
14. *Reynold's Newspaper*, 2 August 1896; *Reynold's Newspaper*, 18 October 1896
15. *Hampshire Advertiser*, 2 June 1897
16. *The Times*, 31 July 1919

Chapter 6: Abandonment
1. *Bristol Mercury and Daily Post*, 14 April 1896
2. *Liverpool Mercury*, 21 April 1896
3. *Morning Post*, 21 September 1898
4. *West London Observer*, 2 October 1869
5. The National Archives
6. *Liverpool Mercury*, 31 October 1896
7. www.ancestry.co.uk, 1911 census

Chapter 7: Children's Homes
1. *The Standard*, 16 September 1871
2. *The Era*, 29 October 1871
3. www.ancestry.co.uk, Hampshire, England, Church of England Baptisms 1813–1921
4. *Western Mail*, 27 October 1871
5. *Liverpool Mercury*, 25 February 1871
6. www.ancestry.co.uk, 1871 census
7. en.wikipedia.org/wiki/Martha_Merington
8. www.learnedsociety.wales/medals/hoggan-medal/frances_hoggan
9. *Daily News*, 27 July 1880; The National Archives, MEPO 3/96
10. *The Star*, 12 August 1873
11. *Bury and Norwich Post and Suffolk Herald*, 12 August 1873
12. *The Standard*, 24 September 1890
13. www.ancestry.co.uk, 1891 census

Chapter 8: Fraud
1. www.ancestry.co.uk, Kent, England, Church of England Baptisms, Marriages, and Burials 1838–1914
2. www.ancestry.co.uk, London, England, Church of England Marriages and Banns 1854–1938

3. *Illustrated Police News*, 29 October 1870; *The Daily Telegraph*, 14 December 1870; www.oldbaileyonline.org, Mary Hall, 12 December 1870
4. The National Archives, MEPO 3/94
5. www.oldbaileyonline.org, Mary Hall, 12 December 1870
6. www.oldbaileyonline.org, Mary Hall, 12 December 1870
7. www.ancestry.co.uk, 1871 census
8. The National Archives, MEPO 3/94
9. *Leeds Mercury*, 17 September 1892; *Leicester Chronicle*, 24 September 1892
10. www.oldbaileyonline.org, Joseph Roadhouse, Annie Roadhouse, 4 May 1891
11. *Huddersfield Chronicle*, 4 August 1900
12. www.ancestry.co.uk, Calendar of Prisoners

Chapter 9: Cruelty
1. *A Pocket History of the NSPCC*
2. *Liverpool Mercury*, 15 November 1879
3. *Liverpool Mercury*, 5 February 1880
4. *Western Mail*, 21 August 1879
5. *Dundee Courier*, 12 November 1880
6. www.oldbaileyonline.org, Margaret Waters, 19 September 1870
7. *Dundee Courier*, 15 October 1880
8. *Dundee Courier*, 22 February 1881
9. *The Hampshire Advertiser*, 17 December 1890
10. *The Morning Post*, 15 January 1891
11. www.oldbaileyonline.org, Alice Reeves, 9 March 1891
12. *The Daily News*, 31 January 1891
13. *Hampshire Telegraph*, 29 October 1894
14. *Leicester Chronicle and Leicestershire Mercury*, 28 September 1895
15. *Bristol Mercury and Daily Post*, 13 April 1895
16. *Bristol Mercury and Daily Post*, 28 March 1895
17. *Illustrated Police News*, 7 October 1899
18. *Eastbourne Gazette*, 27 September 1899
19. www.oldbaileyonline.org, Amy Louisa McNeil Douglas, 12 September 1899
20. *Illustrated Police News*, 23 September 1899
21. *The Standard*, 1 May 1899
22. *Bristol Mercury and Daily Post*, 5 August 1899

Chapter 10: Manslaughter
1. *Reynold's Newspaper*, 29 October 1871
2. www.oldbaileyonline.org, Augusta Gammage, 26 October 1874
3. www.ancestry.co.uk, 1861 census
4. www.ancestry.co.uk, 1871 census
5. *Pall Mall Gazette*, 17 March 1875
6. *Trewman's Exeter Flying Post*, 17 March 1875
7. *The Morning Post*, 23 March 1875
8. www.ancestry.co.uk, 1901, 1911 census
9. The National Archives, HO 144/924/A2946
10. www.ancestry.co.uk, 1871 census
11. *Cheshire Observer*, 4 October 1879

12. *Cheshire Observer*, 27 September 1879
13. *Essex Standard, West Suffolk Gazette and Eastern Counties Advertiser*, 4 October 1879
14. *Cheshire Observer*, 27 September 1879
15. *Cheshire Observer*, 29 November 1879
16. *York Herald*, 1 November 1879
17. The National Archives, HO 144/924/A2946
18. The National Archives, HO 144/924/A2946
19. *Bristol Mercury and Daily Post*, 14 July 1888
20. *Bristol Mercury and Daily Post*, 23 July 1888
21. Berkshire Record Office, D/H 14/D2/2/2
22. *Sheffield and Rotherham Independent*, 28 November 1889
23. *Lancaster Gazette*, 18 January 1890
24. *Liverpool Mercury*, 3 January 1890
25. *Liverpool Mercury*, 13 January 1890
26. *Manchester Times*, 18 January 1890
27. *Blackburn Standard and Weekly Express*, 29 March 1890
28. *Reynold's Newspaper*, 5 March 1893
29. www.oldbaileyonline.org, Ellen Barnard, 6 March 1893
30. *The Times*, 4 August 1919
31. www.ancestry.co.uk, 1911 census
32. *The Times*, 21 August 1919
33. *The Times*, 22 September 1919

Chapter 11: Murder
1. https://en.wikipedia.org/wiki/History_of_Torquay
2. *Life and Trial of the Child Murderess, Charlotte Winsor*, Office of the Illustrated Police News, 1866
3. *Trewman's Exeter Flying Post*, 22 March 1865
4. *Royal Cornwall Gazette*, 4 August 1865
5. *The Pall Mall Gazette*, 2 August 1865
6. *The Morning Post*, 11 August 1865
7. *Pall Mall Gazette*, 7 May 1866
8. *Daily News*, 14 May 1866
9. www.ancestry.co.uk, 1871, 1881, 1991 census
10. The National Archives
11. *Reynold's Newspaper*, 18 February 1866
12. *The Illustrated Police News*, 9 July 1870
13. www.ancestry.co.uk, 1841 census
14. www.ancestry.co.uk, 1851 census
15. www.freebmd.org.uk
16. www.ancestry.co.uk, 1861 census
17. www.freebmd.org.uk
18. www.oldbaileyonline.org, Margaret Waters, Sarah Ellis, 19 September 1870
19. *The Standard*, 12 October 1870
20. *The Illustrated Police News*, 9 July 1870
21. www.oldbaileyonline.org, Margaret Waters, Sarah Ellis, 19 September 1870
22. www.oldbaileyonline.org, Margaret Waters, Sarah Ellis, 19 September 1870
23. *Lloyd's Weekly Newspaper*, 3 July 1870

Notes 213

24. www.oldbaileyonline.org, Margaret Waters, Sarah Ellis, 19 September 1870
25. The National Archives, MEPO 3/96
26. www.oldbaileyonline.org, Margaret Waters, Sarah Ellis, 19 September 1870
27. *The Illustrated Police News*, 9 July 1870
28. *Cheshire Observer*, 2 July 1870
29. www.oldbaileyonline.org, Margaret Waters, Sarah Ellis, 19 September 1870
30. *Reynold's Newspaper*, 3 July 1870
31. www.oldbaileyonline.org, Margaret Waters, Sarah Ellis, 19 September 1870
32. www.oldbaileyonline.org, Sarah Ellis, 19 September 1870
33. www.oldbaileyonline.org, Margaret Waters, Sarah Ellis, 19 September 1870
34. The National Archives, MEPO 3/96
35. *Dundee Courier and Argus*, 12 October 1870
36. *The Standard*, 12 October 1870
37. *The Morning Post*, 16 April 1883
38. *The Morning Post*, 6 May 1873
39. www.ancestry.co.uk, 1881 census
40. *Hull Packet and East Riding Times*, 8 July 1870
41. https://en.wikipedia.org/wiki/Mrs._Winslow%27s_Soothing_Syrup
42. *Manchester Times*, 18 March 1871
43. *Bradford Observer*, 23 March 1871
44. *Manchester Times*, 8 April 1871
45. *Liverpool Mercury*, 31 July 1871; *Manchester Times*, 18 March 1871
46. *Manchester Times*, 5 August 1871
47. *Liverpool Mercury*, 31 July 1871
48. *Manchester Times*, 5 August 1871
49. *Manchester Times*, 5 August 1871
50. www.ancestry.co.uk, 1881 census
51. *Birmingham Daily Post*, 27 March 1877
52. *Freeman's Journal*, 14 August 1877
53. *Lancaster Gazette*, 8 August 1877
54. www.ancestry.co.uk, 1871 census
55. *Lancaster Gazette*, 28 July 1877
56. *Lloyd's Weekly Newspaper*, 5 August 1877; *Lancaster Gazette*, 1 August 1877
57. *Liverpool Mercury*, 3 August 1877; The National Archives, HO144/27/66244 – PCOM 4/51/18
58. The National Archives, HO144/27/66244 – PCOM 4/51/18
59. *Illustrated Police News*, 18 August 1877
60. The National Archives, HO144/27/66244 – PCOM 4/51/18
61. The National Archives, HO144/43/85718
62. *Trewman's Exeter Flying Post*, 13 August 1879
63. *Aberdeen Journal*, 19 February 1889
64. *Glasgow Herald*, 26 February 1889
65. *Glasgow Herald*, 19 February 1889; National Records of Scotland, JC26/1889/179
66. *Northern Echo*, 19 February 1889; National Records of Scotland, JC26/1889/179
67. National Records of Scotland, JC26/1889/179
68. National Records of Scotland, JC26/1889/179
69. National Records of Scotland, JC26/1889/179
70. National Records of Scotland, JC26/1889/179

71. *Aberdeen Weekly Journal*, 11 March 1889
72. *North-Eastern Daily Gazette*, 11 March 1889
73. *Dundee Courier and Argus*, 12 March 1889
74. *Dundee Courier and Argus*, 5 April 1889
75. *Pall Mall Gazette*, 15 August 1889
76. www.ancestry.co.uk, Bristol, England, Church of England Baptisms 1813–1922
77. www.ancestry.co.uk, 1861 census
78. *Lloyd's Weekly Newspaper*, 19 April 1896
79. www.ancestry.co.uk, 1871 census
80. *Lloyd's Weekly Newspaper*, 19 April 1896
81. *Lloyd's Weekly Newspaper*, 19 April 1896
82. www.ancestry.co.uk, 1871 census
83. www.ancestry.co.uk, Bristol, England, Church of England Baptisms 1813–1922
84. www.freebmd.org.uk
85. Alison Rattle and Allison Vale, *Amelia Dyer, Angel Maker: The Woman Who Murdered Babies for Money* (Andre Deutsch, 2007)
86. *Western Mail*, 25 August 1879
87. *Reynold's Newspaper*, 24 August 1879
88. *Dundee Courier and Argus*, 30 August 1879
89. Alison Rattle and Allison Vale, *Amelia Dyer, Angel Maker: The Woman Who Murdered Babies for Money* (Andre Deutsch, 2007)
90. *Lloyd's Weekly Newspaper*, 19 April 1896
91. National Archives, HO 144/267
92. *Bristol Mercury and Daily Post*, 14 April 1896
93. *Bristol Mercury and Daily Post*, 14 April 1896
94. www.ancestry.co.uk, 1891 census
95. *Bristol Mercury and Daily Post*, 17 April 1896
96. *Bristol Mercury and Daily Post*, 17 April 1896
97. *Bristol Mercury and Daily Post*, 17 April 1896
98. *Bristol Mercury and Daily Post*, 27 April 1894
99. Alison Rattle and Allison Vale, *Amelia Dyer, Angel Maker: The Woman Who Murdered Babies for Money* (Andre Deutsch, 2007)
100. National Archives, HO 144/267
101. *Bristol Mercury and Daily Post*, 17 April 1896
102. www.ancestry.co.uk, Bristol, England, Church of England Marriages and Banns 1754–1938
103. *Lloyd's Weekly Newspaper*, 19 April 1896
104. *Bristol Mercury and Daily Post*, 14 April 1896
105. *Bristol Mercury and Daily Post*, 17 April 1896
106. *The Hampshire Telegraph*, 18 April 1896
107. *Lloyd's Weekly Newspaper*, 19 April 1896
108. *Lloyd's Weekly Newspaper*, 19 April 1896
109. Alison Rattle and Allison Vale, *Amelia Dyer, Angel Maker: The Woman Who Murdered Babies for Money* (Andre Deutsch, 2007); *Berkshire Chronicle*
110. *Lloyd's Weekly Newspaper*, 19 April 1896
111. *Illustrated Police News*, 2 May 1896
112. *Lloyd's Weekly Newspaper*, 19 April 1896
113. *Lloyd's Weekly Newspaper*, 3 May 1896

114. *Lloyd's Weekly Newspaper*, 12 April 1896
115. Alison Rattle and Allison Vale, *Amelia Dyer, Angel Maker: The Woman Who Murdered Babies for Money* (Andre Deutsch, 2007)
116. *Lloyd's Weekly Newspaper*, 19 April 1896
117. *Lloyd's Weekly Newspaper*, 19 April 1896
118. *The Standard*, 4 May 1896
119. *Bristol Mercury and Daily Post*, 17 April 1896
120. *Berkshire Chronicle*
121. Alison Rattle and Allison Vale, *Amelia Dyer, Angel Maker: The Woman Who Murdered Babies for Money* (Andre Deutsch, 2007)
122. www.oldbaileyonline.org, Amelia Elizabeth Dyer, 18 May 1896
123. www.oldbaileyonline.org, Amelia Elizabeth Dyer, 18 May 1896
124. *Dundee Courier*, 4 May 1896
125. *Huddersfield Daily Chronicle*, 5 May 1896
126. *Lloyd's Weekly Newspaper*, 3 May 1896
127. www.oldbaileyonline.org, Amelia Elizabeth Dyer, 18 May 1896
128. *Bristol Mercury and Daily Post*, 13 June 1896
129. The National Archives, PCOM 8/44 HO 144/267 CRIM 1/44
130. *Aberdeen Weekly Journal*, 10 June 1896
131. *Bristol Mercury and Daily Post*, 13 June 1896
132. *Sheffield Evening Telegraph*, 18 June 1896
133. *Dundee Courier*, 20 October 1898
134. Jonathan Goodman, *Bloody Versicles: The Rhymes of Crime* (David and Charles, 1971)
135. Walter Wood, *Survivors' Tales of Famous Crimes* (Cassell and Company Ltd, 1916)
136. John O'Connor, Totterdown History
137. www.oldbaileyonline.org, William Chard Williams, Ada Chard Williams, 12 February 1900
138. www.oldbaileyonline.org, William Chard Williams, Ada Chard Williams, 12 February 1900
139. *Lloyd's Weekly Newspaper*, 3 December 1899
140. *Morning Post*, 28 November 1899
141. www.oldbaileyonline.org, William Chard Williams, Ada Chard Williams, 12 February 1900
142. *Morning Post*, 28 November 1899
143. *Liverpool Mercury*, 11 December 1899
144. *Liverpool Mercury*, 11 December 1899
145. The National Archives, CRIM 1/59/4 HO 144/280/A61654
146. *Morning Post*, 17 February 1900
147. *Lloyd's Weekly Newspaper*, 10 December 1899
148. *Reynold's Newspaper*, 18 February 1900
149. www.oldbaileyonline.org, William Chard Williams, Ada Chard Williams, 12 February 1900
150. *Lloyd's Weekly Newspaper*, 4 March 1900
151. *North-Eastern Daily Gazette*, 6 March 1900
152. *Lloyd's Weekly Newspaper*, 8 April 1900
153. www.oldbaileyonline.org, Annie Walters, Amelia Sach, 12 January 1902
154. www.oldbaileyonline.org, Annie Walters, Amelia Sach, 12 January 1903
155. *The Globe*, 10 December 1902

156. www.oldbaileyonline.org, Annie Walters, Amelia Sach, 12 January 1903
157. www.oldbaileyonline.org, Annie Walters, Amelia Sach, 12 January 1903
158. *The Times*, 17 January 1903
159. www.oldbaileyonline.org, Annie Walters, Amelia Sach, 12 January 1903
160. www.oldbaileyonline.org, Annie Walters, Amelia Sach, 12 January 1903
161. www.oldbaileyonline.org, Annie Walters, Amelia Sach, 12 January 1903
162. www.ancestry.co.uk, Surrey, England, Church of England Marriages and Banns 1754–1937
163. The National Archives, CRIM 1/83/2 HO 44/690/104226
164. www.oldbaileyonline.org, Annie Walters, Amelia Sach, 12 January 1903
165. *The Times*, 3 December 1902
166. www.oldbaileyonline.org, Annie Walters, Amelia Sach, 12 January 1903
167. www.oldbaileyonline.org, Annie Walters, Amelia Sach, 12 January 1903
168. www.oldbaileyonline.org, Annie Walters, Amelia Sach, 12 January 1903
169. The National Archives, CRIM 1/83/2 HO 44/690/104226
170. www.oldbaileyonline.org, Annie Walters, Amelia Sach, 12 January 1903
171. www.oldbaileyonline.org, Annie Walters, Amelia Sach, 12 January 1903
172. www.oldbaileyonline.org, Annie Walters, Amelia Sach, 12 January 1903
173. *St James Gazette*, 17 January 1900
174. www.oldbaileyonline.org, Annie Walters, Amelia Sach, 12 January 1903
175. The National Archives, CRIM 1/83/2 HO 44/690/104226
176. The National Archives, CRIM 1/83/2 HO 44/690/104226
177. *The Daily News*, 4 February 1903
178. *Illustrated Police News*, 7 February 1903
179. *The National Archives*, CRIM 1/83/2 HO 44/690/104226
180. www.ancestry.co.uk, 1911 census
181. The National Archives, ASSI 72/33/2 HO 44/861/155396
182. *Western Mail*, 24 July 1907
183. The National Archives, ASSI 72/33/2 HO 44/861/155396
184. *South Wales Daily News*, 25 July 1907
185. The National Archives, ASSI 72/33/2 HO 44/861/155396
186. The National Archives, ASSI 72/33/2 HO 44/861/155396
187. The National Archives, ASSI 72/33/2 HO 44/861/155396
188. *South Wales Daily News*, 25 July 1907
189. The National Archives, ASSI 72/33/2 HO 44/861/155396
190. The National Archives, ASSI 72/33/2 HO 44/861/155396
191. The National Archives, ASSI 72/33/2 HO 44/861/155396
192. The National Archives, ASSI 72/33/2 HO 44/861/155396
193. The National Archives, ASSI 72/33/2 HO 44/861/155396
194. The National Archives, ASSI 72/33/2 HO 44/861/155396
195. *South Wales Daily Post*, 23 July 1907
196. *South Wales Daily News*, 25 July 1907
197. *South Wales Daily News*, 25 July 1907
198. *South Wales Daily Post*, 8 August 1907
199. The National Archives, ASSI 72/33/2 HO 44/861/155396
200. The National Archives, ASSI 72/33/2 HO 44/861/155396
201. *South Wales Daily Post*, 14 August 1907
202. *South Wales Daily Post*, 14 August 1907

203. *South Wales Daily Post*, 14 August 1907
204. The National Archives, ASSI 72/33/2 HO 44/861/155396
205. *South Wales Daily Post*, 14 August 1907
206. *South Wales Daily Post*, 14 August 1907
207. The National Archives, ASSI 72/33/2 HO 44/861/155396

Chapter 12: The Fight to Protect Children
1. *Pall Mall Gazette*, 28 August 1867
2. *The Times*, 1 October 1867
3. *Daily News*, 31 December 1867
4. *Newcastle Courant*, 31 July 1868
5. *Liverpool Mercury*, 9 April 1868
6. James Greenwood, *The Seven Curses of London*, Project Gutenberg eBook
7. J. Brendan Curgenven, *The Waste of Infant Life* (1867)
8. *British Medical Journal*, 1868
9. Curgenven, *On Baby-farming and the Registration of Nurses* (1869)
10. The National Archives, MEPO 3/96
11. www.ancestry.co.uk, 1871 census
12. The National Archives, MEPO 3/96
13. The National Archives, MEPO 3/96
14. Lionel Rose, *Massacre of the Innocents: Infanticide in Great Britain 1800–1939* (Routledge & Kegan Paul 1986)
15. Lionel Rose, *Massacre of the Innocents: Infanticide in Great Britain 1800–1939* (Routledge & Kegan Paul 1986)
16. *Illustrated Police News*, 4 September 1897
17. *Pall Mall Gazette*, 19 August 1889
18. Joanne Pearman, *Bastardy, Baby Farmers, and Social Control in Victorian Britain* (PhD Thesis)
19. Lionel Rose, *Massacre of the Innocents: Infanticide in Great Britain 1800–1939* (Routledge & Kegan Paul 1986)
20. Lionel Rose, *Massacre of the Innocents: Infanticide in Great Britain 1800–1939* (Routledge & Kegan Paul 1986)

Bibliography

Bogart, Dan, Shaw-Taylor, Leigh and You, Xuesheng, 'The development of the railway network in Britain 1825 – 1911' (www.campop.geog.cam.ac.uk, 2018)
Brown, Richard, 'Infanticide: A Case Study' (wordpress.com, 2010)
Buckley, Angela, *Amelia Dyer and The Baby Farm Murders* (Manor Vale Associates, 2016)
Carwardine, Anne, *Disgusted Ladies* (Troubador Publishing, 2018)
Fisher, Pamela Jane, 'The Politics of Sudden Death: The Office and Role of the Coroner in England and Wales 1726–1888' (University of Leicester Doctoral Thesis)
Fowler, Simon, *Workhouse: The People, The Places, The Life Behind Doors* (The National Archives, 2007)
Gladstone, Florence, *Notting Hill in Bygone Days* (T. Fisher Unwin Ltd., 1924)
Greenwood, James, *The Seven Curses of London* (1869)
Grey, Daniel, '"More Ignorant and Stupid than Wilfully Cruel": Homicide Trials and "Baby-farming" in England and Wales in the Wake of the Children Act 1908' (*SOLON Crimes and Misdemeanours: Deviance and the Law in Historical Perspective*, 3(2), 60–77, 2009)
Hall, Catherine, McClelland, Keith and Rendell, Jane, *Defining the Victorian Nation: Class, Race, Gender and the British Reform Act 1867* (Cambridge University Press, 2000)
Haller, Dorothy L., *Bastardy and Baby Farming in Victorian England* (Loyola University, 1989)
Historic England, *Law Courts and Courtrooms 2: Civil and Coroner's Courts* (2018)
Homrighaus, Ruth Ellen, *Baby Farming in British History* (The University of North Carolina at Chapel Hill ProQuest Dissertations Publishing, 2003)
Illustrated Police News, 'Life and Trial of the Child Murderess, Charlotte Winsor' (Office of the Illustrated Police News, 1866)
Martin, Jane, *Women and the Politics of Schooling in Victorian and Edwardian England* (Bloomsbury Publishing, 2010)
Moss, Alan and Skinner, Keith, *Scotland Yard's History of Crime in 100 Objects* (The History Press, 2015)
NSPCC, *A Pocket History of the NSPCC* (2009)
NSPCC, *A History of the NSPCC* (2000)
O'Day, Rosemary and Englander, Davis, *Mayhew: London Labour and the London Poor* (Wordsworth Editions Ltd, 2008)
Pearman, Joanne, 'Bastardy, Baby Farmers, and Social Control in Victorian Britain' (PhD Thesis University of Kent, 2017)
Perrini, Sylvia, 'Baby Farmers of the 19th Century – women who kill' (goldmineguides.com, 2012)
Rattle, Alison and Vale, Allison, *Amelia Dyer, Angel Maker: The Woman Who Murdered Babies for Money* (Andre Deutsch, 2007)
Rose, Lionel, *Massacre of the Innocents: Infanticide in Great Britain 1800–1939* (Routledge & Kegan Paul, 1986)
Seaton, Sarah, *Childhood and Death in Victorian England* (Pen and Sword, 2017)
Sims, George R. (ed.), *Living London*, Vol. 1 (Cassell and Company Ltd., 1902)

Van Wingerden, S., *The Women's Suffrage Movement in Britain 1866–1928* (Palgrave MacMillan, 1999)
Whittington-Egan, Molly, *The Stockbridge Baby-Farmer and other Scottish Murder Stories* (Neil Wilson Publishing, 2001)
Williams, Lucy and Godfrey, Barry, *Criminal Women 1850–1920: Researching the Lives of Britain's Female Offenders* (Pen and Sword, 2018)
Woods, Walter B., *Survivors' Tales of Famous Crimes* (Cassell and Company Ltd., 1906)

Newspapers
Aberdeen Journal, 1881
Aberdeen Weekly Journal, 1879, 1891, 1896
Barnet Press, Finchley and Hendon News, Southgate and Edgware Chronicle, 1903
Belfast Newsletter, 1875, 1888, 1896
Berkshire Chronicle, 1896
Berrow's Worcester Journal, 1879, 1896
Bradford Observer, 1870, 1873, 1875
Birmingham Daily Post, 1867, 1870, 1871, 1874, 1877, 1879, 1892, 1900
Bristol Mercury and Daily Post, 1870, 1873, 1878, 1879, 1881, 1880, 1888, 1895, 1894, 1896
Bury and Ipswich Post and Suffolk Standard, 1873, 1888
Bury and Norwich Post, 1870, 1879, 1888, 1894
Cheshire Observer, 1870, 1874, 1875, 1879, 1896
Daily Gazette, 1877, 1878, 1879
Daily News, 1853, 1866, 1867, 1869, 1870, 1872, 1877, 1879, 1888, 1891, 1896, 1897, 1899, 1902, 1903
Daily Telegraph, 1870
Derby Daily Telegraph, 1907
Derby Mercury, 1896
Dundee Courier and Argos, 1865, 1867, 1870, 1877, 1879, 1880, 1881, 1888, 1896, 1898, 1900
Edmonton and Tottenham Weekly Guardian, 1898
Eastbourne Gazette, 1899
Essex Standard, West Suffolk Gazette and Eastern Counties Advertiser, 1865, 1879
Evening Gazette, 1870
Evening Standard, 1899, 1903
Freeman's Journal and Daily Commercial Advertiser, 1867, 1870, 1877, 1879, 1891, 1895
Glasgow Herald, 1870, 1881, 1896
The Globe, 1899, 1900, 1902, 1903
Gloucester Citizen, 1927
Hampshire Advertiser, 1881, 1890, 1897, 1900
Hampshire Telegraph and Sussex Chronicle, 1890, 1894, 1896
Hendon and Finchley Times, 1901
Huddersfield Chronicle, 1900
Huddersfield Daily Chronicle, 1870, 1873, 1878, 1896, 1900
Hull Daily Mail, 1927
Hull Packet and East Riding Times, 1870
Illustrated Police Budget, 1899
Illustrated Police News, 1867, 1870, 1871, 1877, 1879, 1890, 1896, 1897, 1898, 1899, 1900, 1903, 1927
Ipswich Journal, 1870, 1896
Islington Daily Gazette, 1902, 1903

Lancashire Gazette, 1870, 1873, 1877, 1878, 1879
Leeds Mercury, 1870, 1878, 1879, 1880, 1892, 1894
Leicester Chronicle and Leicestershire Mercury, 1867, 1892, 1895, 1896, 1899
Liverpool Mercury, 1866, 1867, 1871, 1875, 1877, 1879, 1880, 1883, 1896, 1899, 1900
Lloyd's Weekly Newspaper, 1853, 1865, 1869, 1870, 1871, 1875, 1877, 1879, 1880, 1881, 1888, 1889, 1890, 1895, 1896, 1898, 1899, 1900
Manchester Courier (Supplement to), 1907
Manchester Times, 1871, 1880, 1892
Morning Advertiser, 1870
Morning Post, 1853, 1865, 1869, 1870, 1873, 1875, 1883, 1888, 1890, 1891, 1896, 1898, 1899, 1900
Morning Chronicle, 1853
Newcastle Courant, 1853, 1870, 1879, 1899
North-Eastern Daily Gazette, 1888, 1891, 1895, 1896, 1899, 1900
Northern Echo, 1879, 1896
North Wales Chronicle, 1879, 1888
Nottinghamshire Guardian, 1870, 1873, 1896
Oxfordshire Weekly News, 1891
Pall Mall Gazette, 1865, 1867, 1869, 1870, 1874, 1875, 1879, 1881, 1888, 1896, 1900
Pearson's Weekly, 1908
Penny Illustrated Newspaper, 1870, 1879, 1903
The People, 1898, 1899, 1927
Portsmouth Evening News, 1927
Reynold's Newspaper, 1865, 1866, 1870, 1871, 1875, 1879, 1888, 1890, 1894, 1896, 1900
Ross Gazette, 1899
Royal Cornwall Gazette, 1865, 1870, 1879, 1884, 1890, 1900
Sheffield Evening Telegraph, 1896
Sheffield and Rotherham Independent, 1867, 1869, 1870, 1873, 1879, 1880, 1895, 1896, 1900
Southend Telegraph, 1891
South Wales Daily Post, 1907
South Wales Echo, 1899
South Wales Daily News, 1907
The Standard, 1865, 1867, 1869, 1870, 1871, 1878, 1879, 1880, 1888, 1890, 1891, 1895, 1896, 1899, 1900, 1902, 1903
The Star, 1873
The Times, 1889, 1902, 1903, 1919
Trewman's Exeter Flying Post, 1865, 1866, 1875, 1879
Weekly Dispatch, 1896
Weekly Standard and Express, 1895
West Britain and Cornwall Advertiser, 1900
Western Daily Press, 1927
Western Mail, 1870, 1871, 1879, 1880, 1890, 1907
Wrexham Advertiser, 1875, 1880
York Herald, 1869, 1873, 1879, 1881
Yorkshire Herald, 1896

Websites
www.ancestry.co.uk
www.thegenealogist.co.uk
www.theoldbaileyonline.org

Index

Acton, London 44
Acts of Parliament
  Adoption of Children (Regulation) Act 1939 206
  Birth, Death Registration Acts 1836, 1874 20
  Children's and Young Person's Act 1908 206
  Children's Bill 1908 9
  Children's Charter, the 1889 88
  Coroner's Act 1887 19
  Friendly Societies Act 1793–1875 7, 8
  Infant Life Protection Act 1872, 1888 8, 35, 37, 41, 42, 46–47, 53, 59, 69–73, 89, 95, 99, 101, 104, 113–114, 127–129, 155, 168, 172, 205, 206
  Offences against the Persons Act 1861 2
  Poor Law Amendment Act 1834 xii, 1–2
  Prevention of Cruelty to, and Protection of, Children Act 1889 126, 205
    Amendment 1894 206
  Railway Act 1844 6
  Trade Union Amendment Act 1876 8
Adams, James, Dr. 102
Agnew, Thomas 87
Anderson, Agnes 107, 108
Arnold, Jane xiv, 6, 36–42, 54, 206
Ashford, Kent 40
Ashton Keynes, Oxon 38
Assizes
  Berkshire Assizes 181
  Chester Assizes 89
  Glamorgan Assizes Court 197
  Manchester Assizes 72, 147–148
Asylums xiv, 34, 169–171, 180
  Broadmoor Hospital for the Criminally Insane 122
  Bristol Lunatic Asylum 167
  Drouet's Juvenile Pauper Asylum 2
  Gloucestershire Asylum 169, 170
  Magdalene Asylum, Edinburgh 160, 166
  Wells Asylum 170
Augusta, Annie 80, 82

Bailey, Joseph and Agnes 98–100
Bailey, Elizabeth 37, 96
Baker, Sarah 6, 126–128, 130
Baker, Cecilia 107, 108
Baker, Mrs James, *see* Jane Arnold
Baker, Queenie 61, 179

Banks, James 162
Banks, *see* Barnes, John and Catherine
Banks, Mrs, *see* King, Jessie
Barnes, Surrey 185–187
Barnes, John and Catherine 6, 7, 53, 114–120
Barnard, Ellen 6, 126–130
Barton, Abi Joan 95
Barton, Mrs., *see* Maria Castle
Bath, Somerset 7, 98, 111, 118, 120, 122, 170
Battersea, London 11, 57, 69, 139, 140, 173, 184, 186, 188
Beagley, Mrs, *see* Chivers, Ellen, Daisy
Beard, *see* Barnes, John and Catherine
Bell, Fitzroy Mr. 165
Benmore/Binmore, Betsy 110–113
Bermondsey, London 126
Berry, James 166
Beta, Mrs., *see* Baker, Sarah
Bethnal Green, London 21, 25
Betts, Emma 97, 98
Billington, James 181, 189
Billington, William 194
Birkenhead, Cheshire 6, 63, 64, 114, 115, 120, 155
Bithell, Mrs 30, 31
Blackburn, Charlotte 44, 45
Blackburn, Margaret, *see* Waters, Margaret
Blackheath, London 33, 38
Board of Guardians 1, 27, 50
  Chingford Board of Guardians 104
  Kensington Board of Guardians 68
  St Pancras Board of Guardians 14
Bompas, Mr. 113
Bootle, Lancs. 118, 199
Bournemouth, Dorset 9, 37, 42, 58, 145
Bow. London 24, 43, 82
Bowen, Ivor 197
Bowness, Cumbria 153
Brighton, Sussex 50, 80, 82, 186
Brightwell, Caroline 43
Brindley, Richard and Louisa 63–65
Bristol 7, 9, 27, 28, 34, 98, 100, 105, 106, 118, 157, 166–175, 183, 187
Brixton, London xiii, 6, 16, 33, 54, 92, 139–141, 156
Bromley, Kent 42
Buist, James, Mr. 197
Bullen, Henry, St. John, Dr. 143
Burroughs, Mrs 33

Calcraft, William 138
Camborne, Cornwall 157, 158
Camden Town, London 10
Camberwell, London 6, 16, 33, 61, 76, 77, 82, 139–141, 202–204
Campbell, Elizabeth 163, 165
Campbell, Walter, Anderson 165
Cannonmills, Edinburgh 160, 163
Cardiff, Wales 7, 171, 195, 197–199
Carter, Elizabeth xiv, 9, 39, 42
Carter, Mrs., *see* Barnard, Ellen
Castle, Maria 16, 140–141, 143, 144, 155–156, 203–204
Caunter, Lawernce, Mr. 193
Caversham, Berks. 171–173
Central Criminal Court – Old Bailey 83, 93, 179, 182, 188
Chapman, Jessie 36–39, 41
Chard, Mary 201
Chard-Williams, Ada 7, 183–189
Chard-Williams, William 185, 187–189
Chatham, Kent 11, 85
Chester 63, 64, 88
Chew Magna, Somerset 32
Chingford, Essex 48, 104
Chivers, Daisy Ellen 50–51
Clare, *see* Reeves, Alice
Clark, Emily 55
Clarke, Jane 11
Clerkenwell, London 21, 22, 26
Colchester, Essex 79
Cook, Mary 37
Cooper, Mr. & Mrs. William 21
Corbett, Mrs 26
Coroners 20
  Aspinall, Clarke 29
  Baxter, Mr. 42
  Braxton Hicks, Athelston, Mr. 8, 36, 58
  Brewer, W.H. 29, 30, 33
  Browne, M. Mr. 13
  Bunny, Joseph 22
  Churton, H. 30–31
  Coxwell, W., Mr. 35
  Driffield, Mr. 31
  Dudlow, J. N. 30
  Garland, Mr. 27, 28
  Hardwick/e, Dr. 26, 34–35
  Hodgkinson, Alfred, Mr. 44–48
  Humphries/ Humphreys, John Mr. 19, 22, 26
  Langham, Arthur C., Mr. 48
  Luxmore Drew, c., Mr. 45
  MacDonald, Dr. 43
  Reece, E.B. 198
  Richards, Mr. 21, 24, 25
  Wyatt, G. P., Mr. 44
Cotton, Sarah 59
Cowan, Jeanette 17, 141, 143
Cowan, Robert Tassie 6, 140–144
Cox, Mrs., 45, 46
Cox Mrs., *see* Barnard, Ellen
Crabb, Ann 91, 92
Craddock, Frederick, Hurst 170
Crafter, Elizabeth 75, 77
Cruelty x, 37, 54, 87–106, 108, 122, 123, 205, 206
  Liverpool Society for the Prevention of Cruelty to Children 87
  London Society for the Prevention of Cruelty to Children 87
  National Society for the Prevention of Cruelty to Children 87, 88, 91–94, 96–98, 100, 101, 105, 130, 172, 175
  New York Society for the Prevention of Cruelty to Children 87
  Society for the Prevention of Cruelty to Children 53, 95, 105
  National Society for the Prevention of Cruelty to Children Officers
    Akehurst, Mr. 101
    Barker, Mr. 96
    Collard, Insp. 97
    Laiter, George 92
    Ottley, John 98, 105, 108
    Patten, David 92
    Roberts, Ellen 103
    Sygrove, Insp. 130
Cummings, Anne 60–63, 75, 78, 79
Cunningham, Ellen 29
Curgenven, John Brendan, Dr. 200–202

Dalton, *see* Chard-Williams, Ada
Dampier, Matilda 67
Dane, Eleanor 167
Davidson, James, Rev. 157
Davis, Caroline 57
Dawkins, Mary Ann 35
Deal, Kent 85
Denton, Martha Ann, *see* Seville, Joseph and Martha
Dickens, Charles xi, xiv, 1
Douglas, Amy 103–105
Dr. Collis Browne's Compound 190
Driffield, East Yorkshire 58
Drouet, Bartholomew Peter 2
Duckham, May, *see* Measdale, Frances Ruth Naomi
Durdham Down, Bristol 61, 171
Dyer, Amelia, Elizabeth 7, 16, 34, 52, 54, 60, 80, 90, 142, 166–184
Dyer, William 167, 169, 171

Eastbourne, Sussex 9, 101–103
Eastville, Bristol 169, 171
Edgington, Alfred Dudley, Dr. 57
Edmonton, London 48
Ellis, Sarah 6, 78, 139, 141–147, 203
Epping, Essex 95, 104
Evans, David 194, 195, 199
Exeter, Devon 135, 138, 157, 158

Index 223

Finchley, London 190, 191
Finlay, David Ferguson 163, 164
Fisher, N.M., Mr. County Analyst 41
Fisherman's Bend 185
Fishponds, Bristol 169, 171
Fletcher, Mrs 11
Foard, Mr. 152, 153
Folkard, Mr. 135, 137, 138
Ford, Emily 84–86
Fort, *see* Waters, Margaret
Fry, Helena 173, 174, 177
Fulham, London 55, 56, 60, 66, 72, 73, 79, 184
Fulham Model Baby Farm 66, 67
Furley, Mrs., *see* Waters, Margaret

Galley, Ada Charlotte 192–194
Gammage, Augusta 108–110
Gathard, Amy 25
George, Dr. and Mrs. 154–156
George, Mrs, *see* Barton, Abi Joan
Gloucester, Glos. 77, 170, 176
Godfrey's Cordial 168
Gospel Oak, London 14
Gosport, Hants. 37, 96
Goulding, Elizabeth, Miss. 174, 175, 181
Gray, Barbara, *see* Barbara McIntosh
Greenstead Green, Orpington, Kent 77, 78
Greenwood, James 24, 201
Great Yarmouth, Norfolk 38
Griffiths, Alfred Leete, Dr. 129
Grundy, Eva Muriel xiv, 9, 39, 42
Grundy, Sidney 146
Guerra, Caroline 140–142
Gunn, Alexander 161–165
Gunn, Catherine, *see* Whyte, Catherine, Mrs.
Gunn, Robert 163

Hacker, Mrs. 168
Haggerstone, London 26
Hall, *see* Barnes, John and Catherine
Hall, David 75, 78, 82
Hall, Mrs. Jane, *see* Arnold, Jane
Hall, Mary Ann 3, 16, 24, 61–63, 75–83
Hamblin, Mrs. 22
Hamilton, *see* Barnes, John and Catherine
Hammersmith, London 61, 183–185
Harding, Dr., 142
Harding, Mrs, *see* Dyer, Ameilia
Harpur Street Shelter 93, 94
Harris, Mary Jane 133–139
Hatchard, Henry and Beatrice 130–131
Hayes, George and Mary 8, 38, 40, 54
Hede, Mrs. *see* Hosking, Mary
Heley, Elizabeth 7, 46, 47
Henderson, Col. 17
Henderson, Margaret 160, 164
Hengoed, Wales 196
Hereford, Herefordshire 7, 116, 118

Hewetson, Mrs. *see* Chard-Williams, Ada
Higgs, Charlotte 12
Hinam, Mrs 32
Hoggan, Frances Elizabeth, Dr. 68
Holliday, George and Lily 105, 106
Home Secretary 17, 23, 70, 156, 157, 189, 194, 198, 200, 202
  Cross, Richard, Assheton 113, 155, 156
  Gladstone, H. T. 198
  Grey, Sir George 138
Horsfield, Bristol 169
Hosking, Mary 157–159
Howell, Mr. and Mrs., *see* Barnes, John and Catherine
Hull, Yorks. 7, 118
Hurley, *see* Waters, Margaret

Infant Life Protection Act Inspectors
  Babey/Braby, Samuel 46, 53, 54, 73, 74, 127
  Smith, Miss Isobel 57, 58
  Roberts, Ellen 103
Insurance 7–9, 54, 58, 101, 106, 118, 123, 126, 202, 206
  Liverpool Victoria Legal Friendly Society 54
  Pearl Life Assurance Company 8
  Prudential Insurance Company 8, 123
  Victoria Legal Friendly Society 8
Iredale, Mrs. 14
Isleworth, London 12
Islington, London 22, 198, 199

J. W., *see* Waters, Margaret
Jackson, May, *see* Reeves, Alice
Jackson, Mrs, *see* Todd, Sophia, Martha
Jackson, Thomas 153, 156
Jagger, Caroline 19–21, 201
James, Edward 147–149
James, Leslie 194–199
James, Mark and May Jane 9, 58
Jolliffe, Mary Jane 154
Jones, Florence 183, 185, 188
Jones, Mrs., *see* Hall Mary Ann
Jones, Selina Ellen 7, 184, 185

Kane, Jessie, *see* King, Jessie
Kay, Ann 6, 31, 32
Keane, Jessie, *see* King, Jessie
Kensington, London 61, 79, 191, 192, 204, 205
Kentish Town, London 83
Kimberton, Ann 29
King, Jessie 160–166
Kirby, Mrs. 15

Ladywell, Lewisham, London 34
Lamb, Mary Ann 56
Lambeth, London 127
Laming, Mrs. *see* Walters, Annie

Langman, Mrs. 204, 205
Leeds, Yorks. 7, 43, 85, 117, 118
Leonard, Sarah, Annie and Rose 9, 105, 106
Leselles, Rhoda, *see* James, Leslie
Lewisham, London 33
Limehouse, London 25
Liverpool, Lancs. 7, 29, 31, 53, 63–65, 87, 114, 116, 117, 119, 152–155, 169, 188
Loe, Mr. & Mrs. George James 80–82
Loose, Kent 30

M.T., *see* Waters, Margaret
MacKey, Elizabeth 147
MacKenzie 67
MacKenzie, Mrs., 164
MacPherson, Mrs, *see* King, Jessie
MacPherson, Rhoda, *see* James, Leslie
Malvern, Worcs. 12, 13
Manchester, Lancs 71, 82, 117, 147, 148, 152, 174, 196
Manslaughter ix, 35, 46, 53, 58, 59, 72, 74, 91, 93, 95, 103, 107–111, 113, 119, 122–124, 126, 128, 130, 131, 146, 165, 198
Marlborough, Duke of 200
Marmon, Doris 173–175, 177, 179
Marmon, Evalina 175, 177
Marsh, Ann 54
Marshall, Eva 100
Martin, Louisa 16, 17
Marylebone, London 107
McIntosh, Mrs. Barbara 90, 91
Measdale, Frances Ruth Naomi 84–86
Merith, Mrs., *see* Walters, Annie
Merrington, Martha 68–70
Middleton Chaney/Cheney N'ants. 39, 42
Miss Sterling's Destitute Home 161, 164, 165
Mitchell, Ida 92
Morse, Jane 77
Mother Siegle's Syrup 39
Mrs Winslow's Soothing Syrup 147
Muncey, Matilda 72–74
Murder xiii, 3, 16, 36, 54, 62, 63, 66, 78–80, 103, 105, 107, 111, 113, 117–119, 132–199
Murrant, Sarah 11–12

Neave's Food 101
Newbury, Berks. 22
Newcastle-upon-Tyne 7, 171
New Ferry, Cheshire 63, 88, 154
Newport, South Wales 29, 199
Newport Pagnell, Bucks. 41
Newton Abbot 7, 60, 111, 112, 181
Nicholson, Eve 55, 56
Noble, Louisa 120–122
Normanton, Notts. 10
Nottingham, Notts., 13, 139
Notting Hill, London 68, 69, 171, 205

Oakhill, Somerset 27
Old Bailey, *see* Central Criminal Court

Oliver, Mrs. *see* Waters Margaret
Oliver, Ellen Maud (Nellie) 172, 180
Oliver Twist x, xi, xiii, 2
O'Neill, Mary Ann 71, 72

Packer, Mary 48, 49, 100
Painter, Mrs., *see* Barnard, Ellen
Palmer, Arthur and Mary Ann (Polly) 7, 61, 171, 172, 174, 175, 177–181
Pardoe, Rosina 192, 193
Parris, Elizabeth Julia 91
Parsons Green, London 61
Pavitt, Thomas and Annie 9, 101–103
Pearce, Susan 55
Pearson, Thomas 160–166
Pearson, William and Elizabeth 9, 122–126
Penge, London 40
Penkridge, Staffs. 63, 64
Pentreporth, South Wales 33
Peckham, London 33, 55, 139
Perkins, Frank – Public Analyst 159
Petre, Lady Mary 201
Petty Sessions
    Edmonton 205
    Epping 95
    Gosport 96
Pierrepoint, Henry 198
Plymouth, Devon 7, 60, 136, 158, 171, 178, 179
Police xiv, 6, 11, 14, 16, 17, 20, 25, 28, 30, 34, 36, 41, 45, 53, 54, 56, 60–64, 67, 69, 71, 75–83, 85, 86, 88, 94, 104, 105, 109, 114–118, 120, 123, 127, 132–135, 143, 147, 149, 150, 152, 155–159, 162, 165, 167, 168, 170–174, 176–179 184–187, 189–192, 195, 197, 200, 203, 204
    Birkenhead Police 114, 115, 118
    Cardiff Police 198, 199
    Edinburgh Police 90
    Metropolitan Police 11, 203
    Liverpool Police 65
    Staffordshire Police 64, 65
    Thames Police 172
Police Courts
    Birkenhead Police Court 118
    Cannock Police Court 65
    Lambeth Police Court 143
    Loughborough Police Court 97
    Marlborough Street Court 10
    Reading Police Court 177
    South-Western Police Court 58
    West London Police Court 128
Police Officers
    Abberline, Detective Chief Inspector Frederick 83
    Anderson, James, Detective Constable 173, 174
    Clark, James, Detective 162
    Clarke, Inspector 156

Index 225

Clarke, George, Chief Inspector 11, 203, 204
Cross, Inspector 123
Davey, William Inspector 198
Daw, Inspector 82
Edwards, John, Sergeant 133
Ford, W., Police Constable 133, 134
Haslam, Police Constable 148
Igoe, Sergeant 32
James, Harry, Sergeant 173, 174
King, Sergeant 96
Kyd, Detective Constable 193
Marsh, W., Inspector 69
Meade, Police Inspector 71
Mullard, Sergeant 11
Nelson, Detective 155
New, Police Constable 58
Nicholls, Police Constable 112
Pegg, Police Constable 97
Pearson, Detective Inspector 63
Relf, Richard, Sergeant/Inspector 6, 16, 78, 79, 141–143, 145–147, 156, 203
Scott, Detective Inspector 186, 187
Seal, Police Constable 190
Sheppard, Inspector 34
Slater, Police Constable 148, 149
Strettell, Detective 152
Tewsley, Chief Constable 174
Troughton, Sergeant 61
Voice, David, Police Constable 184
White, Police Sergeant 191
Williamson, Superintendent 11
Windmill, Sergeant 98
Wright, Detective 191
Pontypool, Wales 194
Poor Law xii, 68, 200, 201
Portobello, Scotland 67, 68, 90
Pratt, Mrs., *see* Pavitt, Annie
Pratt, Charlotte Selina 134–136
Price, Hannah 29, 30
Prisons
  Aylesbury Prison 120
  Calton Gaol 165
  Dartmoor Prison 120
  Devon County Gaol 159
  Edinburgh Prison 163
  Exeter Prison 138
  Fulham Women's Prison 152, 156
  Horsemonger Lane Gaol 146
  Newgate Prison ix, 181
  Wandsworth Prison 78, 82
  Woking Prison 122, 138, 147
Puckle, George, Dr. 77, 142–144
Putney, Surrey 110
Pyle Marsh, Bristol 167

Quarter Sessions
  Devon Quarter Sessions 181
  West Riding Quarter Sessions 86
Queen Victoria x, 87, 138

Railway 3–7, 37, 43, 60, 63, 79, 126, 133, 153, 176, 181
Railway Stations
  Abbeyhill 165
  Brighton 102
  Birkenhead 6, 31
  Bristol 170
  Brixton 6, 140
  Camberwell New Road 6, 141
  Cheltenham 7, 176
  Gloucester 7
  Hereford 6, 116
  Liverpool Exchange Station 6, 115
  London Bishop's Road Underground 62
  London Charing Cross 184
  London Euston 6
  London Liverpool Street 7, 42
  London Paddington 7, 177–179
  London Victoria 6, 126, 128
  Newton Abbot 7
  South Kensington Underground 7, 191
  Walworth Road 6, 140
  Wolverton 6, 37
  Woolwich 7, 183
Reading, Berks. 7, 33, 34, 171–177, 179
Rees, Ann 33, 34
Reeves, Alice 92–95
Roadhouse, Joseph and Annie 83, 84
Robinson, John 152, 155
Robinson, Lydia 126–129
Rogers, Frances 147–151
Rudolf, Edward 87
Russell, Elizabeth 26, 27

St. Luke's, London 22, 78
St. Pancras, London 34
Sach, Amelia 3, 16, 189–194
Salvation Army 47, 48, 130, 195
Sargeant, Amelia Hannah 176–178
Saville, Caroline 24, 82, 201
Seville, Joseph and Martha 88, 89
Secretary of State for Scotland 165
Shaftesbury, Lord 82, 201
Shepherd's Bush, London 45, 175
Sheppard, Mary Ann 34, 35
Short, Ann 42, 43
Sileby, Leics. 97
Simmonds, Harry 173, 175–177, 179
Smith, *see* Reeves, Alice
Smith, Jane 171, 179
Smith, Mary, Mrs., *see* Dyer, Amelia
Smith, Mrs., *see* Pavitt, Annie
Smith, Rose 195, 196
Smith, Samuel, M.P. 87
Smith, Sarah/Suannah 25, 26
Snelling, George and Sarah 105
Southampton, Hampshire 35, 114
South Kensington, London 68, 190
Southport, Lancs. 85, 122, 123, 167

Soho, London 16, 17
Sophia Nursery, Fulham, *see* Fulham Model Baby Farm
Spencer, Mary 77
Spicer, Charlotte 44, 45
Spinks, Ann 47, 48
Spurgeon, Mrs., 30
Staite, George, Rev. 87
Stansfield, Mrs., *see* Dyer Amelia
Stephens, Mary Ann 57
Stevenson, Eva 43
Stevenson, Thomas, Dr., Government Analyst 40
Stewart, *see* Waters, Margaret
Stewart, Mr. and Miss., *see* King, Jessie and Pearson, Thomas
Stockbridge, Edinburgh 161, 163
Stockwell, London 55
Southport, Lancs. 85, 122, 123, 167
Stretton, Charles Marston 146
Surbiton, Surrey 146
Swindon, Wilts. 40, 54

Tarbeth, Mrs 12–13
Taylor, Jessie 160
Thames, River 172, 184, 185
Thomas, George 167
Thomas, Mrs., *see* Dyer, Amelia
Thompson, Elizabeth 53, 54, 155, 169
Thompson, George Henry 155
Thompson, Henry 152, 156
Thorne, Matilda 22, 23, 200
Thorne, Nurse, *see* Sach, Amelia
Thorpe, Oscar Rev. 202–204
Thorpe, Richard, Rev. 16
Thornton, Willie 171, 172, 179
Tilston, Cheshire 30, 31
Todd, Sophia Martha 17, 152–157, 203
Toller, John 173
Tomlinson, Alice Maria Jane Stewart 162, 163
Tomlinson, Violet 162, 163, 165
Tonkins, Elizabeth 157
Tooke, Annie 157–159
Tooting, Surrey 2, 15, 37, 85
Torquay, Devon 111, 117, 118, 132–134
Tottenham, London 19, 44–48, 100
Totterdown, Bristol 54, 80, 167, 169, 183
Tranmere, Cheshire 115, 117–119
Treasure, Maud 196–198
Tremain, Davidstowe, Cornwall 36

Upper Broughton, Leics. 43
Upper Knowle, Somerset 98
Uxbridge, Middx. 55

Vauxhall, London 11, 92
Vincent, Mrs., *see* Pavitt, Annie

Walham Green, London 73
Waller, Mary Ann 52, 53
Walpole, Mrs., *see* Arnold, Jane
Walters, Annie 7, 189–194
Walthamstow, London 103
Walthen, *see* Dyer, Amelia
Walworth, London 44, 127
Wandsworth, London 36, 37, 105
Waters, Margaret xii, 6, 11, 16, 63, 67, 75–78, 90, 92, 139–147, 156, 167, 202, 203
Watson, *see* Waters, Margaret
Waugh, Benjamin, Rev. 88, 205, 206
Wavertree, Liverpool 31
Wells, Somerset 121
West Ham, London 103
Weston, Mrs., *see* Baker, Sarah
Weston-Super-Mare 33
West Kensington, London 45, 186
White, Mrs., *see* Waters, Margaret
Whitechapel, London 190
Whyte, Catherine 160, 161, 163, 164
Wigan, Lancs. 7, 117, 118
Willesden, London 38, 129, 174, 177, 179
Williams, Mrs. 168
Willis, Mrs., *see* Waters, Margaret and Ellis, Sarah
Willis, Rhoda, *see* James, Leslie
Wilson, Hannah 195–197
Wilson, Martha, Sophia, O. *see* Todd Sophia, Martha
Winsor, Charlotte xiv, 132–139, 200
Woking, Surrey 17, 194, 205
Workhouses x, xi, xii, xiii, 1–2, 11–12, 14, 27, 29, 36, 39, 45, 49, 61, 71, 73, 89, 99–101, 103, 106, 107, 111, 112, 116–120, 143, 145, 150, 151, 158, 171, 195, 199, 202
  Barton Regis Workhouse 170, 171
  Birkenhead Workhouse 115, 117
  Bourton Workhouse 100
  Brownlow Hill Workhouse 64
  Camelford Workhouse 36
  Clatterbridge Workhouse 89
  Crumpsall Workhouse 150
  Edmonton Union Workhouse 48, 49
  Holborn Workhouse 107
  Kensington Workhouse 60, 69
  Lambeth Workhouse 143
  Leeds Workhouse 85
  Newton Abbot Union Workhouse 111
  Wandsworth Workhouse 15
Wotton, Mrs. 27, 28